Cultural Encounters in the Age of Globalism

Nicholas J. Barnett

Cultural Encounters in the Age of Globalism

1945 to the Present

Nicholas J. Barnett
University of Salford
Manchester, UK

ISBN 978-3-031-68796-9   ISBN 978-3-031-68797-6 (eBook)
https://doi.org/10.1007/978-3-031-68797-6

© The Editor(s) (if applicable) and The Author(s), under exclusive license to Springer Nature Switzerland AG 2024

This work is subject to copyright. All rights are solely and exclusively licensed by the Publisher, whether the whole or part of the material is concerned, specifically the rights of translation, reprinting, reuse of illustrations, recitation, broadcasting, reproduction on microfilms or in any other physical way, and transmission or information storage and retrieval, electronic adaptation, computer software, or by similar or dissimilar methodology now known or hereafter developed.
The use of general descriptive names, registered names, trademarks, service marks, etc. in this publication does not imply, even in the absence of a specific statement, that such names are exempt from the relevant protective laws and regulations and therefore free for general use.
The publisher, the authors and the editors are safe to assume that the advice and information in this book are believed to be true and accurate at the date of publication. Neither the publisher nor the authors or the editors give a warranty, expressed or implied, with respect to the material contained herein or for any errors or omissions that may have been made. The publisher remains neutral with regard to jurisdictional claims in published maps and institutional affiliations.

This Palgrave Macmillan imprint is published by the registered company Springer Nature Switzerland AG
The registered company address is: Gewerbestrasse 11, 6330 Cham, Switzerland

If disposing of this product, please recycle the paper.

For Catrin Owen

Preface

As a youth I was more ignorant than today. I eschewed education, left school at sixteen and pursued a career in the belief that 'people like me' did not need a degree, nor did we belong in the university system. Over the years some sparks began to enlighten me to the possibilities of culture and adventure. In the early 2000s a friend and I took a trip to China. Once there my mind was open to a new world. Taking in the tourist sites, I saw the Great Wall of China, flew a kite in Tiananmen Square, a site I had previously associated with terror and repression, visited sites like the Forbidden City, Summer Palace and the tomb of Mao Tse Tung, a man about who I knew little. During this time I immersed myself in Chinese food culture, something which I felt I was familiar with from visits to British Chinese restaurants. How wrong I was; insects, noodle soups and sweet and sour fish served on the bone changed my view of Chinese food. The street stalls and shopping centres challenged my impressions of a communist state. On my last afternoon in Beijing my friend and I sat in the lobby of our hotel and played cards with the hotel porter. He spoke no English and we no Chinese but the common language of gameplay helped us to communicate while the receptionist helpfully translated a few words.

These experiences amounted to one of my first memorable cultural encounters. They spurred me on to learn more about the nation of which I still returned so ignorant. I began to read about other cultures and history. A few years later I had decided to enter the world of Higher Education and undertook a history degree in my late-twenties. My encounters with Chinese culture, however fleeting, influenced my later decisions to pursue education, which I was able to turn into a career. While I look back on my cultural encounter with China as an enriching and a positive experience (save for the upset stomach that drove me to my bed for several days) other encounters sometimes prove to be the opposite. This book examines some of the positive and negative outcomes of encounters between people of different cultures during the Age of Globalism.

Manchester, UK   Nicholas J. Barnett

Acknowledgments

The writing timespan of this book spans the Covid-19 pandemic, which was a challenging time for all, and delayed me as I became accustomed to new writing habits. The book's themes came from a module that I taught at Swansea University and the topics have now been incorporated into the International History module at University of Salford. At both universities I have relished discussing the topics with students and a lot of the thought process has come from this. I would also like to thank the colleagues at both universities who have offered support along the way including Professor Martyn Johns, Dr. Steve Ward, Dr. Ben Williams, Dr. Richard Worrall & Dr. Simon Hill. I would also like to thank the staff at Palgrave especially Lucy Kidwell. Last and most importantly is my wife Cat Owen who has helped through the process of writing this book in many ways.

Contents

1 **Introduction: Broadening the Mind?** 1
  The Age of Globalism 2
  Cultural Encounters 6
  Transnationalism 8
  Diversity and Identity 9
  Resurgent Nationalism 10

2 **Migration and Encounter** 15
  The Post-war Movement of Peoples 16
  Migration into and Around Europe During the 'Economic Miracle' 24
  The USA and Post-war Migration 37
  Change from the 1970s 41
  Migration in the Post-Cold War Era 45

3 **Tourism as a Cultural Encounter** 59
  Tourism Before World War Two 60
  The Growth of Tourism in the Post-war Period 63
  The Eastern Bloc 70
  Beyond Europe 74
  Problematising Travel 78
  The End of Mass Tourism? 84

4	**Globalising Activism**	87
	International Anti-apartheid Activism	88
	Women's Liberation	98
	Environmentalism	107
	Globalising Activism	123
5	**Encounters at the International Expositions**	125
	World War Two and the Early Post-war Period	129
	International Expositions in the 1960s and 1970s	139
	International Expositions in the Post-Cold War World	148
6	**Olympian Encounters at the Summer Games**	157
	The Austerity-Era Olympics	161
	The Games Confront the Past	165
	The Olympics and the Coming of Neo-liberalism	176
	The Olympics in the Twenty-First Century	183
	Do the Olympics Provide a Global Encounter?	187
	Conclusion	191
7	**Conclusion: An Age of Encounter?**	193
	References	207
	Index	221

About the Author

Nicholas J. Barnett is Lecturer in Contemporary History and Politics at University of Salford. His previous work explores the cultural cold war.

ABBREVIATIONS

A8	Ascension Eight Nations
AAM	Anti-Apartheid Movement
ANC	African National Congress
BHE	*Bund der Heimatvertriebenen und Entrechteten*
CCTV	China Central Television
ECSC	European Coal and Steel Community
EEC	European Economic Community
EU	European Union
EVW	European Voluntary Workers
FRG	Federal Republic of Germany
G8	Group of Eight
GDR	German Democratic Republic
HART	Halt All Racist Tours
HUAC	House Un-American Activities Committee
ICC	International Cricket Conference
IOC	International Olympic Committee
IMF	International Monetary Fund
IPC	International Paralympic Committee
IRO	International Refugee Organisation
IYHF	International Youth Hostel Federation
MCC	Marylebone Cricket Club
MOIP	Moscow Society of Naturalists
MTA	*Mouvement des Travailleurs Arabes*
NGO	Non-Governmental Organisation
PAC	Pan-African Congress
PRC	People's Republic of China
PRI	National Revolutionary Party
UN	United Nations
UNRRA	United Nations Relief and Rehabilitation Agency
VOOP	All-Russia Society for the Protection of Nature
VOSOPiONOP	All-Russia Society for the Protection of Nature and the Greening of Population Centres
WIDF	Women's International Democratic Federation

List of Figures

Fig. 3.1	'On the Adriatic', poster for Yugoslavian tourism, 1950s	74
Fig. 4.1	Racial Segregation: Apartheid in South Africa	89
Fig. 4.2	Earthrise. *Source*: NASA/Bill Anders	113
Fig. 5.1	The Atomium, Brussels	131
Fig. 6.1	After the Games: The empty Barcelona Olympic Stadium	182

CHAPTER 1

Introduction: Broadening the Mind?

The 2010s and early 2020s may be labelled an era of deglobalisation. Britain's vote to leave the European Union on 23 June 2016 followed by the election of Donald Trump in the USA later that year marked the beginning of a series of victories for anti-globalising voices. The target of these political campaigns was not the economic free trade agenda and the free movement of capital that had represented globalisation, although both targeted geographic areas of industrial decline and off-shoring of jobs. Rather they focussed on the mobility of people: immigration was the key driver for many voters. Anti-immigration politicians have come to power in many European nations including Britain and Italy. Even the economic side of globalisation has sometimes been challenged by the era's politicians. The Covid-19 pandemic that began in 2020, moreover, severely limited the mobility of tourists as many nations or states entered partial or full lockdown to stop the spread of the deadly illness. It caused the delay of sporting events like the 2020 Tokyo Olympics. Global trade was severely impacted with supply chains failing and demand for many goods falling while others like medical supplies peaked. The interconnectedness of the world was upset further in February 2022 when Russia invaded Ukraine. In response the USA, Britain and the EU began to decouple their economies from Russia's, divesting and seeking to block Russia's global trading connections. Food, fuel and fertiliser exports from Ukraine and Russia, on which much of Europe and beyond had based their economic strategies, declined. Yet, world trade has recovered with both the Western nations and Russia tilting towards other geographic areas. The mobility of people has not declined despite policies designed to hinder immigration. Globalisation, it seems, is hard to stop.

© The Author(s), under exclusive license to Springer Nature Switzerland AG 2024
N. J. Barnett, *Cultural Encounters in the Age of Globalism*,
https://doi.org/10.1007/978-3-031-68797-6_1

This book is about the encounters that result from globalisation: the everyday engagements with other cultures or more political engagements driven by states. Interconnections were formed through travel, migration and globalised activism, but they also came through the globalised 'cultural supermarket' that brought physical and cultural products from far and wide into new areas, raising people's awareness of other cultures.[1] All forms of encounter can also cause people to react with anxiety and withdraw, feeling the need to protect 'their' culture. However, this book also examines the role of governments and corporations in mediating these encounters, suggesting that the global citizen is not as free to explore and discover as they may believe.

The book draws on literature about cultural encounters by scholars in a broad range of disciplines including history, politics, anthropology, sociology, geography and economics. This interdisciplinary and transnational approach allows a fuller range of the cultural impacts of globalisation to be explored than a solely historical approach. The book will interest students and scholars in an extensive range of subjects beyond Contemporary History.

THE AGE OF GLOBALISM

Economic and cultural globalism have existed for centuries if not millennia. The age of European Imperialism that peaked in the nineteenth century shared many features with globalisation: world economies and supply chains extended as never before, often through building exploitative relations between peoples. Improvements in transport and communications technology such as the railway, steamship and the telegraph made interconnections ever greater. The early twentieth century saw these links speed up with transport and mass communications improving, especially with road and early air travel, radio and cinema enabling people, goods and ideas to become more mobile.

Yet the roots of globalisation are far older. Globalisation has been a process that has been ongoing for centuries but which grew exponentially from the onset of capitalism in the sixteenth century. The European empires in the nineteenth century embodied a wave of globalisation that was enabled by new technologies such as the steamship, the Maxim gun and the telegraph. In the second half of the twentieth century the process sped up again. Victoria de Grazia sees the seeds for post-war globalisation being set by Woodrow Wilson in the early twentieth century. Wilson's desire to create an empire of trade where values accompanied the sale of commodities led to what she sees as a peaceful conquest of the world.[2] This positivist approach ignores the role of American force throughout the twentieth century, often subverting democracy and sponsoring coups in foreign lands. American ideological and economic

---

[1] Gordon Matthews, *Global Culture/Individual Identity: Searching for Home in the Cultural Supermarket* (London: Routledge, 2000).

[2] Victoria de Grazia, *Irresistible Empire: America's Advance through 20th Century Europe* (Ann Arbor, MI: University of Michigan Press, 2005).

hegemony in Europe, however, did not come about through the barrel of a gun, and the American 'way of life', or mass consumption, was often tied to financial aid or came through imports of culture. Globalisation has been a feature of the world since at least the sixteenth century. The post-1945 globalisation may have had different technologies and appeared revolutionary, but it was built on previous waves.

The European Recovery Programme or Marshall Plan of 1947, which provided recapitalisation funds for the Western European nations, was tied to economic liberalisation. A number of historians see this plan as saving Europe from poverty and the rising threat of communism after it struggled to recover from the war.[3] Certainly, the investment was followed by growth in Europe leading to a widespread belief in a post-war 'economic miracle' in several economies until the 1980s. Yet, others dispute this claim. Alan Milward sees the plan as something of a red herring, suggesting that growth had already occurred and that the merely resolved a short-term crisis caused by the exceptionally harsh winter of 1946–47.[4] He contends that the plan aimed to support the world trading system which had been envisioned at the Bretton Woods conference but was not yet realised. Furthermore, Ferenc Jánossy suggested that the miracles of European growth were merely a return to a previous upward trend that the war had interrupted.[5] By the 1960s growth slowed as the expected economic size based on interwar trends was reached.

The period after 1945, however, saw rapid changes in politics, economies and culture that brought the arrival of the global era. The economic arrangements made at the end of World War Two at the Bretton Woods conference heralded in a new economic system which promoted greater integration of economies and supply chains. It created the International Monetary Fund (IMF) and the World Bank, two institutions that later became central to the economic liberalism and free trade underpinning globalisation. The Marshall Plan enabled American goods and credit to flow throughout Europe. At the same time, European politicians implemented their own plans to integrate their economies to prevent future wars. The European Coal and Steel Community (ECSC) formed in 1952 with the nations of France, Germany, Belgium, Netherlands, Luxembourg and Italy, but it gradually expanded and deepened into the institution that became the European Union (EU).

---

[3] Harry Price, *The Marshall Plan and its Meaning* (Ithaca, NY: Cornell University Press, 1955); Michael Hogan, *The Marshall Plan: America, Britain and the Reconstruction of Western Europe, 1947–52* (Cambridge: Cambridge University Press, 1987); Barry Eichengreen, *Europe's Postwar Recovery* (Cambridge: Cambridge University Press, 1995).

[4] Alan Milward, *The Reconstruction of Western Europe 1945–51* (London: Routledge, 1984), 5.

[5] Ferenc Jánossy, *The End of the Economic Miracle: Appearance and Reality in Economic Development* (New York: International Arts & Science Press, 1971), cited in Mark Harrison, 'The Soviet Union after 1945: Economic Recovery and Political Repression', *Past and Present* (2011) Sup 6, 111.

The institutions of globalisation also included political formations. With the failure of the interwar League of Nations, a new institution, the United Nations (UN), aimed to prevent conflict and maintain the balance between the global powers, especially the United States of America and the Soviet Union. While a major part of its operations were in international relations, the UN quickly became involved in relief and aid. As it became more established its various committees and institutions have developed to act as a concert of nations able to respond to crises but also enabling smaller nations to work together to protect their interests.

The processes discussed in this book have all been enabled by what is commonly termed 'globalisation'. Scholars have debated this concept. The sociologist Anthony Giddens suggests that globalisation is 'the intensification of worldwide social relations which link distant localities in such a way that local happenings are shaped by events occurring many miles away and vice versa'.[6] This definition, which is supportive of globalisation, points towards the interconnections that are discussed in this book. Giddens' definition, however, neglects the capitalist imperative that drives globalisation. The ever-increasing search for global markets and the desire to maximise profits has led to the integration of supply chains and their diffusion across several nations. The sociologist Michael Mann is more critical. He writes,

> what is generally called globalization involved the extension of distinct relations of ideological, economic, military, and political power across the world. Concretely, in the period after 1945 this means the diffusion of ideologies like liberalism and socialism, the spread of the capitalist mode of production, the extension of military striking ranges, and the extension of nation-states across the world, at first with two empires and then with just one surviving.[7]

This definition is more similar to what has, traditionally, been labelled 'imperialism'. However, Mann also discusses how ideology is tied into globalisation and sees it as very much the spreading of neo-liberal policies across the globe. The term neo-liberal, an ideology whose existence is often dismissed by media commentators,[8] refers to the attempts to disrupt the social welfare systems which were put in place after World War Two. Philip Mirowski and Quinn Slobodian have both charted the rise of neo-liberalism as a distinct

---

[6] Anthony Giddens, *Consequences of Modernity* (Cambridge: Polity, 1994), 64.

[7] Michael Mann, *The Sources of Social Power: Volume 4, Globalizations, 1945–2011* (Cambridge: Cambridge University Press, 2013), 11.

[8] Ed Conway, 'Sky Views: What is Neoliberalism and why is it an Insult?', *Sky News*, 15 May 2018, https://news.sky.com/story/sky-views-what-is-neoliberalism-and-why-is-it-an-insult-11373031, accessed 1 July 2023; Bill Scher 'Is this the stupidest book ever written about socialism', *Politico Magazine*, 28 Aug 2018, https://www.politico.com/magazine/story/2018/08/28/chapo-trap-house-book-review-219596, accessed 1 July 2017; Jonathan Chait, 'How "Neoliberalism" became the left's favourite insult of liberals', *New York*, 16 July 2017, https://nymag.com/intelligencer/2017/07/how-neoliberalism-became-the-lefts-favorite-insult.html accessed 1 July 2023.

collection of ideas that its adherents aimed to spread.[9] Mirowski pays particular attention to the development of the ideology through the Mont Pelerin Society, which included economists such as Friedrich Hayek and Milton Friedman. These thinkers differed from the classical liberals who believed that the state should be minimalist and a 'watch-man'. Hayek, Friedman and other economists proposed the take-over of the state to transform society into their ideal form of 'pure freedom'. It is that maintenance and use of the strong state which sets neo-liberalism apart from liberalism. Neo-liberalism has been associated with post-war globalisation through organisations like the IMF and World Bank often ensuring frictionless trade between borders.

Along with economic growth came improvements in communications technology. The expansion and globalisation of television, radio and press (accompanied by improvements in literacy, translation and the spread of lingua francas such as English), and later the invention of the internet, all contributed to people hearing about other cultures and spread consumer capitalism around the world. These were accompanied by increases also in travel speeds and the affordability of both mass communications and travel, meaning that people were more in touch with those of other nations than ever before.

As these economic and political changes took place, opportunities began to appear for people around the world to engage with other cultures. With labour shortages in many European nations, recruitment of foreign workers spurred the mobility of people on a temporary or permanent basis. Over time governments made agreements with one another to take labour, with emigrants often sending remittances home and improving their nations' wealth. Migration was far from new but in the second half of the twentieth and early twenty-first centuries it became a central aspect of cultural change and economic growth and at times its impacts became the target of politicians and communities. One of the key industries that was deemed to both help economies and to build better relationships between people was tourism. With Americans and Europeans encouraged to travel and mix with each other and better availability of air travel, more of the world became accessible to more people than ever before. A number of European and non-European nations built vast tourist industries and people of all ages took holidays in search of sun, culture or to broaden their horizons. Increased communication, migration and travel enabled people to learn about and communicate with people far and wide; it was not long before international affiliations were built. Political activism and ideologies had existed for hundreds of years but the single-issue nature of these groups or collaborations brought people from different nations together in movements and campaigns on a greater scale. An event in one part of the world would often cause a response from populations in other countries. As industries grew past their pre-war levels, governments, businesses and

---

[9] Philip Mirowski, *Never Let A Good Crisis Go To Waste*, (London: Verso, 2014); Quinn Slobodian, *Globalists: The End of Empire and the Birth of Neoliberalism* (Cambridge, MA: Harvard University Press, 2018).

non-governmental organisations worked to promote their nations overseas. Nations used large-scale events to promote their values and to build relationships with other governments and global audiences. The Olympic Games returned at London in 1948 and over the next decades grew into a festival of physical prowess that gave host and visiting nations alike the opportunity to impress the world and sell their global 'brand'. The cultural equivalent of the Games are the International Expositions, which had been regular events since the late nineteenth century. Their return, beginning in the 1950s, allowed organisations and governments to present their cultures, beliefs and scientific inventions globally, drawing millions of visitors to explore these national presentations. These cultural encounters, the development of their structures and their impact on populations are the focus of this book.

Cultural Encounters

When scholars discuss cultural encounters they have often referred to the meetings of relatively isolated communities from the ancient world onwards.[10] The focus of cultural encounters has been on contacts and interactions between different peoples, friendly or unfriendly. Since 1945 the scale of these encounters has increased. But it is important to see cultural encounters as part of a larger historical process in which globalisation and imperialism have expanded in waves, which are punctuated by other periods where connections might be broken by isolationism or war. Cultural encounters are often examined using a specific language about the flows, transfers and interconnections, referring to the ability of people, ideas and goods to cross borders. From these interactions we often see the emergence of hybrid cultures.

Sociologist Gerard Delanty has identified six types of encounter that are useful when considering how populations have responded to the mixing of cultures in the post-war period. Delanty's scale ranges from hostility to embrace.[11] First, the rejection of other cultures leads to disputes, mistrust and conflict, for example, the Cold War or the terrorist attacks of 11 September 2001 and ensuing war on terror. These encounters often led to the rejection of other cultures: anti-Russianness or Anti-Islamism in Western film, literature and other media. The second is 'cultural divergence'. In this type of encounter different cultures emerge from a single entity. New autonomous

---

[10] John Thares Davidann & Marc Jason Gilbert, *Cross-Cultural Encounters in Modern World History* (Abingdon: Routledge, 2013); Michelle Ying Ling Huang (ed.), *Beyond Boundaries: East and West Cross-Cultural Encounters* (Newcastle-Upon-Tyne: Cambridge Scholars Publishing, 2011); Charles Issawi, *Cross-Cultural Encounters and Conflicts* (Oxford: Oxford University Press, 1998); Özlem Çaykent & Luca Zavagno, *Islands of the East Mediterranean: A History of Cross-Cultural Encounters* (London: I. B. Tauris, 2014).

[11] Gerard Delanty, 'Cultural diversity, democracy and the prospects of cosmopolitanism: a theory of cultural encounters', *The British Journal of Sociology*, 62.4 (2011), 633–656.

cultures are created from the new communities, each having differing interpretations of culture and history. An example is the division of the Christian church into Catholic and orthodox in 1054. Later further religious divergence became important in the late twentieth century in Northern Ireland, which saw tensions emerging along religious and nationalist lines. These divisions caused conflict between a Catholic nationalist community, which saw itself as part of the Irish Republic, and the Protestant Unionist community, which saw itself as part of Great Britain. Some cultural encounters lead to or embed divisiveness between communities.

Third, Delanty identifies 'cultural assimilation' as a type of encounter. This term appears more positive than the previous two and does not lead directly to conflict. Instead, one culture is absorbed by the other. The absorbing culture does not change, but the assimilated loses its characteristics or language. An example might be a migrant community that is fully integrated by the host nation, with no recognition or celebration of its previous culture, or as Delanty suggests, religious conversion. Assimilation might, however, be problematic for communities who have lost traces of their identity and the rejection of diversity.

Fourth is 'acceptance'. In this encounter cultures have limited contact, for example through trading relations. There are still divisions and there can be some forms of conflict between the cultures, notably competition between them. There might be some acceptance of the foreign culture, but this is limited to aspects like food or fashion. An example of this might be the period of the Cold War known as peaceful co-existence from the mid-1950s. Eastern and Western nations, especially those outside the USA, increased their trading with each other and aspects of culture like fashion were tentatively brought across the Iron Curtain. However, the two sides were very much in a period of conflict through the competition of ideologies and sought to influence worldwide public opinion.

The fifth of Delanty's encounters is 'cultural diffusion' or adaptation. Two or more cultures interact and the divisions between them begin to become blurred. There are some forms of cross-fertilisation but each culture maintains its key aspects of individuality. Diffusion means learning about other cultures and increasing awareness of the diversity within and outside societies. The keyword here is integration, as opposed to the assimilation of his third category. Some of the key examples of cultural diffusion are the availability of global foodstuffs, music or film in their original form as opposed to more Westernised variations of these which would fit more into his final category.

Delanty's final encounter is cultural fusion, which contains many elements that scholars term 'hybridity'. Fusion implies the mixing of elements of two or more cultures to produce a new identity that contains aspects of the older versions. British national identity is formed from elements of its constituent nations; it is a combination of English, Welsh, Scottish and Northern Irish identities but also aspects of other migrant identities from Europe and beyond.

Similarly the USA is made of a mixture of Protestant and Catholic communities that originate from various northern and southern European nations and have at times struggled with each other as well the native American culture that the Europeans decimated. Latterly, influences from Asia and Africa have diversified American culture, making it ever more hybridised through the mixing of traditions. These hybrid identities are the result of the fusion of many different cultures. There are numerous forms of cultural encounter; most of them do not neatly fit into a model, taking an aspect of several—conflict may be followed by acceptance and later assimilation or hybridity. Delanty's framework shows how cultural encounters fit along this scale of responses.

Transnationalism

Many encounters which are discussed in this book are transnational in outlook. They go beyond the idea of the nation state and show how individuals can be either empowered by aspects of globalisation or internationalism or constrained by these new structures and encounters emerging from them. For Ulf Hannerz,

> The term transnational is in a way more humble [than globalisation], and often a more adequate label for phenomena which can be of quite variable scale and distribution, even when they do share the characteristic of being within a state. It also makes the point that many of the linkages in question are not "international," in the strictest sense of involving national – actually, states – as corporate actors. In the transnational arena, the actors may be individuals, groups, movements, business enterprises.[12]

Therefore the linkages and encounters examined here are not always about the nation state; they concern how individuals form encounters on their own terms. Pierre-Yves Saunier suggests that transnational history creates a perspective that 'enhances [history's] capacity by adding the history of entanglements between countries to the checklist of national history writing'.[13] It is argued that the ability to make connections beyond borders shapes everything that we do but that the nation remains important. This book is a history of globalisation which examines how everyday people are affected by the structures created by global businesses, nation states and supranational organisations rather than an examination of those institutions.

---

[12] Ulf Hannerz, *Transnational Connections: Culture, People, Places* (London: Routledge, 1996), 7.

[13] Pierre-Yves Saunier, *Transnational History* (London: Bloomsbury, 2013), 2.

DIVERSITY AND IDENTITY

The increasing prevalence of global encounters has led to societies and cultures becoming more diverse. For large parts of the Age of Globalism those from outside the majority culture, religion or linguistic group were waging a contest for acceptance. The issue of diversity has become a current political issue often relating to immigration or foreign influences impacting on domestic cultures. The recent global surge of the far right has led some scholars to question the benefits of diversity and frame it as a threat to national cultures (by which they mean 'white' national cultures in the West). Many of these books have helped white nationalist politicians to legitimise their brand of identity politics.[14] Conversely, in the global era, many people have adopted what they consider a cosmopolitan identity. They are able to move around the world for work or leisure; they sample a range of diverse cultural products through ever-increasing mass media including print, broadcasting and the internet. Many build friendships around the world, some without leaving their home.

Identity in the twenty-first century is highly contested. When reaffirming her decision to withdraw the UK from the European Union on the basis of a slim referendum majority, the Prime Minister, Theresa May, made an attack on cosmopolitanism in an attempt to win working-class votes for the Conservative Party:

> Today, too many people in positions of power behave as though they have more in common with international elites than with the people down the road, the people they employ, the people they pass in the street.
>
> But if you believe you're a citizen of the world, you're a citizen of nowhere. You don't understand what the very word 'citizenship' means.[15]

The speech aimed to appeal to those who believed they had been left behind by globalisation and that their societies and economies had deteriorated because of migration. The radical right, who had gained traction during the referendum campaign, had attacked those who wanted to remain in the EU as the 'elite'. Many people, therefore, who identified as something other than an imagined conception of a homogeneous white British majority felt under attack. It was not just certain ethnicities or groups but the idea of cosmopolitanism which was threatened by May's rhetoric. Much of the press and her political opponents focussed on the phrase 'citizen of nowhere'. The Liberal Democrat politician Vince Cable declared the phrase to be 'quite evil ... it could have been taken out of *Mein Kampf*. I think that's where

---

[14] Matthew Goodwin, *Values, Voices and Virtue: The New British Politics* (London: Penguin, 2023); Eric Kaufman, *Whiteshift: Populism, Immigration and the Future of White Majorities* (London: Allen Lane, 2018).

[15] Theressa May, 'Speech to Conservative Party Conference', 4 October 2016.

it came from, wasn't it "Rootless Cosmopolitanism"'.[16] The link with antisemitic phrases of the 1930s clearly had an impact on many who felt that they were 'citizens of the world' who were now being made stateless. Letters to *The Guardian* by several writers criticised this 'insular nationalism' as a rejection of ideas of cosmopolitanism that were embedded in enlightenment values.[17] These people felt attacked by May because the government had responded to what they felt was a minority xenophobic streak in Britain that was directing policy. Others bore the slogan 'citizen of nowhere' with pride. The National Theatre of Scotland held a Citizen of Nowhere festival that celebrated a diverse civil society.[18] T-shirts bearing the slogan were sold and a book was published that aimed to remake Europe on more democratic lines.[19] This hegemonic contest for the values of cosmopolitanism showed that identities are fractured and diverse and can cause conflict within individual societies. The response also showed that the power of the nation state had weakened for some people who drew allegiances across borders as part of what is sometimes termed the 'transnational civil society'.[20] While this term often refers to organised advocacy groups and non-governmental organisations it also implies the building of communities with interconnections across borders and shared values that diverge from those of political leaders.

Resurgent Nationalism

Discussion of concepts like transnationalism, cosmopolitanism, globalisation or hybridity could lead observers to conclude that the nation state and nationalism are outdated. In some ways this is true: a more interconnected world has allowed citizens to think beyond borders. Identities have changed with ideas like the 'global melange', the spread of hybrid cultures resulting from globalisation, and the 'cultural supermarket', the exposure to and ability to engage with previously separated cultures, enabling people to choose values and ideas that matter to them.[21] Institutions created throughout the twentieth century

---

[16] Quoted in, 'Theresa May Speech could have been taken out of Mein Kampf' *Independent*, 5 July 2017, https://www.independent.co.uk/news/uk/politics/theresa-may-mein-kampf-adolf-hitler-nazi-vince-cable-liberal-democrat-conservatives-a7825381.html accessed 7 Feb 2019.

[17] See Phillip Murphy et al. 'Theresa May's rejection of Enlightenment Values', 9 Oct 2016, https://www.theguardian.com/politics/2016/oct/09/theresa-may-rejection-of-enlightenment-values accessed 8 Feb 2019.

[18] National Theatre of Scotland 'Citizen of Nowhere'. https://www.nationaltheatrescotland.com/production/citizen-of-nowhere/ accessed 8 Feb 2019.

[19] Lorenzo Marsili & Niccolo Milanese, *Citizens of Nowhere: How Europe Can be Saved from Itself* (London: Zed, 2018).

[20] Thomas Davies, *NGOs: A New History of Transnational Civil Society* (Oxford: Oxford University Press, 2014).

[21] Jan Nederveen Pieterse, *Globalization and Culture: Global Mélange, 2nd Edition* (Plymouth: Rowman & Littlefield, 2009); Matthews, *Global Culture*.

from the League of Nations, UN, NATO, EU, and the African Union to the World Bank and IMF have ensured that leaders think beyond the confines of their borders and realise that isolationism cannot easily be adopted as foreign policy. By the end of the twentieth century it seemed to many observers that nations were becoming less important in an integrated world where citizenship was multi-directional.

But nationalism matters. The turn of the millennium has seen a resurgence of this ideology that had sometimes seemed destined for the dustbin of history. Ethnic conflicts characterised the 1990s and continued into the 2000s. As Anthony Smith points out, the globalised labour market has witnessed a return to anxieties and prejudices thought to have disappeared.[22] New nationalist movements emerged and solidified in many nations throughout the early twenty-first century. The victories of Brexit, Trump and Jair Bolsonaro in Brazil, and semi-authoritarian leaders in Poland, Hungary and Russia seemed to herald a new era of far-right domination of world politics. Behind many of these movements of the 2010s seemed to be the orchestrating voices of internet campaigners, such as the Breitbart News Network and its former chairperson Steve Bannon, who advised Trump, Leave.eu, one of Britain's anti-EU groups, and Bolsonaro and built political networks throughout Europe. In many ways far-right populism acted as a transnational community of mutual support. While nationalist movements using transnational networks for their reciprocal benefit might appear contradictory, it should not surprise us. In the 1930s fascist parties were interconnected and mutually supporting, and this international support for other movements has influenced the new nationalist parties.[23] For Smith, nationalism remains popular because of the quasi-religious nature of the ideology that feeds off the ability of populations to 'imagine' in-groups and out-groups based on historical narratives, symbols and culture which globalisation and cosmopolitanism have been unable to dislodge. The ideology of nationalism grew in the twenty-first century and its anti-globalising agenda influenced policy makers.

Nationalism has long been a feature of cultural encounters. The political scientist Mary Kaldor suggests that it is here to stay despite the weakening of ties to the nation state in the global era. In 2004 she prophetically wrote:

> I do not think that nationalism will necessarily go away in an era of globalisation. We are in the midst of a period of political experimentation, as earlier political ideas and institutions have been eroded by dramatic socio-economic and cultural change. Various political ideologies are currently in competition, including market fundamentalism, global Islam, cosmopolitanism, Europeanism and, of course, nationalism. Some of these ideologies are forward-looking or reformist ... others are backward-looking or regressive, appealing to an imagined

[22] Anthony Smith, *Nations and Nationalism in a Global Era* (Cambridge: Polity, 2007).
[23] Arad Bauerkamper and Grzegorz Rossolinski-Liebe (eds), *Fascism without Borders: Transnational Connections between Movements and Regimes in Europe, 1918–1945*, (Oxford: Berghahn, 2017).

past, and proposing to reverse at least some aspects of the current changes... Unfortunately, there is no ... reason to suggest that the more forward-looking ideologies will triumph over the backward-looking ideologies.[24]

The following decade saw many, perhaps backward-looking, ideologies like nationalism intensify. It saw them grow as political forces that captivated many. The politics of nationalism offered a convenient scapegoat that disguised the excesses and inequalities caused by three decades of market fundamentalism. In addition, right-wing movements of the twenty-first century utilised the discourses of anti-Islamism that had predominated since the start of the War on Terror. And yet very often the scapegoats were not Muslims alone. The inflated fears of EU, African, Middle Eastern and Central American migrants, combined with the aforementioned cosmopolitan 'elites', offered politicians a convenient group against whom to unite their supporters.

Kaldor has written about how nations continue to present a form of identity through mass co-ordinated performances that would not be out of place in the former USSR or Nazi Germany. This 'spectacle nationalism' can be seen in royal parades and celebrations, Olympic opening ceremonies and the singing of national anthems at sporting events. She observes that very often these and similar rituals aim to cement nationalism as an official legitimising ideology. She sees the passion as performed by those who join the crowd or watch on television; they are driven by a sense of obligation rather than a real urge to celebrate their nation. But by taking the message on board they accept the role of the state and the obligations, such as paying taxes, that come with it. She distinguishes between this spectacle nationalism and extreme nationalism in which participants take up the cause with a sense of religious fervour. A form of the latter has been invoked by the government of Ukraine to encourage its people to participate in repelling the Russian army, with some units, including the Azov Battalion, highly influenced by far-right ideology. But febrile nationalism does not need to be linked to war. The Proud Boys, an American neo-fascist organisation that combined nationalism with misogyny and were strong supporters of Donald Trump, mobilised in street actions aimed at creating conflict. Nationalism has taken different forms, from actions against elements of globalisation such as migration, to participation in festivals and ceremonies. Spectacle nationalism has taken on a global face, which has expanded in the twentieth and twenty-first centuries. Here it is examined in the context of the International Expositions and the Olympics, with a particular focus on how states mediate these encounters and governments use them to spread their values among their own population and beyond.

The chapters of this book are each formed around a type of cultural encounter. Migration has been the most notable encounter of the Age of Globalism, discussed in Chapter 2. At times assimilation, hybridity or conflict

---

[24] Mary Kaldor, 'Nationalism and Globalisation', *Nations and Nationalism*, 10 (2004), 161–177.

have arisen in societies which experience migration. Chapter 3 examines tourism, a boom industry of the later twentieth century, which has allowed people to travel even on relatively low budgets. Their ability to encounter other cultures is questioned and the impact of tourism on host nations is weighed against its cultural and economic impacts. Chapter 4 focuses on transnational activism, where groups of activists and non-governmental organisations coalesced around single issues. Three of the more prominent are examined here: the anti-Apartheid movement against South Africa's National Party government, the women's movement and environmentalism. Each balanced their national campaigning with international actions but often tensions emerged between different groups. The cultural encounters that enabled common aims and values sometimes came up against differences that hindered collaboration. The International Expositions, or World's Fairs, are the subject of Chapter 5. These events acted as 'spectacle nationalism', but also aimed to expand trade and promote national cultures. Certain host and exhibiting nations used them to position themselves globally and to build better international relations. Finally, the book examines the summer Olympic Games. These sporting mega-events bring thousands of participants and spectators into close contact, but they also create a global media audience. Different international and domestic cultures interact at these events. They are mediated by governments, city authorities and the International Olympic Committee, but often participants have found a way to have their 'off-brand' messages heard. These are far from the only types of encounters enabled by globalisation but they bring millions of people around the world into direct and indirect contact with each other, creating mobility and interconnectedness between different cultures.

CHAPTER 2

Migration and Encounter

The Age of Globalism from 1945 was an era of high mobility and migration. War, the economic inequality caused by globalisation and climate disaster became driving factors in migration. Migration became a contentious driver of policy with migrants the world over becoming the target of press sensationalism. Throughout the era governments implemented policies to encourage or discourage migration as it suited their agendas. The Cold War divided most of the world between communist governments and liberal democracies and the movement of peoples became an international issue. In the communist states preventing emigration became the central economic and security concern. In the twenty-first century political action against immigration increased following the economic downturn from 2008, with the rise of populism in developed nations including Trumpism in the USA, Brexit in the UK, the Italian *Fratelli d'Italia*, *Fiedesz* in Hungary and The Freedom Party (Freiheitliche Partei Österreichs) in Austria. Stopping immigration became one of the central aims of these deglobalising movements.

Migrants spread their culture and traditions around the world. They mixed and bred with existing populations and created more diverse societies and hybrid cultures that amalgamated old and new identities. Others shed their old identities to adopt new naturalised ones. Before the 1990s most migrants were either post-colonial emigrants heading to the 'mother country', economic migrants or Cold War refugees. Many were seeking a living but they were also pulled by the globalised world, national promotions and the political desire for a 'flexible' workforce consisting of cheap expendable labour. The world's wealthiest regions of North America, Europe and Australia were the main receivers of immigrants. In 2000 the UN found that these were the destinations for 56 per cent of all migrants.[1] Immigration helped cities like New York, London, Singapore, Amsterdam, Hong Kong, Tokyo and Paris grow into global cities. However, from the late 1990s new regions attracted migrants, for instance Southern European and Middle Eastern nations sought to plug labour gaps. Migration brings hybridisation and is possibly the biggest creator of new cultures and creole languages, but the old cultures of both host and migrant remain and sometimes come into conflict.

This chapter explores some of the key patterns of migration after World War Two. It examines the political impact of migration as nations struggled to adapt to a globalising world. The chapter also covers some of the cultural adaptations that migrants brought to their new nations. In exploring some of the main flows related to globalisation, decolonisation, the Cold War and the post-Cold War world, it suggests that during the global age migration was vital for the growth of Western economies, but that politicians opened and closed the door as it suited them. Migrants provided one of the clearest encounters between nations, but this was not always seamless. Migrants had to force their own space in their host nations; they created new hybrid cultures and identities, often combining their culture with that of their new nation.

THE POST-WAR MOVEMENT OF PEOPLES

The immediate story of post-war migration is one of displacement, return and refuge. At the end of World War Two there were around eleven million displaced persons in Europe, eight million of those in Germany.[2] Additionally, there were around eight million displaced persons in Asia, mainly Japanese civilians. A huge change in international relations, which included the decline of European empires and the onset of the Cold War, meant that during the initial post-war period many language communities were no longer welcome where they lived, as ethnic cleansing took place around Europe and part of Asia.

In the 1930s Germans had been encouraged to settle newly annexed European territories. Alongside these *Reichsdeutsche*, other ethnic Germans or *Volksdeutsche*, had from the Middle Ages onwards inhabited parts of present-day Czechia, Poland, Hungary, Romania and the territory that made up the post-war USSR.[3] The *Reichsdeutsche* and *Volksdeutsche* totalled around eleven million persons and many of them had supported Hitler's expansionism. During the last days of the war the Allies discussed how to deal with ethnic Germans in occupied lands, with Winston Churchill recommending a 'clean

---

[1] Cited in 'Introduction', *Migration in a Globalised World: New Research Issues and Prospects* edited by Cedric Audelbert and Mohamed Kamel Dorai (Amsterdam: Amsterdam University Press, 2010), 8.

[2] Ian Buruma, *Year Zero: A History of 1945* (London: Atlantic Books, 2013), 121.

[3] Ian Connor, *Refugees and Expellees in Postwar Germany* (Manchester: Manchester University Press, 2014), 8.

sweep' take place in Poland. As the Allies advanced the new governments of Czechoslovakia and Poland ordered their militias and police forces to begin to eject ethnic Germans (including up to a tenth of them who did not speak German).[4] Colonists and generations-long inhabitants were forcibly, and often brutally, moved in what have been labelled "wild expulsions".[5]

At the Potsdam Conference in the summer of 1945 the Allied leaders made the decision to cede one-quarter of Germany's Eastern territory, mainly to Poland in compensation for its loss of lands to the Soviet Union. The eleven million German speakers were to be 'returned' to Germany 'in an orderly and humane manner', with the occupying powers able to prepare for the arrivals.[6] These transfers, as shown by Raymond Douglas, were anything but orderly: local governments took the opportunity of the disorganised expulsions to rid themselves of remaining Jewish and other minority populations, while racketeers profited by selling space on the transports.[7] The route of German expellees, moreover, was perilous: the breakdown in law and order left them subject to looting and violence by the Red Army and local gangs seeking plunder or revenge. German women were seen as legitimate targets and often subjected to sexual violence. Between 500,000 and a million Germans are believed to have died during the 'repatriation'. Allied authorities lacked the resources to check or process the deportees and often could not provide food and shelter on their arrival. The expulsion of Germans worked to create less ethnically diverse populations in Europe; in the case of the Czechoslovakian regions of Bohemia and Moravia the proportion of German speakers fell from 29 per cent in 1930 to just 1.8 per cent by 1950.[8]

When the expellees reached Germany, life remained problematic. Over 23 per cent of Germany's pre-war housing was destroyed or severely damaged.[9] Expellees were often forced into cramped housing, with around ten per cent initially housed in government camps. The expectation was that new arrivals would move to rural areas where housing was less damaged: Bavaria, Lower Saxony, Westphalia and Schleswig–Holstein became the main destinations in West Germany. Expellees arriving in either section of Germany took what manual work was available. Most worked in lower-skilled jobs than they held previously. They were the first to be laid off when turmoil hit, such as the currency reforms in 1948. Migrants were seen as outsiders in their new

---

[4] Peter Gatrell, *The Unsettling of Europe: How Migration Reshaped a Continent* (London: Basic Books, 2019), 23, 251.

[5] Raymond Douglas, *Orderly and Humane: The Expulsion of the Germans after the Second World War* (New Haven, CT: Yale University Press, 2012), 84–5.

[6] Foreign Relations of the United States: Diplomatic Papers, The Conference of Berlin (The Potsdam Conference), 1945, Volume II https://history.state.gov/historicaldocuments/frus1945Berlinv02/d1383 Accessed 11 Aug 2022.

[7] Douglas, *Orderly and Humane*, 136–146.

[8] Tony Judt, *Postwar: A History of Europe Since 1945* (London: Pimlico, 2007), 26.

[9] Connor, *Refugees and Expellees*, 30–32.

communities, especially in rural areas, and were derogatorily referred to as 'Gypsies', 'Slavs' or 'Polaks', with the hang-overs of racialised terminology persisting. These attitudes were often reinforced by political elites. The mayor of Feuchtwangen, Bavaria referred to the newcomers as a 'foreign rabble', while local officials refused to enforce laws guaranteeing equality between both populations.[10] Sometimes Catholic expellees ended up in predominantly Protestant towns and vice versa, leaving religious differences that cast them as outsiders. The port town of Lübeck had escaped heavy bombing (just 8.5 per cent of its housing was destroyed) but the arrival of 97,000 German refugees, equal to 40 per cent of the town's population, caused tension between newcomers and their hosts. A mediation office soon opened to resolve difficulties.[11] The integration of German-speaking expellees proved less than harmonious and the attitudes of both sides led to prejudice and acrimony.

With integration into the West German community proving difficult, expellees found ways to make their voices heard. The *Bund der Heimatvertriebenen und Entrechteten* (BHE) or League of Expellees and Deprived of Rights was established in 1950. The organisation had links to German nationalists and contained former Nazi Party members. It gained success in areas where expellees were prominent, winning 23 per cent in Schleswig–Holstein in 1953. Its success was short lived: as material conditions for Germans in general improved, expellees turned away from this group. The expellee groups sometimes pushed an agenda of revanchism, hoping to regain the lost German territory. During their brief period of popularity, they appealed to those who had found integration difficult. Expellees, however, became more integrated into West German society throughout the 1960s, despite some residual tensions between the migrant Germans and others, especially for older age groups. Integration was especially common in younger age groups, with mixed marriages increasing and participation in sports and societies allowing them to form a new German identity.[12]

The post-war remaking of Europe's borders led to further forcible expulsions and the homogenisation of populations in Central and Eastern Europe. From 1947 around 500,000 ethnic Hungarians were transferred from Czechoslovakia with the aim of providing land for poor farmers. In return Czechoslovakia received around 100,000 people deemed Czech or Slovak from Yugoslavia and around 60,000 from the USSR.[13] Other exchanges of populations included from Bulgaria to Turkey (numbering 160,000); Poland, Hungary and the Soviet Union. The deportations were decided on language, turning nations more ethnically homogeneous. New arrivals, however, often found little common culture other than language similarities. Transferees often arrived to poor conditions: farmers relocated from Czechoslovakia to Hungary

---

[10] Connor, *Refugees and Expellees*, 40–47, 67.

[11] Connor, *Refugees and Expellees*, 63–64.

[12] Connor, *Refugees and Expellees*, 150–164.

[13] Gatrell, *Unsettling*, 26.

complained of the less fertile soil on their new plots. Yet for others conditions were better. The Finnish government worked to improve the lives of people from Karelia (a former province ceded to the USSR in 1940), who were transferred from Russia, while German expellees who settled in Sweden were able to improve their standard of living over time.[14] The homogenisation of nations led to population transfers and transformed the lives of millions.

The war had forced millions from their homelands and their return became an important concern for governments and aid agencies. All nations required labour to rebuild, especially the USSR and Poland, who had suffered the worst of the wartime displacements. The Allies agreed that those classed as displaced persons would either be returned to their homeland or found new homes, which the United Nations Relief and Rehabilitation Agency (UNRRA) aimed to facilitate. Displaced persons' camps acted as temporary housing. However, the lack of resources and transport slowed the return process. Many were reluctant to return, including a large proportion of the 1.2 million displaced Poles who were fearful of the Red Army and increasing communist influence on their government. The Western Allies returned hundreds of thousands of Soviet citizens to the USSR, where many were executed or imprisoned; the British justified the return to themselves by stating that these people, including women and children, had fought for the Nazis.[15] Repatriation often meant retribution for wartime conduct, whether real or imagined; for many displaced persons home no longer existed. By 1946 the International Refugee Organisation (IRO, the successor to UNRRA) was attempting to find homes for the 'last million' displaced persons. These were a fluctuating group of around 1.2 million. Around ten per cent of them were Jewish survivors of the Final Solution; the rest were anti-communist refugees from Poland, Estonia, Latvia, Lithuania and Ukraine, many of whom had been Wehrmacht fighters, forced labourers and displaced persons from Hungary, Czechoslovakia and Yugoslavia. All now felt that they had nowhere to go.[16]

The displaced persons represented around ten per cent of Europe's postwar refugee population and authorities questioned how to humanely rehouse them. Questions of war crimes, retribution and suitability impacted the process of refuge. The IRO was often suspicious of refugees, as many lacked documentation, leading to many being rejected for resettlement. Others chose to stay with family members who had been rejected. Several governments sent selectors to handpick compliant workers from the displaced persons camps. The British government recruited around 90,000 Eastern European men and women to boost their reconstruction efforts and the French around 80,000.[17] The British designated them European Voluntary Workers (EVW),

---

[14] Gatrell, *Unsettling*, 20–30.

[15] Buruma, *Year Zero*, 148.

[16] Gerard Daniel Cohen, *In War's Wake: Europe's Displaced Persons in the Post-war Order* (Oxford: Oxford University Press, 2022), 5.

[17] Gatrell, *Unsettling*, 71–76.

a term which added an appearance of temporality to the migrants' status. The complexity of providing settlement for stateless people meant that some camps remained active until 1956.

The plight of Jewish people did not end with the Holocaust. Many were initially housed in displaced persons camps. Sometimes their lodgings were near or with other displaced persons who had been part of the Nazi apparatus. The Jewish survivors organised themselves immediately, forming the Central Committee of Liberated Jews, to which the US Army gave official status in October 1946.[18] Some camps became Jewish villages where the culture of the European Jews could be re-established. Yiddish emerged as a popular language; Jewish orchestras and theatre companies began the process of recreating the culture destroyed under the Nazis. Jewish camp residents produced their own newspapers; among other subjects these debated where home was. The camps became the focus of new Jewish ideas around identity.

Those that chose to return to their Eastern European homes often found unfriendly receptions. Yankel Pomerantz returned to Poland and recalls receiving comments from neighbours including 'What, are you still alive?' and 'What are you doing here?'[19] At times the hostility turned to violence. Far-right groups spread anti-Semitic propaganda, often accusing Jews of supporting Bolshevism. In July 1946 at Kielce, 42 Jews were murdered and 50 more wounded by a local Polish mob.[20] This pogrom and other subsequent outrages in places such as in Topol'čany, Czechoslovakia and Kunmadaras, Hungary led to the deaths of around 1,500–2,000 Jews. In response many Jews fled Central Europe to the displaced persons camps, including around 150,000 "infiltrees" who stayed in the displaced persons camps because of the hostile atmosphere in post-war Central Europe.[21] They, along with 63,387 Jews, preferred to remain in temporary sanctuary in displaced persons camps in Germany under the occupation of the American army.[22]

In this 'waiting room' survivors questioned where the Jewish home might be. The USA was attractive, but placed limits on migration of Jews until 1949. Since the end of the nineteenth century Jewish people had bought land and attempted to migrate to Palestine. Support increased for the idea of establishing a Jewish homeland in Palestine.[23] One proponent of this idea, David Ben-Gurion, toured displaced persons camps where he lectured survivors. Zionism became solidified and popularised in these camps, with survivors making plans to migrate to Palestine by whatever means necessary.

---

[18] Lloyd Gartner, *History of the Jews in Modern Times* (Oxford: Oxford University Press, 2001), 380.

[19] Ruth Gay, *Safe Among the Germans: Liberated Jews after World War II* (New Haven: Yale University Press, 2002), 52.

[20] Gay, *Among the Germans*, 53.

[21] Cohen, *In Wars Wake*, 126.

[22] Judt, *Postwar*, 24.

[23] Gay, *Among the Germans*, 59–66.

The British occupiers, however, continued their 1930s policy of limiting Jewish migration to Palestine because they had a 'dual obligation' to Jewish settlers and Arab Palestinians. The British hoped to maintain favour with Arab nationalists so they could uphold their presence in the Middle East. They allowed more Jews to migrate to mainland Britain instead. Zionists organised migration routes to Palestine regardless. Often the British navy forcibly seized vessels interning the migrants in Cyprus or returned them to Germany. From the end of 1945 Zionists used terrorism against the British to attempt to change their policy of blocking Jewish migration. The British had little appetite for a war against the Jewish population of Palestine and left the territory on 14 May 1948. The departure allowed the state of Israel to be formally founded but led to further conflict between the Jews and Arabs. The Arab nations of Jordan, Syria and Egypt invaded immediately. The ensuing war created a wave of emigration from Israel with around 750,000 Palestinian Arabs forced to leave by the war's end in March 1949.[24] The new state of Israel was founded on the migration of the Jewish exiles from Europe, but it led to the displacement of many of the Palestinian Arab population.

The territorial changes of World War Two led to huge population displacement. Stalin used forced migration based on nationality against the newest states of the USSR. The attempt to Russify the Baltic states of Latvia, Lithuania and Estonia and other parts of the USSR continued from the war's end amid fighting from anti-communist rebels. Potentially rebellious peoples who might develop nationalist tendencies were selected, with over 75,000 displaced from Lithuania and Western Ukraine by May 1947.[25] From February 1948 their families were included in these deportations along with those believed to be supporting them. On 22 May 1948 Operation *Vesna* was launched in Vilnius and Kaunas resulting in the deportation of 49,331 people who were sent eastwards to special settlements to work in the timber industry. By early 1949 these numbers increased when Operation *Priboi* led to the round-up of around 95,000 people from the Baltic states who were deemed to be supporters of the guerrilla warfare against the Soviet occupation. By 1953 over 200,000 people had been deported from the Baltic states to be 'internally' exiled and other Soviet peoples were also forcibly moved. Many deportees either died in transit or within a year of arrival. Expellees from the Baltics were replaced by Russian speakers who were sent westwards to ensure the linguistic domination of the internal Soviet Empire. Following deportation, these national groups maintained their identity and language by forming tightly knit communities, organising social events where national customs including dancing and singing were performed by people who had made new national costumes while in exile. Exiles associated together and talked of home, keeping the idea of the

---

[24] Gartner, *History of the Jews*, 344, 389, 395.
[25] Pavel Polian, *Against their Will: The History and Geography of Forced Migrations in the USSR* (Budapest: CEU Press, 2004), 166.

homeland in theirs and their children's heads.[26] Occasionally packages from relatives were received, allowing some connections with their homelands to be maintained.

The special settlements contained several different groupings who were considered suspicious. Those 'repatriated' to the USSR were often accused of collaboration with the Germans, others were suspect because the regime feared that returnees had been exposed to Western ideas. In February 1948 the Supreme Soviet Presidium banished those deemed 'dangerous special state offenders' to remote areas like Kolyma, Siberia or certain areas of Kazakhstan.[27] Many people who had begun to live among the general Soviet population were arrested and internally exiled to areas that required a labour influx. Further expulsions from Moldavia, Georgia, Armenia, Azerbaijan, Ukraine and Russia followed. By 1953 the USSR had around 2.8 million 'special settlers', around 1.2 million of these being Germans who had lived in areas like the Volga before the war. The rules deemed their period of exile to be 'eternal' with no right to return.[28] Some forced settlers began to buy or build new homes. Estonian Arne Valja recalled that in the early 1950s his mother bought a small wooden house that his brother renovated, including building a sauna, thereby expressing the cultural heritage of his homeland. Ella Tursk recalled how the Baltic deportees helped to improve conditions for locals, 'We taught them that the building of a house should begin from the foundation … and that a soil hut was damper and colder than a log house'.[29] Even in the darkest of conditions mixed cultures and societies were formed.

Following Stalin's death in 1953 settlers' civil rights were gradually reinstated and some were able to return to their homelands, although not Volga Germans or Crimean Tartars. The registered numbers of settlers reduced to around 154,000.[30] Settlers had to apply for the right to return. Certain areas remained off limits. Estonians were usually not permitted to live in Tallin, frontier zones or the towns from which they had been deported. Many returnees felt out of place; Adau Tomson moved to Mõisaküla, Estonia (not their original hometown) but found, 'The local atmosphere was not friendly: "Why did you come here?"'[31] The sense of exile continued for many ex-settlers even after the loosening of restrictions.

---

[26] Tomas Balkelis, 'Ethnicity, Identity and Imaginings of Home in the Memoirs of Lithuanian Child Deportees, 1941–53', in *Displaced Children in Russia and Eastern Europe, 1915–53: Ideologies, Identities, Experiences*, edited by Nick Baron (London: Brill, 2017), 267–269.

[27] Polian, *Against their Will*, 165.

[28] Polian, *Against their Will*, 182–3.

[29] Aigi Rahi-Tamm 'Homeless Forever: Home and Homelessness among Deportees from Estonia', *Narratives of Exile and Identity: Soviet Deportation Memoirs from the Baltic States*, ed. Violeta Davoliūtė and Tomas Bakelis, (Budapest: Central European Press, 2018), 65–84, 75.

[30] Polian, *Against their Will*, 186.

[31] Rahi-Tamm 'Homeless Forever', 79.

Involuntary migration also resulted from the decolonisation of European empires. When India became independent of British rule in 1947 the ensuing ethnic cleansing exacerbated religious differences between Muslims, Hindus and Sikhs. It turned into one of the largest involuntary migrations of the twentieth century. Previously there were some tensions between communities, but many remember peaceful relations. Hindu Raj Diswani, who now lives in the UK, recalls 'We used to live like brothers. There was no discrimination'.[32] Gurbaksh Garcha, a Sikh living in the UK, remembered that 'At the Eid they would send sweets to our house, and at Diwali we'd send sweets to theirs... it was a fairly close relationship'. Ultimately the violence was driven by the political quest for power and territory. The British governments of the 1930s implemented a divide and rule strategy to attempt to stifle the Indian National Congress's demand for independence. The British classified groups according to religion and, while giving Indians political concessions and representation at provincial level, they provided quotas for different communities beyond the Hindu elites, who had done most to agitate for independence.[33] This political tactic facilitated the growth of the All-India Muslim League under Muhammad Ali Jinnah who called for a separate Muslim state of Pakistan. Instead of forming alliances, the two religious groups vied for political power. Amidst discussion between Indian politicians and the British occupiers about the future of India, violence between communities escalated. The British agreed to the division of India to prevent a civil war. The borders of the separate states of India and Pakistan were hurriedly drawn up with little consideration of community cohesion.

The decision to divide the provinces of Punjab and Bengal was heralded by the *Times of India* as a great decision that would 'avoid bloodshed',[34] but it ended in catastrophic communal violence. Rioting and raids between the communities, who suddenly found themselves in a foreign country, led many on either side to flee their homes. The movement of Muslims from East Punjab and Sikhs from West Punjab, totalling around ten million refugees, turned into large-scale brutality as monsoon rains drenched expellees while they were attacked by people from either side. Garcha remembers witnessing one such attack, 'It was really horrific... We started seeing trains going really slowly, doors open, bodies hanging out. Some dead. Some dying. Smeared in blood.'[35] The scale of killings is disputed but it may have been as high as two million people.[36] Women became targets for sexual violence and dismemberment. Sawa Sultana, a Muslim fleeing Indian territory, witnessed one such

---

[32] *Partition Voices*, Ep. 1 'Division', broadcast 6 Aug 2017, BBC Radio 4.

[33] Joya Chatterjee, *The Spoils of Partition: Bengal and India 1947–1967* (Cambridge: Cambridge University Press, 2007), 11.

[34] Yasmin Khan, *The Great Partition: The Making of India and Pakistan* (London: Yale University Press, 2017), 5.

[35] *Partition Voices*, Ep. 2 'Aftermath', Broadcast 7 Aug 2017, BBC Radio 4.

[36] Ian Talbot and Gurharpal Singh, *The Partition of India* (Cambridge: CUP, 2009), 2.

atrocity, 'I saw it myself from the bus. They stripped them naked and then they also cut them up with their knives ... and beheaded the corpses ... Our bus somehow managed to drive past'.[37] This ethnic cleansing caused as many as fifteen million people to flee their homes and move to one or other of the new states. The divisive effects of this encounter led to more homogenised communities, divided along religious lines, and tensions between the two nation states. But it also acted to aggravate people of other communities who felt that they were part of neither Pakistan nor India and that their identities were side-lined.

The partition led to a prolonged period of involuntary migration of people from all communities in Indian and Pakistani territory which lasted well into the 1950s. Likewise the division of Bengal meant that around four million Muslims were in West Bengal and eleven million Hindus were in East Bengal (modern-day Bangladesh). While the migration was less sudden (and less violent) than that of Punjab, the movement of people began almost immediately and continued well into the 1960s, by which time the West Bengali authorities had stopped aiding new arrivals.[38] Many of the refugees took several years to find permanent residence, reducing them to living itinerantly. Some remained in refugee camps for many years and the route out of poverty was difficult, despite the West Bengali government providing some loans to build homes and purchase agricultural equipment. The government of India labelled subsequent waves as 'economic migrants' and effectively cut short the support that refugees could receive. In response refugees formed squatter colonies, often trespassing on land in order to cultivate it and survive. The immediate post-war period saw migration as one of the key concerns: it led to nation creation and expansion but also turmoil and catastrophe with forced human movement on a hitherto unprecedented scale.

MIGRATION INTO AND AROUND EUROPE DURING THE 'ECONOMIC MIRACLE'

Once the shock of the war had receded migration became integral to European reconstruction efforts and economic growth through the 1950s and 1960s. The governments of Britain, Germany, Switzerland, Belgium and France especially saw a need to replace lost manpower and encourage migration, usually of other Europeans, to help reconstruct their economies. In 1951 the first steps towards European integration were taken with the inception of the European Coal and Steel Community. The members, France, Italy, Belgium, Germany, Luxembourg and the Netherlands, wrote regular labour exchanges into the founding Treaty of Paris. The economic recovery and subsequent boom increased demand for labour all over Northern Europe. Almost immediately movement of peoples between the six nations increased. The post-war

---

[37] *Partition Voices*, Ep. 2 'Aftermath', Broadcast 7 Aug 2017, BBC Radio 4.
[38] Talbot and Singh, *Partition*, 101.

Italian government, anomalously for a European state, promoted emigration due to its high rate of unemployment and risk of radicalisation.[39] Contingents of Italian workers moved to Belgium in special convoys to work in its mines.[40] The closer co-operation embedded in the European Economic Community with the Treaty of Rome in 1957 allowed freedom of movement for certain categories of workers between member states, which would begin after a transition period to 1970. The more liberal migration policy set the framework for the later development of the European Union.

The Federal Republic of Germany (FRG) admitted over fourteen million guest workers between the end of World War Two and the fall of the Berlin Wall.[41] A series of treaties with Italy, Spain, Greece, Turkey, Portugal, Yugoslavia, Morocco and Tunisia provided a steady supply of labour throughout the 1960s and 1970s. Their guest status implied that they would not be permanent migrants. Around eleven million guest workers eventually returned to their country of origin. They helped Germany to build its leading position in the European economy. Initially the aim was to plug agricultural gaps with Italian workers, who arrived to poor living conditions with many housed in barracks with a curfew. From 1961 Turkish workers, including Kurds and Albanians, travelled to Germany on cramped and insanitary trains in conditions that journalists compared to cattle carts. The guest workers were usually well-educated individuals saving Germany their training costs. The immigrants' willingness to undertake menial work kept wage growth sustainable and allowed Germans to move into more skilled employment.

The Turkish government expected workers to send money home. Certainly Turkey's foreign remittances were helped, with over 273 million dollars paid into Turkish bank accounts from Germany in 1970 alone.[42] These sums soon made up around 90 per cent of Turkey's export earnings.[43] Many of these workers saw themselves as improving Turkey's and their family's well-being by working outside the homeland and sending money and consumer goods home. Throughout the period, however, discrimination against Turkish workers abounded, and the cramped and often insanitary conditions in which they lived helped to reinforce a myth of them being unclean. Scholars investigating the German reception of Turkish migrants suggest that they and their children born in Germany have remained rejected by parts of the German community on account of their Muslim religion. This prejudice during the 1970s, 1980s and 1990s, especially among landlords, led to ghettoisation of

---

[39] Gatrell, *Unsettling*, 78–9.
[40] Judt, *Postwar*, 333.
[41] Saskia Sassen, *Guests and Aliens* (New York: Norton, 1993), 99.
[42] Gatrell, *Unsettling*, 155.
[43] Judt, *Postwar*, 334.

Turks and their families in terms of housing, but communities still mixed and maintained contacts.[44]

Germany was also a Cold War migration hotspot. The West German state claimed to be the legal representative of all Germans and encouraged migration from the communist German Democratic Republic (GDR). While the border became increasingly hard to cross during the 1950s, the East German state suffered from depopulation amidst an ongoing economic crisis caused by its decision to 'build the foundations of socialism' from 1952. Tightening border restrictions in 1954 and 1957 did little to stem the flow. The piecemeal approach appeared to encourage those who were in two minds to move.[45] Over 3 million made this journey throughout the 1950s, with many leaving their families behind. Further spikes in emigration followed other policy announcements such as in 1960 when the state announced the collectivisation of agriculture, which adversely impacted the food supply. Demographics did not work in the GDR's favour: of around 550,000 refugees from 1959 to 1961 just under half were under the age of 25.[46] After much discussion between the East German leader Walter Ulbricht and the Soviet leadership it was decided that the border between East and West would be permanently closed, cutting off not only migration to the West but also casual encounters between Germans from the two states and often breaking family ties. The building of the Berlin Wall from 13 August 1961 symbolised the division between East and West; the physical barrier to prevent emigration remained in place for 28 years.

Many European nations received migrants from their former colonies which had begun to win their freedom. Elites and colonial administrators, including many descendants of those who had moved to the empire, were repatriated to their 'homeland'. Furthermore, locals who had collaborated and enabled the empires to function now found themselves unwelcome. Others were offered the opportunity to travel, often to fill labour gaps and through imperial citizenship laws. Indians, West Africans and Caribbeans migrated to the UK, while Algerians and other North Africans to France. The Netherlands experienced Indonesian migration from the Moluccans who had collaborated with the Dutch. The latter brought their politics with them and throughout the 1960s and 1970s agitated from afar for independence of the Moluccan islands. From 1951 Surinamese migrants were admitted to the Netherlands under citizenship laws and their numbers multiplied with those fleeing the dictatorship from 1975 and subsequent civil war during the 1980s. Their numbers totalled over 200,000 by the early 1990s, around a third of the South American nation's overall population. The European empires, and the attempts of governments

---

[44] Faruk Şen, 'The Historical Situation of Turkish Migrants in Germany', *Immigrants & Minorities*, 22.2–3 (2003), 208–227, 214–219.

[45] Manfred Wilke, *The Path to the Berlin Wall: Critical Stages in the History of Divided Germany* (Berlin: Berghahn, 2014), 48.

[46] Wilke, *Berlin Wall*, 189.

to maintain them while colonies won their freedoms, caused migration from periphery to metropole.

The post-war flow of non-white migration to Britain began in a fit of absence of mind. The apparently permissive approach was part of the justification for the continuation of empire. British governments favoured 'white' European labour to fill the worker shortage. In 1949 a Royal Commission reported that 140,000 immigrants per year were needed to make up the shortfall.[47] Irish workers who shared a common language and European displaced persons were initially welcomed as guest workers. The 1948 British Nationality Act attempted to ensure that all 600,000,000 subjects of the British Empire enjoyed equal rights of citizenship regardless of where they were born. On 22 June 1948 the *Empire Windrush*, a converted troopship, docked at Tilbury Docks. On board were 500 mainly young men from the Caribbean and around 100 Polish displaced persons. The media initially responded positively. *Pathé* newsreel showed Aldwyn Roberts, known as Lord Kitchener, singing a calypso,[48] while the *London Evening Standard*'s headline read 'Welcome Home'.[49] This response suggests that the idea of equivalence of citizenship was accepted before immigration numbers grew; although it may also have been because around half had served in the UK forces or worked in munitions factories during the war. During this early post-war period there were few restrictions on immigration from the Empire and Commonwealth into the UK.

By 1953 around 3,000 Caribbean migrants were arriving in the UK annually; these were dwarfed by the 40,000 from Ireland every year throughout the 1950s.[50] The devastating effects of Hurricane Charlie in 1951 and the limitation of Caribbean migration to the USA under the McCarran-Walter Act (1952) spurred Caribbean migrants towards Britain. The numbers peaked in 1961 at 66,000, following news of the forthcoming tightening of migration laws. But during the 1950s and 1960s immigration did not generally keep up with emigration and the only years until the 1990s when Britain was not a net exporter of people were 1958–62.[51] At the peak of Britain's post-war immigration in 1961 a quarter of the foreign-born labour force were Italian,[52] and the numbers of Irish living in Britain increased from around 500,000 in

---

[47] 'Report of the Royal Commission on Population', 1949 cited in Dominic Sandbrook, *Having it So Good: A History of Britain from the Suez to the Beatles* (London: Abacus, 2005), 313.

[48] 'Pathé Reporter Meets' (1948), Pathé News, https://www.youtube.com/watch?v=QDH4IBeZF-M, Accessed 22 Aug 2022.

[49] Quoted in David Olusoga, *Black and British: A Forgotten History* (London: Pan Macmillan, 2016), 489.

[50] Clair Wills, *Lovers and Strangers: An Immigrant History of Post-War Britain* (London: Penguin, 2017), xii.

[51] Sandbrook, *Having it So Good*, 308.

[52] Gatrell, *Unsettling*, 161.

1951 to around one million by 1971. The European migrants had been somewhat invisible, and in the case of the Irish, more easily assimilated because of the common language, although many of these still experienced discrimination. One area where Britain required a ready-made workforce was its newly socialised National Health Service. In 1963 the Conservative Minister for Health, Enoch Powell, launched a campaign for medically trained Commonwealth citizens. This migration saved Britain's training costs and deprived the sending country of doctors that they had paid to educate. Other large-scale campaigns for Commonwealth migrants were rarer.[53]

Britain's migrant policy was Janus-faced. A Chinese community had lived in Liverpool since 1834, one of Europe's oldest, with a Chinatown formed close to the waterfront district. In the interwar years this community, mainly of seafarers, numbered in the hundreds and many started families with local women. During World War Two the Chinese community of Liverpool boomed to around 20,000 as seafarers answered the call to work in the merchant navy.[54] After the war and into 1947 these men were subject to forced repatriation with police officers hunting Chinese sailors and strong-arming them onto ships. With China embroiled in a civil war these repatriations endangered a great number of lives. Their wives and children were left in limbo, never knowing what had happened to their husbands and fathers. The Home Office denied all involvement in the secret deportations until 2022, despite the emergence of memos to Liverpool City Police and immigration officers that referred to 'roundups'.[55] Elsewhere parliamentarians and press opposed early post-war migration; often they cited the burden on the new welfare state, despite migrants largely being young, healthy and in many cases those who enabled the National Health Service to function.[56]

Many British politicians expressed anxieties about migration. Harold Macmillan recorded in his diary a 1955 conversation with the Prime Minister Winston Churchill, 'More discussion about West Indian migrants. A bill is being drafted—but it is not an easy problem. PM thinks "Keep England White" a good slogan.'[57] While this slogan was eventually discarded, Oswald Mosely's Union Movement (the successor to the British Union of Fascists) campaigned using 'Keep Britain White' in 1959. Such expressions of racism

---

[53] Randall Hansen, *Citizenship and Immigration in Post-war Britain: The Institutional Origins of a Multicultural Nation* (Oxford: Oxford University Press, 2000), 8.

[54] Gregor Benton and Edmund Terrance Gomez, *The Chinese in Britain, 1800-Present: Economy, Transnationalism, Identity* (Basingstoke: Palgrave, 2008), 29.

[55] Dan Hancox 'Chinese Seafairers were coerced into leaving UK after war, Home Office admits', *Guardian*, 2 Aug 2022. https://www.theguardian.com/world/2022/aug/02/chinese-seafarers-were-coerced-into-leaving-uk-after-war-home-office-admits?CMP=share_btn_fb&fbclid=IwAR0trI2t1-V1Mz6cRRucfuXjFLKHIBfp8gTC3_-O9pkkIwkR6Mo6kIKA--8. Accessed 4 January 2023.

[56] Gatrell, *Unsettling*, 166.

[57] *Diary of Harold Macmillan*, 20 Jan 1955, cited by David Kynaston, *Family Britain 1951–57* (London: Bloomsbury, 2009), 455.

from politicians and policy that turned immigration into a racialised issue has led a number of scholars to conclude that discrimination in Britain was primarily directed by politicians who instigated a campaign via the press that made skin colour central to immigration policy.[58]

Broader public opinion about immigration was mixed. In 1955 in response to the Gallup opinion poll question 'Do you think it is right or wrong for people to refuse to work with coloured men and women?', 79 per cent answered in the negative. However, a *Daily Sketch* poll in January found that 81 per cent favoured stopping 'all West Indian Migration'.[59] Often the prejudice was less well expressed: it came in the form of refusal of housing or lack of friendliness in the workplace. It is this contested attitude that historian Randall Hansen argues showed that anti-migrant feeling predominated among the public, with politicians generally following their electorates' attitudes.[60] Yet perhaps it was less clear. In 1959 sociologist Michael Blanton found that at least two-thirds of the British population did not openly express racist views and that often individuals were drawn to discriminate to maintain face with other white people, although this does not excuse discriminatory behaviour. According to Blanton, 71 per cent believed that Commonwealth citizens should be given preference over those from European nations.[61] It is fair to say that discrimination against migrants and the longer-standing black population was not something that the majority of the population indulged in but that the actions of those, including many politicians, who held those views created a negative experience for many migrants to Britain.

Opposition to Commonwealth migrants sometimes became violent. In 1949, 1,000 white people besieged a hotel in Deptford Broadway and in 1950 two houses in Camden were set alight as locals tried to force out the West Indian immigrants. Immigrants were often forced to take cheap housing that was dilapidated and overcrowded in areas like London's Notting Hill. These homes had previously been occupied by white working-class people. But as general prosperity rose throughout the 1950s, more moved away in a process termed 'white flight'. Those who remained, either through choice or poverty, tended to blame the decay of the area on immigration. In 1958 these simmering tensions boiled over causing the Notting Hill riots, where white people, often from outside the area, attacked and intimidated black people, causing them to mobilise and fight back. The press roundly condemned the violence but sometimes presented immigration as a problem; *Pathé* stated that

---

[58] Cf. Kathleen Paul, *Whitewashing Britain: Race and Citizenship in the Postwar Era* (Ithica, NY: Cornell University Press, 1997; Kehinde Andrews, *The New Age of Empire: How Racism and Colonialism Still Rule the World* (London: Penguin, 2021).

[59] Cited in Kynaston, *Family Britain*, 456–7.

[60] Hansen, *Citizenship and Immigration*, 10–15.

[61] Michael Blanton, *White and Coloured: The Behaviour of British People towards Coloured Migrants* (New Jersey: Rutgers University Press, 1959) 17: Olusoga., *Black and British*, 503–4.

'opinions differ on how to solve Britain's racial problems'.[62] This type of coverage maintained that there was a legitimate complaint against immigrants.

Violence and prejudice could have led to a sense of embattlement among migrant communities but some used it to produce positive outcomes. Claudia Jones, a Trinidadian communist, campaigned for black peoples' right to be visible in British public space. Following the riots in Notting Hill and the 1959 murder of Kelso Cochrane, an Antiguan migrant, she founded the annual Notting Hill Carnival, which celebrates the Caribbean community and its contribution to the UK. A hybrid culture later emerged in Notting Hill, with many white people eventually being drawn to the area by its cosmopolitan reputation.

This generation of migrants contributed economically and culturally to their new homes. Immigrants worked throughout Britain's industries including the National Health Service. Many created their own culture and networks. Black writers like Sam Selvon produced literary classics, which explored new migrant identities. *The Lonely Londoners* follows a group of Caribbean and African migrants who struggle to adapt to life in London while facing a mixture of support and hostility but form new friendship groups and communities.[63] Partly written in a Jamaican patois it shows how this new adaptation was fusing aspects of Caribbean life with their new surroundings and producing a hybrid culture. Elsewhere, Stuart Hall migrated from Jamaica in the 1950s. His role in the Centre for Contemporary Cultural Studies at the University of Birmingham, of which he was director from 1968, allowed him to examine how issues of race affected representation. His work criticised how the media reinforced negative stereotypes about black people and how the justice system criminalised this group.[64] Hall was one of the black migrant Britons who became part of the educational establishment and shaped the ideas of many academics while forcing Britain to think critically about how it perceived and responded to issues of race and criminality.

Patrick Weight argues that during this period black migrants' dual identities were eroded, with a distinct Caribbean-British identity emerging that was influenced by the Caribbean and Black American cultures.[65] But American and Caribbean influences facilitated the creation of hybrid cultures. Musical styles like reggae and ska became popular in Britain in the 1960s and 1970s and their influence continued into the twenty-first century. Literary influences have also been strong, Candice Carty-Williams' 2019 novel *Queenie*, about a British-Jamaican woman's experiences in London, could be seen as a modern-day successor of authors like Sam Selvon. Veronica Ryan's sculptures dedicated

---

[62] 'Shameful Episode', *Pathé*, 4 Aug 1958.

[63] Samuel Selvon, *The Lonely Londoners*, (London: Longman's, 1956).

[64] Paul Gilroy (ed.), *Without Guarantees: In Honour of Stuart Hall* (London: Verso, 2000).

[65] Richard Weight, *Patriots: National Identity in Britain 1940–2000* (London: Macmillan, 2002), 293.

to the Windrush Generation winning of the Turner Prize in 2022 cemented Britain's Caribbean heritage as part of mainstream British culture.

While some Commonwealth and European migrants arrived in Britain the nation experienced a period of emigration, many going to 'old Commonwealth' nations like Australia, New Zealand and Canada. In 1950, Australian immigration minister Harold Holt introduced an Assisted Passage scheme. For adults the journey would cost £10 while accompanying children travelled free. At a time of post-war austerity the chance to make a new life appealed to many Britons. The increasing prosperity and rise of consumerism in the late 1950s and 1960s did not dim the appeal of Australia. Over one and a half million Britons departed for Australia between the end of World War Two and 1975, with these migrants becoming known as 'Ten Pound Poms'.[66] Australian governments preferred Britons as the type of immigrant who would fit into its predominantly white, English-speaking way of life. They prioritised this more easily assimilated form of immigration until 1975. The guidance became known as the 'White Australia' policy. In the post-war period this involved tasking immigration officers with deciding who was white enough to enter Australia, rather than formally stating that entry was limited to white people.[67] However, the numbers were never quite high enough and Australia later sought migrants from non-English speaking countries of Central, Western and Southern Europe. These migrants along with later flows from Asia changed the ethnic make-up of Australians and facilitated the development of hybrid cultures in ways that the British emigrants rarely did.

Migrants from Britain's Commonwealth had moved to Britain as citizens. When they arrived the British state, as Robert Gildea argues, reimposed colonial hierarchies and racial segregation.[68] Often this meant the introduction of informal 'colour bars' in many industries to protect the jobs of white people and the ghettoisation of former imperial subjects. Migrants felt the need to fight against discriminatory laws or regulations. In April 1963 black rights campaigners Paul Stephenson and Roy Hackett organised a boycott of Bristol's bus network because black workers were barred from working as conductors. The boycott ran until August when a negotiated end to the colour bar was reached. This assertion of citizenship was part of migrants finding a voice and demonstrating against their treatment as second-class citizens. Public pressure campaigns such as the Bristol boycott eventually made politicians realise the need to ban discrimination based on skin colour.

The Labour government of the late 1960s introduced laws that integrated immigrants into British society, giving them formal rights, but also limited

---

[66] A. James Hammerton & Alistair Thomson, *Ten Pound Poms: Australia's Invisible Migrants* (Manchester: MUP, 2005), 9.

[67] James Jupp, *From White Australia to Woomera: The Story of Australian Immigration* (Cambridge: Cambridge University Press, 2002), 9.

[68] Robert Gildea, *Empires of the Mind: The Colonial Past and the Politics of the Present* (Cambridge: Cambridge University Press, 2019), 4.

future Commonwealth migration. The 1965 Race Relations Act banned open discrimination in public places and in written publications. A 1968 amendment outlawed the denial of housing, employment or public services on grounds of colour. The Labour Party, however, also introduced the Commonwealth Migrants Act, 1968. The act followed the migration to the UK of 20,000 Asians who had been removed from employment in Kenya under Jono Kenyatta's 'Africanisation' policy. From now on British Commonwealth passport holders would need a pre-existing 'qualifying connection' to the UK, effectively limiting migration to those born in the UK or children seeking family reunion.[69] It was designed specifically to halt non-white people from fleeing to Britain under similar tumults. While politicians sought to limit non-white migration, their efforts to make Britain fairer for those who had already arrived soon met with opposition.

On 20 April 1968 Enoch Powell, Conservative MP for Wolverhampton, made a speech to Birmingham Conservatives. He claimed that the Race Relations Act would prevent people in his constituency from letting out rooms, forcing them into poverty. He said one lady had suffered dog dirt forced through her windows as she was the only white person in the area. At the end of the speech he said, 'As I look ahead I am filled with foreboding, like the Roman I seem to see "the River Tiber foaming with much blood"'.[70] Powell's speech was deemed shocking and he was sacked as Shadow Defence Secretary by the Conservative leader Edward Heath. He gained some popular support, however, with marches and thousands of supportive letters sent to him.[71] While Powell was put in the political wilderness, Conservative immigration policy in the 1970s was notably stricter.[72] For Camila Schofield, Powell's speech marked a moment where racism in Britain became less influenced by ideas of pseudo-scientific racism and focussed on preserving a culture that was perceived to be under threat. This new form of racism challenged the ideas of cosmopolitanism and many parts of society remained hostile to immigration. Powell staked out new ground in the politicisation of racism in Britain and became a rallying figure for those that opposed immigration well into the twenty-first century.

Black people had to fight for equal rights and for better treatment; they often came up against an institutionally racist legal and civil system. The British state perceived political activism by black people as criminality. In Notting Hill a restaurant called The Mangrove became an important part of the British-Caribbean community, offering advice to immigrants. It attracted intellectuals and radical activists like C. L. R. James and Angela Davis; musicians including Jimi Hendrix, Nina Simone and Marvin Gaye; celebrities like

[69] Hansen, *Citizenship and Immigration*, 153–6.

[70] Enoch Powell, 'The Birmingham Speech', 20 April 1968.

[71] Camilla Schofield, *Enoch Powell and the Making of Postcolonial Britain* (Cambridge: Cambridge University Press, 2013), 209.

[72] Hansen, *Citizenship and Immigration*, 182.

Vanessa Redgrave; and the staff of the satirical counter-cultural *Oz* magazine, whose content had led its editors to be prosecuted for obscenity. The restaurant boasted a mixture of black working class, black intellectuals and radical whites becoming the genus of a hybrid community.[73] The police targeted The Mangrove with a series of raids over 1969 and 1970 each time claiming to be searching for drugs, but finding none. In response, activist Darcus Howe began a campaign against police oppression of the black community.

On 9 August 1970 Howe organised a demonstration against the police's actions. Some protesters wore berets, dark glasses and leather jackets, a style borrowed from the American Black Panther movement. The march became marred by violence as the large numbers of police attempted to disperse the crowd.[74] Nineteen activists including Howe were arrested and nine were charged with riot and incitement to riot. Their ensuing trial lasted 55 days and pitted the activists against a state which viewed black activism as criminal. Howe and the defendants dismissed their appointed legal counsel and defended themselves. By doing so they were able to show the paucity of the case against them and to get the state to admit that the police were racially prejudiced against the activists. The British state often acted to prevent the integration of former colonial immigrants, causing them to have to fight the system for acceptance.

France also required an influx of labour to aid reconstruction and growth. Initially the majority of its immigrants came from Italy, Poland, Spain and Belgium. France also drew immigrants from its African colonies, mainly Algeria, from where there were 240,000 incomers by 1954.[75] Others came from Senegal, Guinea and the former French Indo-China. This labour power helped to boost the French economy through the three decades of economic growth, to around 1975, that acquired the mythological status of *Les Trente Glorieuses*. Migration was often temporary with workers following a long tradition of spending a few months or years in France before returning home or moving elsewhere. During this time France's population became increasingly urban with the manufacturing and service sectors steadily growing; migrant workers fuelled these sectors or worked in more unskilled posts allowing the French to upskill. In return, post-colonial France asked that migrants assimilate and adopt its principle of secularism in civic life.

Colonial divisions continued following the French withdrawal from Algeria in 1962, after eight years of warfare. Around one million *pieds-noirs*, the European settler population; over 140,000 African auxiliary troops, who fought with the French against Algerian independence; and other collaborators, the so-called Harkis, fled to France. The latter were herded into internment camps. But these population transfers threatened to recreate the Algerian situation in

---

[73] Robin Bunce and Paul Field, *Darcus Howe: A Political Biography* (London: Bloomsbury, 2014), 98.

[74] Bunce and Field, *Darcus Howe*, 109–110.

[75] Gildea, *Empires of the Mind*, p. 129.

mainland France. Algerian migrants sometimes faced hostility from local populations and many felt unable to express their political opinion. They tended to live in ghettos formed in poor suburbs on the outskirts of cities. By 1969 over 600,000 Algerians lived in depopulated French villages, housing blocks or slum suburbs which included temporary huts and became known as the *bidonvilles*. Some of the inhabitants of the *bidonvilles* became Arab activists and, by the end of the 1960s, were agitating for the Palestinian cause in the escalating Arab–Israeli conflict. These slums, and their inhabitants, were undesirable to many French municipalities who began to flatten the *bidonvilles* in the late 1960s to make way for more affluent residents. Newly homeless migrants responded by occupying empty houses, with squatting movements springing up in Paris, Dijon and Strasbourg.

Some European nations experienced population decline. Italy's workforce dropped by seven million between 1945 and 1970.[76] Greece's labour force declined by around 25 per cent in the same period leading to labour shortages. Ireland, Spain, Portugal and Yugoslavia all saw depopulation as labour moved to other European nations. Spain, Greece, Poland, Czechoslovakia and Hungary experienced more emigration in mid-century but by the end of the century became net receivers of immigrants, often from outside Europe. Throughout the post-war period migration levels were determined by economic conditions. During the early 1970s, economies slowed or fell into recession, which reduced the need for industrial labour, leading many Western European nations to restrict immigration.[77] Many immigrants who settled began to assimilate into communities or formed new expatriate organisations. Often these networks helped to maintain aspects of their home culture and helped other immigrants to obtain goods from their home nation.

The communist nations also required labour to continue their post-war reconstruction and economic growth; the experience of forced migrants was not the whole story. Initially migration inside Soviet nations was strictly controlled but industrial cities required an influx of labour. Worker shortages were eased with labour from German prisoners of war, the last of whom were repatriated in 1955. After the death of Stalin in 1953 workers were able to move within the nation after giving notice. Others moved without the official permissions.[78] Many were attracted from the Caucasus and Central Asian republics to Moscow and Leningrad by the availability of consumer goods, study, better pay and the modernity of these cities. Migrants including Bolat Oruzbaev were optimistic about their opportunities. Moving from Kara-Suu in Kyrgyzstan to study in Leningrad he felt that advancement was open: 'all you needed was to have a will and use your head'.[79] For Jeff Sahadeo these

---

[76] Judt, *Postwar*, 334.

[77] Sassen, *Guests and Aliens*, 102.

[78] Gatrell, *Unsettling*, 90.

[79] Quoted in Jeff Sahadeo, *Voices from the Edge: Southern Migrants in Leningrad and Moscow* (Ithaca: Cornell University Press, 2019), 74.

metropoles became global cities as they became multi-ethnic, similar to many Western cities. Some newcomers recalled a welcoming atmosphere and kindness from locals.[80] Others experienced racism, often in the form of staring or the use of racist phrases. The arrival of Muslims from Central Asia conflicted with the state's official atheist status. In Moscow worshippers gathered at the city's single mosque for Friday prayers and Leningrad's mosque was reopened in 1955 in response to migrant demand.[81] Custom and tradition changed with these incomers and they often found ways to make this compatible with urban Soviet life. This partial mobility continued for the rest of the Union's existence but increased with Mikhail Gorbachev's liberalising reforms in the 1980s.

Incentives such as higher wages, better housing and consumer goods were offered to entice workers to newly industrial areas that were sparsely populated. These enticements continued after the post-1953 piecemeal release of many *gulag* prisoners. The return of forced settlers increased the pool of available industrial labour in the cities but left remote regions in something of a worker crisis. Many people used migration, often within a collection of states such as the USSR, as an opportunity to gain education and move up the structured society that the communists had retained. Peasants who moved to cities and factory sites in other communist nations, like Bulgaria and Romania, could become upwardly mobile. Others took advantage of opportunities in Siberia and the Central Asian republics as economic development took place at a great pace throughout the first few post-war decades.

The most famous mass movement of Soviet labour was the Virgin Lands Campaign instigated by Nikita Khrushchev in 1954. Hundreds of thousands of Soviet citizens, members of the party's youth wing, former soldiers, seasonal workers or former wartime deportees, joined official schemes to move to Central Asia, the Urals and Western Siberia to bring the land into agricultural use. The first arrivals had to build huts and barracks. But development soon led to the creation of communities and amenities. Siegelbaum and Moch see Soviet resettlement, forced or otherwise, as part of a colonial project to mobilise populations to make use of underpopulated areas.[82] The sheer number of migrants, who were expecting a deserted land, sometimes caused conflict and violence with existing inhabitants. Several riots broke out between groups of settlers and collective farmers.[83] However, this violence dissipated after the first few years. While 1956 delivered a bumper crop, other years did not fare so well. Following the end of the mass campaign in 1956 workers

[80] Sahadeo, *Voices*, 79.

[81] Sahadeo, *Voices*, 24.

[82] Lewis Siegelbaum and Leslie Page Moch, *Broad is My Native Land: Repertoires and Regimes of Migration in Russia's Twentieth Century* (Ithaca: Cornell University Press, 2014), 62.

[83] Michael Pohl, 'The "Planet of One Hundred Languages": Ethnic Relations and Soviet Identity in the Virgin Lands', in *Peopling the Russian Periphery: Borderland Colonization in Eurasian History* edited by Nicholas Breyfogle, Abby Schrader and Willard Sunderland (Abingdon: Routledge, 2007), 246.

continued to arrive in Kazakhstan into the mid-1960s, but these were more likely to become permanent residents. One estimate suggests between one and two million migrated from Western USSR to Kazakhstan because of the campaign, including Russians, Balts, Chechens, Germans and Ingush people.[84]

The second half of the twentieth century saw regular refugee flows, sometimes across the Iron Curtain, caused by conflict. When the Czechoslovakian Communist Party took over the government in February 1948 some Czechoslovakians attempted to flee the regime and evade a new ban on emigration. In September 1951 a group of Czechs hijacked a train to take them from Czechoslovakia to the American-occupied sector of Germany. Around twenty conspirators planned the hijacking and the main plotters, the train driver František Kovalinka and three others, acquired guns.[85] They rerouted the train to an abandoned line that linked to Germany. They were hailed as lovers of freedom by the Western media. Out of the other 90 passengers only seven took up the offer of asylum in Germany with the rest returning to Czechoslovakia.[86] Throughout the Cold War stories of escapes from the Eastern Bloc led to dramatic headlines in the West and the welcoming of refugees fleeing communism.

Cold War flashpoints often led to mass migrations. In October 1956 Hungarians protested against their hard-line communist government, leading to an armed uprising. The protesters demanded the return of the reform-minded communist Prime Minister Imre Nagy. He asked the Soviets to withdraw their troops from Hungary, which they appeared to do. When Nagy announced that Hungary was to leave the Warsaw Pact the Soviet government invaded. The suppression of the uprising led to over 200,000 people fleeing, mainly via neighbouring Austria. Those that stayed in Austria were initially welcomed, but once they became active in the economy some Austrians turned against them.[87] Other nations offered refuge to Hungarians, notably the USA, Australia, Canada, the Netherlands and Great Britain. When Hungarians did move to other nations they sometimes became disillusioned with their new surroundings. A group who became students in Britain reported issues with isolation and their inability to speak the language. Others found the food problematic, especially unfamiliar dishes like smoked kippers and overcooked cabbage. Nevertheless, many were able to assimilate and play a full part in British life. One refugee, Laszlo Antal, represented Britain in shooting events including at the Olympics.[88] The USA eventually accepted around 115,000

---

[84] Pohl, 'The "Planet of One Hundred Languages"', 238.

[85] Timothy Phillips, *The Curtain and the Wall: A Modern Journey Along Europe's Cold War Border* (London: Granta, 2022), 241–246.

[86] Tara Zahra, *The Great Departure: Mass Migration from Eastern Europe and the Making of the Modern World* (London: Norton, 2016), 216–218.

[87] Gatrell, *Unsettling*, 66.

[88] Magda Czigany, *"Just Like Other Students": Reception of the 1956 Hungarian Refugee Students in Britain* (Newcastle: Cambridge Scholars Publishing, 2009), 178.

Hungarians with many aided by the Rockefeller Foundation to study in American universities. Other Hungarians used their fame to escape, such as the 46 Olympians who defected to Australia at the 1956 Melbourne Olympics or the footballer Ferenc Puskas, who sought refuge in Franco's authoritarian Spain, where he became one of the world's best-known players of the game. Migration became one of the key crises of the Central European communist states. In Eastern Europe migration tended to be limited to within their nations' borders, or sometimes between the communist nations. Many of those who migrated away from communism, whether under crisis conditions or otherwise, went to Western European nations, others followed a long legacy of Eastern European migration and sought a new life in America.

THE USA AND POST-WAR MIGRATION

Immigration is central to the USA's foundation myth. Generations retell the story of their immigrant ancestors sailing past the Statue of Liberty to dock at Ellis Island, where they were processed by immigration officials before building a better life through hard work. They became the Americans who built the USA. Modern American success has been the story of immigration: the founders of Google, eBay, Intel and Yahoo were all migrants to the USA.[89] The story feeds on the presentation of the USA as a welcoming country that allows hard-working people to succeed and become wealthy, known as the American Dream. This myth, however, focusses on white European immigrants. As David Gerber points out, much less retold is the experience of Chinese and other Asian immigrants docking at Angel Island, San Francisco, where treatment was often cruel and the rejection rate over 25 per cent compared to around one per cent for Europeans.[90] Chinese immigration was essentially illegal from 1882 and only gradually opened after World War Two. American history is one of race division, forced migration and slavery whose legacy impacted migration in the twentieth century.

While the popular Ellis Island myth tells only a fraction of America's migration story, it is a vital part of our understanding of population movements to America, which experienced over 30 million immigrants in the century between 1820 and 1920. These migrants helped to turn America from a rural into an industrial nation. Yet, even during this time, public conversations around migration raised suspicions of immigrants. In the nineteenth century Chinese migrants were regularly portrayed as opium-smoking gamblers who habitually cheated on business deals, while Irish and Italian immigrants were labelled as lazy, poverty-stricken burdens on America who threatened the unity of the nation with their Catholic religion. Immigration was as much a target

---

[89] Darrell West, *Brain Gain: Rethinking U. S. Immigration Policy* (Washington, DC: Brookings Institution Press, 2010), 16–17.

[90] David Gerber, *American Immigration: A Very Short Introduction* (Oxford: OUP, 2011), 10.

for the gutter press as it is today.[91] From the early twentieth century to the 1960s around 74.5 per cent of migrants to America were European. This was because the National Origins Quotas Acts of 1921 and 1924 effectively barred migration from countries in the Eastern hemisphere, with Latin Americans and Asians making up only around 14.4 per cent of immigrants to the USA. The 1930s depression and American isolationism also made the nation less of a draw for migrants.

At the end of World War Two the USA was an attractive destination for migrants. Displaced persons, expellees and refugees were soon followed by those fleeing the turbulence caused by decolonisation and the Cold War. Furthermore, undocumented migrants had worked within the American economy throughout the post-war period; during the 1950s many of these workers regularly crossed from Mexico for seasonal work and then returned to their families. By forming a transnational workforce they began to create a hybrid culture blending Mexican and American influences. Often these irregular migrants worked in low-wage jobs but began to integrate with Spanish-speaking communities, with some enrolling their children into schools and taking jobs outside the traditional agricultural sector of such migrants, including construction, catering or domestic work. Often, however, American media and society threw back the racialised 'wetback' stereotype at Mexicans and implied they were destitute and criminal.[92] At times the American government recognised the need for this labour and gave formal guest worker status, including through the Bracero programme which operated between 1942 and 1965. This scheme permitted the seasonal migration of Mexicans, giving temporary legal status to around 200,000 workers per year. The system operated mainly on industrial-scale farms and, despite reassurances to the contrary, these corporations often also used seasonal irregular labour to lower agricultural wages and working conditions.[93] In 1955 Ricardo Velasquez, a married man with five children, hoped to increase his wages from around 65 cents per day in Mexico to a rumoured 50 cents per hour via Bracero. On arrival at a melon farm in Edinburg, Texas he found the conditions, which included sharing a room with five other men, so uncomfortable that none could sleep. On deployment to the field they were told that wages were only 30 cents per hour. The six men talked it over and decided to walk away from the programme, becoming irregular workers until they were either caught or able to return home. While the scheme aimed to reduce undocumented migration, it often encouraged it due to the way workers were treated or because companies wanted to pay lower wages.[94] Undocumented migrants became

---

[91] West, *Brain Gain*, 3, 69–74.

[92] Mai Ngai, *Impossible Subjects: Illegal Aliens and the Making of Modern American* (Princeton: Princeton University Press, 2004), 149.

[93] Ngai, *Impossible Subjects*, 138.

[94] Ngai, *Impossible Subjects*, 163.

a mainstay of the American economy, with many companies exploiting their labour to help depress wages.

During the Cold War the American Chinese community, who had been granted some legal status and rights during World War Two, was subject to investigation. The hunt for communist sympathisers in American society, led by Senator Joseph McCarthy, created a climate of suspicion. In 1955 fears of a Chinese 'fifth column' were exacerbated when the American consul general in Hong Kong, Everett F. Drumright, claimed to have uncovered a communist conspiracy to use the American Chinese community as spies. They were accused of blackmail or giving benefits to family members of migrants in China and the threat of withholding these.[95] The report essentially aimed to bar Chinese immigration to America and repeated racialised rhetoric about the Chinese as fraudsters. As Mae Ngai reveals, however, State Department officials were uneasy with the report because they did not want to alienate Chinese nationalists in Taipei or the British authorities in Hong Kong. This suspicion was repeated in the United States, where in February 1956 immigration officials in San Francisco and New York raided Chinese communities to find irregular migrants and to impel official citizens to prove the legitimacy of their citizenship. The Cold War and the paranoid atmosphere in America led to discrimination against the American Chinese community.

By the late 1950s the American limitation of official migration to white people was increasingly dubious. The failure to protect Europe's Jews before World War Two led to new moral thinking, as groups like the Anti-Defamation League challenged America's refusal to open its doors to people in need. In the 1950s they appealed to the American senator for Massachusetts, John F. Kennedy. In response Kennedy published *A Nation of immigrants* (1958), which outlined how America's origins were tied to immigration and how 'some had come to America in search of riches, some in flight from poverty and some because they were bought and sold and had no choice'.[96] Moreover, he stated that immigrants had enhanced every aspect of American life. He criticised the existing immigration policy which, he claimed, 'violates the spirit expressed in the Declaration of Independence that "all men are created equal"'.[97] Kennedy sketched out his future aim to eliminate the national origins quota system. With America as the most prosperous nation on earth during the 1950s and 1960s, industry and agricultural businesses needed labour to maintain their output, and trade unions, who had previously feared the undercutting of wages, felt that changes were no longer a threat. As the USA's segregationist policies were slowly rolled away, reformers applied pressure to change the racist quota system.

The Immigration and Naturalization Act of 1965 changed much. The law was promoted by Massachusetts senator Edward Kennedy who dedicated

---

[95] Ngai, *Impossible Subjects*, 228–9.
[96] John F Kennedy, *A Nation of Immigrants* (New York: Harper, 2008 [1958]), 9.
[97] Kennedy, *Immigrants*, 56.

his effort to his murdered brother John. It is described by Margaret Sands Orchowski as 'the most liberal national migration law in the world'[98]; it ended the quotas and prioritised family reunification. National origins no longer mattered in granting residency in the USA and the door was now opened to Asian immigrants. Over the next 40 years the USA's offer of permanent residency to immigrants and a pathway to citizenship offered stability for many. Faster airline travel and improving communication networks, combined with the idea of America as 'a nation of immigrants' with a large economy that continued to grow proportionately, made the USA become the top destination for highly skilled individuals including Nobel Prize winners. These range from Felix Bloch, a Swiss-born migrant who fled the Nazis in 1933, and later won the Nobel Prize for physics, to Maria Ressa, born in the Philippines, who won the Nobel Peace Prize in 2021.

Throughout the 1970s and 1980s migrants were drawn to America. The globalisation of culture meant that Hollywood and other mass media promoted American ideals, increasing its appeal. The numbers of legal immigrants per year increased from 267,967 in 1965 to a peak of 1,266,129 in 2006.[99] Europeans were less inclined to migrate because of rising affluence in their own nations. By 2006 only 15.3 per cent were from Europe, 25.5 per cent were Asian and 51 per cent were Latin American. Many of these people left their homelands at a time of increasing population; they were searching for a better standard of living that the USA appeared to promise, especially to the highly educated. Before the twenty-first century a major draw to America was the relative ease of gaining a visa. At the same time the undocumented migrant population increased, with estimates suggesting that this reached 11,600,000 by 2006. This increase can be attributed to America's global role and its economic pre-eminence, which disrupted global labour markets and displaced work, while the abundance of jobs in the USA drew many migrants. Immigration therefore changed American society from a bi-ethnic (white and African American) to a multi-ethnic state, causing American identity to diversify, incorporating a range of cultures. Despite this change, many areas of the USA were, for much of the twentieth century, relatively untouched by immigration, with California, New York, Texas, Florida, New Jersey and Illinois absorbing around 70 per cent of incomers. The USA's reliance on immigration throughout its history meant the main visible impact of late twentieth-century migration was changes in ethnic make-up, language and religion.

---

[98] Margaret Sands Orchowski, *The Law that Changed the Face of America: The Immigration and Nationality Act of 1965* (London: Rowman and Littlefield, 2015), vii.

[99] The data in this paragraph is from Michael Sobczak, *American Attitudes Toward Immigrants and Immigration Policy* (El Paso, TX: LFB Scholarly publishing, 2010), 7–8.

Change from the 1970s

In Europe the position of migrants was often insecure. The guest status of many migrant labourers appeased local populations. They worked in low-skill jobs and were easily dispensed with when the post-war boom ended during the 1970s. The oil shocks that began in 1973 pushed Western Europe and North America into a series of recessions. Inflation and interest rates grew while unemployment rose from a manageable rate of around 3 per cent to over 10 per cent in many nations. The Netherlands, France, West Germany and Switzerland, among others, cut the numbers of guest workers, reducing the size of this transitory workforce.

The simmering tensions between Algerian immigrants and local French populations spread when politicians sought to limit immigration amid the visible politicisation of Muslim Algerian migrants. The 'Marcellin-Fontanet Circular' of September 1972 limited the right of immigrants to apply for jobs, while making deportations easier. The immigrant population in Grasse protested in response but they were met by police with fire hoses, with the town's mayor labelling them an 'invasion'.[100] With the press heavily opposed to Algerian migrants, racial hatred and violence became commonplace, especially in areas with large immigrant communities like Paris or Marseilles, which had populations of both Algerians and the *Pieds-Noirs*. Gildea argues that colonial structures were recreated in France, with former colonists often joining the police. Vigilante gangs often attacked immigrants: the Marseilles Defence Committee murdered ten Algerians in the early 1970s. Changes in the economic situation exacerbated underlying disquiet with immigration.

In the 1970s French right-wing groups spread, among them the *Front National*, founded by Jean-Marie Le Pen in 1972. Le Pen focussed on turning his fringe political movement into a mainstream party. In response French governments turned increasingly anti-migrant, especially as economic conditions worsened. In 1974 the government of Valéry Giscard d'Estaing banned the recruitment of overseas workers and established funds to promote remigration. This incentive was aimed primarily at North African migrants and the flow slowed, especially from Morocco and Yugoslavia. But workers from Portugal and Spain were most likely to take these funds as their countries of origin emerged from dictatorship, making return home more attractive.[101]

Outward anti-migrant and racist sentiments increased in many nations of the West throughout the 1970s, but it also led to the emergence of new anti-racist cultures that included immigrants and native populations. On 5 August 1976 the guitarist Eric Clapton announced on stage that Enoch Powell

---

[100] Gildea, *Empires*, 133.
[101] Gatrell, *Unsettling*, 199.

had been right and that he wanted to 'Keep Britain White'.[102] Clapton's support for Powell prompted Red Saunders, a freelance photographer, to write to various national music newspapers calling for 'a rank-and-file movement against the racist poison in rock music'.[103] Musicians and activists responded to his appeal and within weeks a new movement called Rock Against Racism was created. Popular bands including The Clash, Steel Pulse, The Specials, X-Ray Spex and The Selector joined the organisation. It became a musical movement that was constructed out of hybrid styles including punk, reggae, ska and two-tone that gave music created by immigrants and their children a place in the United Kingdom. But it was also a street movement that held anti-fascist carnivals and concerts, which could draw tens of thousands of people onto the streets to showcase Britain's diverse culture and fight the far right's influence.

Through the 1970s politicians used anti-black migration statements to increase support. In 1978 the Conservative Party leader Margaret Thatcher stoked anti-immigrant feeling, stating that with up to four million migrants from the 'new Commonwealth or Pakistan … this country might be rather swamped by people with a different culture', leading to a less welcoming atmosphere for immigrants.[104] Thatcher's speech was reminiscent of Powell's earlier claim that immigration would inflame racial tensions. Her politicisation of immigration helped to draw support away from the far right during her successful 1979 election campaign. Under Thatcher's premiership the British state continued to treat immigrants and their children differently to the white population. Institutionalised racism in many police forces saw the so-called 'sus laws', a 19th-century law against vagrancy, which allowed anybody suspected of intending to commit crime to be detained, disproportionately applied against the black population. This discrimination by the British police led to social tensions and outbreaks of rioting in Bristol, Liverpool and Brixton during the early years of Thatcher's first government. The official *Scarman Report* on the riots in London tied institutional racism to the recession. Amid a poor economic climate, Thatcher introduced neo-liberal economic policies such as cutting tax on higher incomes and raising interest rates. The impact was increasing unemployment, which spiked at over 10 per cent in 1982.[105] Black people and immigrants were disproportionately impacted, with unemployment reaching 25 per cent in Brixton, which had a large Caribbean community. Despite legal protections from 1968, employers often prioritised

---

[102] Mike Roberts and Ryan Moore, 'Peace Punks and Punks Against Racism: Resource Mobilisation and Frame Construction in the Punk Movement', *Music and Arts in Action*, 2.1 (2009), 25.

[103] Quoted in Daniel Rachel, *Walls Come Tumbling Down: The Music and Politics of Rock against Racism, 2 Tone and Red Wedge* (London: Picador, 2016) xix.

[104] Margaret Thatcher, cited in Jenny Bourne, '"May we bring harmony'? Thatcher's legacy on 'race'", *Race and Class*, 55: 1 (2013), 87–91, 87.

[105] Lord Scarman, *The Scarman Report: The Brixton Disorders, 10–12 April 1981* (London: Pelican, 1982).

white people in employment. The actions of the population and government in many European nations made it difficult for immigrants and their children to integrate, leaving groups of young people disillusioned, without hope or prospects, leading some to become involved in petty crime.

Several Western nations, especially France, Germany and Britain, saw the size of their Muslim populations grow from the late twentieth century, raising questions around integration. Many governments promoted multicultural policies ensuring the co-existence of different cultures instead of integration. Effectively this meant the marginalisation of migrant groups, especially Muslims.[106] When this discrimination was combined with the rise of political Islam in the 1980s in nations like Iran and Saudi Arabia, some European and Western Muslims saw themselves more as an Islamic diaspora than as adopting a hybridised identity. While European nations became more secular, religiosity remained strong for a large proportion of Muslim immigrants and their children, often as part of an attempt to retain their previous identity.

In France North African immigrants fought back against their marginalisation and exclusion from mainstream politics by forming activist groups throughout the 1970s. They united around their common Maghrebi identity. The Arab Workers Movement (*Mouvement des Travailleurs Arabes, MTA*) aimed to defend all Arabs against neo-colonialism and followed the tendency for Western movements to be inspired by Maoism. However, it rejected the French and Western cultures that its members saw as oppressive and which alienated Arab workers. This nationalist identity was therefore tied to class struggle but based on Arab workers winning equal rights in France. When faced with the deportation of immigrants in the early 1970s the *MTA* and other groups adopted tactics such as hunger strikes to draw attention to their plight. They received solidarity action from areas of the French public, including some in the Catholic Church: in December 1972 four Catholic priests in Valence refused to perform midnight mass in solidarity with nineteen Tunisians who were facing deportation.[107] The *MTA* and other migrant rights groups, therefore, saw their struggle not against the values of the French, with whom the Arab workers shared commonalities, despite their cultural distinctiveness, but against the discrimination of the state which was rooted in French colonialism.

In the 1980s France's socialist president François Mitterrand was more sympathetic. In 1981 he granted equal rights of association to immigrants. However, these were rights in name only and the police in particular gave rough treatment to many Algerians. Many of the force had formerly fought against Algerians and often their discrimination stemmed from this. At the

---

[106] Gerard Delanty, 'Dilemmas of Secularism: Europe, Religion and the problem of pluralism', in *Migration, Discrimination and Belonging in Europe* edited by Gerard Delanty, Ruth Wodak and Paul Jones (Liverpool: Liverpool University Press, 2008), 78–98, 79.

[107] Rabah Aissaoui, *Immigration and National Identity: North African Political Movements in Colonial and Postcolonial France* (London: Tauris, 2009), 170.

same time Le Pen's *Front National* began to gain ground. Their rise was a reaction to Mitterrand's integrationist policy and a weakened centre right. Their electoral growth from 1983 brought airtime and Le Pen's book *Les Français d'abord* (The French First), in which he predicted the takeover of France by outsiders, helped to spread his views.[108] The *Front National* soon won their first ten National Assembly seats. In a similar fashion to the British mainstream right, the response of the French centre-right parties was to try to outflank the extremists. During the power-sharing government from 1986, with Jacques Chirac as Prime Minister, harsh migration laws were introduced in a bid to show that the government stood for the homogeneous French culture. From the early 1990s, when the French right began to gain more power, Minister for the Interior Charles Pasqua sought to deport undocumented Algerians living in France. These measures only emboldened the extreme right, with their support growing to 15 per cent.

Anti-migrant parties targeted the wearing of certain kinds of head coverings by Muslim women. The French principle of *laïcité* ensures religious neutrality in public and education. This secular ideal was developed to protect the republic against Catholicism, but from the late 1980s it increasingly became invoked to defend French national identity against intrusion from other cultures. In 1989 three schoolgirls were excluded from their school in Criel, a town with a high Muslim population, for refusing to remove their *hijabs*. The incident prompted widespread discussion with many politicians and media siding with the headmaster's decision, but French Muslims marched on 22 October against what they saw as an intrusion of their rights.[109] This was the opening salvo in a battle over Muslims' freedom of expression; the issue of head coverings would remain contentious in French society into the twenty-first century.

Political Islam became a global force, and fundamentalist governments like revolutionary Iran and militias such as the Mujahedeen in Afghanistan attempted to politicise the Islamic diaspora. In 1989 these events made their first impact in Britain. The British-Indian author Salman Rushdie had published his book *The Satanic Verses* in 1988 to critical acclaim.[110] A group of Muslims from Bradford petitioned the publisher Penguin when they learned that the book contained passages that apparently mocked the prophet Mohammad. With no action taken a group organised by one of the clerics publicly burned copies of the book on 14 January 1989. The issue soon spread beyond Bradford and similar burnings occurred in Bombay, Decca and Islamabad. These protests were followed a month later by the issuing of a *fatwa* by Ayatollah Khomeini of Iran with a promise of martyrdom for his killers. Rushdie, a lapsed Muslim, was forced into hiding and needed police

---

[108] Jean-Marie Le Pen, *Les Français D'abord* (Neuilly-sur-Seine: Michel Lafon, 1984).

[109] Gildea, *Empires*, 171–3.

[110] Salman Rushdie, *The Satanic Verses* (London: Viking Penguin, 1988).

protection.[111] He was stabbed when speaking at an event in 2022. The right wing claimed that multiculturalism had caused the outrage and that Islam was incompatible with Western culture. For many Muslims, however, the controversy raised questions about their freedom to practice their religion without feeling rejected by the British state and a population whose conception of Britishness often remained rooted in a homogeneous populace and the imperial past. The globalised cultures created by migration sometimes challenged the values of traditional cultures, bringing communities into conflict.

As European nations erected barriers to immigration by non-Europeans during the 1980s, they reduced obstacles between members of the European Economic Community. The 'ever closer union' enshrined in the Treaty of Rome (1957) paved the way for frictionless travel between those nations. The 1980s saw the emergence of opposition to the union and mobility for its citizens. On 20 September 1988 British Prime Minister Margaret Thatcher spoke in Bruges; comparing the EEC to the Soviet Union she stated, 'We have not successfully rolled back the frontiers of the state in Britain only to see them reimposed at a European Level with a European super-state exercising a new dominance from Brussels'.[112] The speech paved the way for the resurgence of the xenophobic-Eurosceptic wing of the Conservative Party, which would dominate British politics in the 2010s and 2020s.

MIGRATION IN THE POST-COLD WAR ERA

The end of the 1980s saw important geopolitical developments with the end of communist regimes in Central Europe, followed by the dissolution of the Soviet Union in 1991. The communist bloc had controlled the movement of people. There had, however, been some leeway. Older people from Poland were allowed to reunite with family in either German state. Other groups moved between the Eastern Bloc countries as part of labour-intensive schemes like building the Baikal–Amur Mainline in the 1970s. The Eastern Bloc had required its population to increase to maintain economic growth during the 1960s and 1970s. They recruited workers, often from the communist 'global South' including Cuba, Vietnam and Mozambique. From the 1960s to 1980s nations including Czechoslovakia, Hungary and the GDR ran schemes to employ Vietnamese people on short-term contracts with an emphasis on building socialist solidarity while providing training and literacy as well as employing their labour.[113] The globalisation of labour did not stop at the Iron Curtain; migration was essential to economies on either side.

After 1991 many newly independent nations had sizeable Russian minorities. A relatively free right of movement between Soviet states had been in

---

[111] Gildea, *Empires*, 165.

[112] Margaret Thatcher, 'Speech to the College of Europe', 20 Sept 1988, https://www.margaretthatcher.org/document/107332 Accessed 6 Oct 2022.

[113] Gatrell, *Unsettling*, 189.

place under Gorbachev. But the establishment of new nations created hard borders which lessened those everyday crossings and increased the potential for discrimination against minorities. Moscow and Leningrad had been centres of migration; Russians had moved to the constituent Soviet republics such as the Baltic states or Ukraine. Many of these immigrants and their offspring suddenly found themselves less welcome. Russia became a net receiver of migrants from the former Soviet republics. Most of the migrants were ethnic Russians, but these were often treated as outsiders, with the media raising suspicions of the newcomers and the government worried about a potential deluge of migrants.[114] The migration of ethnic Russians after the Cold War lacked the violence and intensity of the post-war movement of German speakers, but they often received a similarly cold reception.

Through the 1990s and 2000s migration to Western Europe from former communist nations increased. Following the collapse of European communism the newly democratising nations applied to join the European Union. The first nation to be integrated was the former GDR, which was reunited with the rest of Germany in 1990. As Saskia Sassen argues, in reunified Germany migrants from the East were racialised and treated like a different ethnic group.[115] This outsider status followed the pattern of German speakers in the 1940s. Western European nations developed a high demand for Eastern European labour as their economies grew steadily from the late 1990s up to 2007. Nations like Italy and Spain, which had previously sent their labour abroad, now attracted immigrants.

But it was not only migration from other EU nations that increased during this time. Albanians and Africans migrated to Greece and Italy. Both permitted migration from African nations, with Italy's total number of immigrants, either regular or irregular, at around 2.4 million in 2003, most from outside the EU. In 2004 Spain had around 1.4 million immigrants working mainly in agriculture, tourism or the black market.[116] The Southern European nations were experiencing a reversal of their post-war depopulation, enabling their economies to grow in the first decade of the twenty-first century. Spain's enclaves of Ceuta and Melilla provided a direct land border with Morocco and migrants travelled there from Northern and Central African nations to claim asylum. During the early 1990s there was little opposition to immigration and authorities in some Spanish towns such as Aguaviva used non-European incomers to repopulate their towns. A number of regions adopted a Janus-faced strategy to immigration: in 2001 Italy's conservative Veneto region applied for funding to assist the integration of migrants, but at the same time allocated funding to assist the return of Italian emigrants. Both strategies

---

[114] Hilary Pilkington, *Migration, Displacement and Identity in Post-Soviet Russia* (Abingdon: Routledge, 1997).

[115] Sassen, *Guests and Aliens*, xvi.

[116] Kitty Calavita, *Immigrants at the Margins: Law, Race, and Exclusion in Southern Europe* (Cambridge: Cambridge University Press, 2005), 3.

meant ensuring that Venetian values were not challenged.[117] Such policies, however, did not prevent the rise of political anti-migration movements such as the *Lega Nord* (Northern League). In response the Italian government passed the Bossi-Fini Law in 2002, which limited immigration from outside the EU.[118] In the early 2000s governments used immigration to sustain economic growth but discontent had emerged in some quarters, and it was set to grow.

In the late 1990s and early 2000s many Eastern Europeans felt that a decline in their living standards had happened since the ending of communism: in Poland unemployment increased to 20 per cent. Huge numbers moved to Western Europe in search of a decent living.[119] The make-up of immigrant populations often changed. In Germany Turkish guest workers were replaced by Romanians, Russians, Poles and those from the former GDR. Low wages paid to these migrants helped sustain economic growth. In Britain the tabloid press created scare stories around immigration with both Europeans and non-Europeans being targeted. They claimed that immigrants were unfairly competing for jobs, but also that they were benefits 'scroungers' (which was disproven by official statistics). Other scare stories claimed that Polish people were eating swans.[120] The response from some members of the population ranged from anti-Polish sentiment to physical attacks on Polish people.[121] Yet other areas of British society welcomed immigrants. The West Wiltshire–Elblag Twinning Association sought to welcome new residents to Trowbridge and councils like Bristol published welcome brochures in Polish, while police and health services sought to build community relations.[122] Many Poles appreciated commonalities of culture such as the availability of Catholic schools and locals shopping in Polish delicatessens, creating a feeling of mutual appreciation. Yet others, especially those without higher education and English language skills, felt isolated. The experience and ability of migrants to feel at home was mixed but community cohesion began to develop.

The height of the global era in the 1990s had seen Western mainstream political parties of left and right move towards 'the third way' of neo-liberalism combined with social democracy. By embracing globalisation these parties often liberalised migration laws, seeking to aid overall economic growth. However, resentment simmered in some former industrial areas as the lack of opportunities allowed myths about immigrants infringing on the job market to proliferate. These fears were exploited by both extremists and traditional conservatives, with parties of both types spreading a new narrative about the

[117] Calavita, *Immigrants at the Margins*, 88–91.

[118] Gatrell, *Unsettling*, 328–9.

[119] Gatrell, *Unsettling*, 382.

[120] Phillipe Legrain, *Immigrants: Your Country Needs Them* (London: Abacus, 2004), 11.

[121] Anne White, *Polish Families and Migration Since EU accession* (London: Policy, 2010), 147.

[122] White, *Polish Families*, 144.

decline of nationhood. New far-right movements emerged in most Western European countries in the 1990s, while others formed across Central and Eastern Europe in the first decades of the twenty-first century. They generally avoided the discourse of biological racism that had been used in the colonial era. Instead they used 'cultural racism', which involved setting 'others' or outsiders against domestic communities by suggesting that the other posed a threat to the way of life of the nation or 'stole' jobs and welfare payments.[123] The racism became a code that disguised the belief in an homogeneous and often monolinguistic population. As their popularity has increased these parties have often denied their racism, with some organisations, and even the British government, declaring that structural racism does not exist.[124] Very often racism displays itself in attacking the cultural aspects of other religions: animal slaughter rituals, treatment of women, treatment of homosexuals and the symbols of religious expression like the headscarf and veil, despite the movements very often displaying no prior support for women's and gay rights until it came to using these issues to criticise Muslim communities.

Elsewhere, immigrants and their children merged aspects of British culture with their parents' culture, with some engaging with issues of integration. The British band Cornershop contains Asian and white members. They produced a hybrid of Indian music, indie and dance music and were most successful during the Britpop era of the late 1990s. Their collaborations with mainstream stars such as Noel Gallagher and musicians from the Asian subcontinent such as Bubbley Kaur shows the development of post-colonial identity. Moreover, the radio and television comedy sketch show *Goodness Gracious Me* (1996–2001) was written by and starred a cast of Asian descent. The show made light of the attempts of immigrants to integrate into British society and parodied the attitude of British people towards Asians. One sketch 'Going for an English' showed a group of Indians entering a late-night English restaurant. They continually mispronounced the waiter's name, asked for the 'blandest' thing on the menu, and ordered too many portions of chips. Such behaviour mocked the conduct of many British people in Indian restaurants. Another sketch featured the Kapoors, whose surname has mutated to Cooper, and claim to be native English, despite getting many of the customs wrong. The show mocked both the attitudes of white British to immigrants and those of migrants who rejected their own culture in the rush to assimilate. These hybrids became popular when the New Labour government was hoping to

---

[123] Gerard Delanty, Paul Jones and Ruth Wodak, 'Introduction' in *Migration, Discrimination and Belonging in Europe*, 1.

[124] Cf Tony Sewell et al., *Commission on Race and Ethnic Disparities: The Report* (London: HM Stationery Office, 2021); Jacqueline Yi et al., 'Ignoring Race and Denying Racism', *Journal of Counselling Psychology*, 2022; Roland Clark, 'What Happens When Governments Deny that Racism Exists', Open Democracy, 22 April 2021 https://www.opendemocracy.net/en/countering-radical-right/what-happens-when-governments-deny-racism-exists/, accessed 8 Nov 2022.

redefine what it meant to be British and when migrant communities were increasingly part of British culture.

The USA's popularity among migrants also increased because of its position as the economic and popular culture global hegemon of the late twentieth century. The lure of European nations was also strong as the economies rebounded in the post-war period. Previously personal letters, newspapers, exhibitions and books facilitated engagement between old and new cultures. These gave way to the cinema and television in the post-war period and email, internet and social media into the twenty-first century. With faster communications enabling better connectivity in the Age of Globalism, migrants could keep in contact with family and friends at home as well as building networks in their new nation. Many, as discussed above, sent money home to families. Others grouped together in associations set up to raise money for their hometown.

Migration has often been depicted as creating cultural change, including more diverse food in shops and restaurants and more languages spoken in schools and other civic places. Orchowski has pointed out that these are sanitised versions that depart from the original culture.[125] Many new migrants are unable to find opportunities in the industries in which they are skilled and open restaurants or shops. A creole form of the culture is sold to their new nation, often using more available foodstuffs as substitutes for more exotic varieties, making them more palatable to people in the new nation and maximising sales. General Tso's Chicken is popular in American restaurants as a traditional Chinese dish, yet it is not known in Hunan. The dish was created by Taiwanese migrants to suit the tastes of American people.[126] The meal has become a classic dish of American Chinese cuisine and has been taken up by the Taiwanese as part of their traditional food culture. The creation of such hybrids often impacts on both the host culture and the migrants' native culture.

In late twentieth-century America, immigrants were concentrated in a few major cities. California had long been the centre for trans-Pacific migration, with Los Angeles having the largest concentration of East Asians: around 47 per cent of its population were Hispanic. In Miami Cubans became prominent throughout the later decades of the twentieth century, with many fleeing the Castro government which seized power in 1959. During the 1980s the Cubans became firmly established in the city. While Spanish was always spoken in the American Southern states, immigrants from Cuba and other Hispanophone countries like Puerto Rico and Mexico spread its usage. But it was when they used English with a distinct Cuban influence that success came: stars like Gloria Estevan, who emigrated to the USA as a child, brought

---

[125] Orchowski, *Nationality Act*, 80.

[126] Fuschia Dunlop, 'The Strange tale of General Tso's Chicken', *Authenticity in the Kitchen: Proceedings on the Oxford Symposium on Food and Cookery, 2005*, edited by Richard Hosking (Totnes: Prosect Books, 2005), 165–177.

a uniquely Cuban-American musical culture to the world.[127] Her success was followed by the growth of reggaeton, a musical style that emerged in Central and South America, becoming popular in the USA through the 2000s and 2010s. By 2000, Cubans had become Miami's largest ethnic group, reaching 57 per cent of the city's population. This change has been exacerbated by differences in the birth rate; migrant groups tend to reproduce faster than the existing population. With fewer industrial jobs in America workers often feel that they are in competition with these migrant workers domestically and internationally as a result of globalisation.[128] The debates that 'nativists' have pushed have focussed on the lower wages and competition that they claim migration brings.

During the presidency of Bill Clinton from 1993 to 2001 the neo-liberal model of globalisation expanded in the USA with the liberalisation of banking and information technology driving growth. Clinton saw this economic model as complementary to a cosmopolitan society that was multi-ethnic and allowed a relatively high rate of immigration with few security measures.[129] Attitudes and policy changed, however, following the terrorist attacks in New York on 11 September 2001. The attacks were carried out by nineteen men, mainly from Saudi Arabia, who had arrived in America on business and tourist visas and formed a cell of the Al Qaida terrorist organisation. They hijacked four planes, flying two into the towers of the World Trade Centre, one into the Pentagon and the fourth was brought down by passengers in a field in Pennsylvania. Following the attacks narratives around immigration, particularly in the USA, became linked with the rhetoric of security. President George W. Bush (2001–2009) militarised the southern border with Mexico and erected a huge fence in sections to deter border crossings.[130] The World Trade Centre attacks and subsequent War on Terror changed the USA's immigration policy.

Following the attacks on the World Trade Centre, Western attitudes towards Muslims and immigrants generally became more hostile. The USA and many of its allies declared 'War on Terror'. The subsequent invasions of Afghanistan and Iraq and bombing campaigns in Yemen, Pakistan and Syria increased the flows of refugees. During the 1990s wars in the Gulf, the former Yugoslav states, Congo, Somalia and Rwanda were among those that increased the global refugee population to eighteen million in 1993 (from fifteen million in 1990 and 2.4 million in 1975). By the end of the century the number of refugees had decreased to twelve million. In the 2000s new waves of refugees fled conflict including the War on Terror. By 2008 it was estimated that refugees numbered 42 million worldwide including sixteen

---

[127] Gustavo Pérez Firmat, *Life on the Hyphen: The Cuban-American Way* (Austin, TX: University of Texas Press, 2012, 118–125.

[128] Gerber, *American Immigration*, 4.

[129] Gary Gerstle, *The Rise and Fall of the Neoliberal Order* (Oxford: OUP, 2022), 152–188.

[130] Gerber, *American Immigration*, 63.

million asylum seekers and 26 million who were displaced within their own countries.[131] Simultaneously anti-Islamic tensions grew following attacks by extremists in Western cities such as Madrid in 2004 and London 2005. The terror campaigns continued into the 2010s with the 2015 attack on the Paris office of satirical newspaper *Charlie Hebdo,* actions that led to terrorism by white nationalists against Muslim immigrants and those sympathetic to refugees during the 2010s and 2020s.

Immediately following the 11 September attacks the USA instigated a review of male visa applicants from predominantly Muslim countries under the code name Condor. Muslims living in the USA were targeted by its security apparatus with thousands arrested and questioned. A Homeland Security presidential directive in October 2001 and the Patriot Act of the same month tied American security to immigration policy.[132] Thousands of people hoping to work, study or holiday in the USA were delayed while the CIA and FBI ambled through their paperwork. The climate of fear that prevailed in the USA impacted on many who had lived there for years. These included the heart surgeon Dr Fiaz Bhora, a Pakistani national, who had just completed medical training in the USA. He was appointed as a clinical practitioner in America, but regulations meant that he had to return to Pakistan before starting his job. He was forced to wait in Pakistan for over a year before being allowed to take up his role as a surgeon.[133] Others, including students and scientists who worked in the USA but left for conferences or holidays, found themselves unable to re-enter because of the ethnicity-based security review. The introduction of a new system involving interviews for visa applications from residents of most nations, not just predominantly Muslim ones, added further delays and bureaucracy. The number of visas issued for all types of travel reduced and foreign investment in the USA shrank because of the perceived unwelcoming atmosphere.[134]

Under this climate of fear and suspicion certain sections of the American population turned against Muslims, with the right being particularly vitriolic: televangelists such as Pat Robertson and Franklin Graham preached hatred against Islam. Hate crimes against Muslims, including physical attacks and murders, subsequently increased with members of these communities reporting feeling more marginalised in the decade after the attack.[135] The use of immigration enforcement to prevent terrorist infiltration of the USA

---

[131] Maggie O'Neil, *Asylum, Migration and Community* (London: Polity, 2010), 3.

[132] John Tirman, 'Introduction: The Movement of People and the Security of States', in *The Maze of Fear: Security and Migration after 9/11* edited by John Tirman (New York: New Press, 2004), 1–17.

[133] Edward H. Alden, *The Closing of the American Border: Terrorism, Immigration and Security Since 9/11* (New York: Harper, 2008), 2–3.

[134] Alden, *American Border*, 15.

[135] Louise Cainkar, 'The Impact of September 11 Attacks on Arab and Muslim Communities in the United States' in *The Maze of Fear,* edited by John Tirman, 215–239.

soon expanded. Media and politicians demanded action against immigration and 'illegal' immigration from Mexico in particular. Over the next decade the USA implemented a system of securitisation of its borders including that with Mexico. From 2005 a 'virtual fence' of observation posts, cameras and drones acted to reduce crossings from Mexico. From 2006 President Bush legislated to have this fence made physical.

The 2000s were a decade of increased migration. The opening of Europe in 2004 to the Ascension Eight (A8) nations of six former communist states—Czech Republic, Estonia, Hungary, Latvia, Lithuania, Poland, Slovakia and Slovenia—plus Cyprus and Malta increased the movement of people within the European Union. Migration from these countries was already considerable with around 3.2 million leaving before 2004.[136] The expansion continued in 2007 with Romania and Bulgaria joining. Some existing EU nations secured an exemption to limit the number of entrants from new nations. Around 60 per cent of the A8 migrants to the UK saw their move as permanent and sought to integrate into British society.[137] In Britain alone statistics showed that among the Central European migrants age and high employment rates meant that they were less likely to use services like the NHS or unemployment benefits.[138] Western Europeans also took advantage of the opportunities to travel. Business and opportunities for study or a formative experience for young people drew them to work overseas. London, Amsterdam, Brussels and Berlin became the leading 'Euro-cities' and built reputations for cosmopolitanism and tolerance. Adrian Favell discusses how this movement, which often involved regular commuting between numerous global cities, meant that many of the 'professional foreigners' no longer felt part of their original nation. For high-achieving individuals the 'Eurostar' tag might be employed—a new class of nationless metropolitans who felt at home in the globalised cities of Europe and beyond.[139]

The immigration enabled by the EU and the emergence of a mobile and ethnically diverse cosmopolitan class, who were deemed to have benefitted from globalisation while others were left behind, led to a backlash. European and non-European immigrants alike became the target of right-wing politicians looking to exploit fears over jobs and wages. While many of these parties

[136] Mansoor and Quillan cited in Godfried Engberson, Marek Okólski, Richard Black & Christina Pant ru, 'Introduction' in their *A Continent moving West: EU Enlargement and Migration from Central and Eastern Europe* (Amsterdam: Amsterdam University Press, 2010), 10.

[137] White, *Polish Families*, 138.

[138] Mariña Fernández-Reino & Cinzia Rienzo, 'Migrants in the UK Labour Market: An Overview', *The Migration Observatory*, 6 Jan 2022 https://migrationobservatory.ox.ac.uk/resources/briefings/migrants-in-the-uk-labour-market-an-overview/ accessed 9 Nov 2022; Mariña Fernández-Reino, 'The Health of Migrants in the UK', *The Migration Observatory*, 21 Aug 2020, https://migrationobservatory.ox.ac.uk/resources/briefings/the-health-of-migrants-in-the-uk/ accessed 9 Nov 2022.

[139] Adrian Favell, *Eurostars and Eurocities: Free Movement and Mobility in an Integrating Europe* (London: Blackwell, 2008).

had their origins in the twentieth century and had grown in popularity during the neo-liberal-dominated 1990s, the shock of the 11 September attacks allowed them to further exploit fears. The far-right parties increased their share of votes in several European nations including Italy, Austria, France, Germany, the UK and the Netherlands. When the target became specifically Muslims, the vitriol and sometimes the violence worsened. The Netherlands had long been seen (perhaps inaccurately) as the bastion of social liberalism in Europe because of metropolitan Amsterdam's global city status. Pim Fortuyn was a right-wing politician who claimed to lead the Dutch equivalent of the American neo-Conservatives and was highly critical of Islam and immigration.[140] When he was murdered by a political opponent in 2002 his previously marginal party, Lijst Pim Fortuyn, gained an immediate electoral boost. In the following years the Party for Freedom, led by Gert Wilders, attempted to capitalise on this support and made non-European migration its key target, winning double per centage figures in elections throughout most of the 2010s before winning the 2023 general election.

While anti-migration rhetoric was a feature of political discourse towards the end of the twentieth century, the 'War on Terror' turned xenophobia into a mainstream political subject. Into this charged atmosphere the influential neo-conservative academic Samuel P. Huntington wrote that the new generation of immigrants do not make good Americans because they lack the 'Anglo-protestant' values of the 'original' settlers who, he contends, created American identity, and often choose not to assimilate into American society because of their transitory status.[141] While this publication used reductionist views of national identity, which were never truly reflective of the make-up of the American population, they were a shot across the bow of those who saw little need for restrictions on migration. These debates might still have been considered views held by a minority of polemicists and controversialists were it not for the global economic depression from 2008.

The era of neo-liberal globalisation from the late 1970s had been founded on extending home ownership. It was hoped that this would tie working-class people to the capitalist system and make them part of a property-owning democracy. The USA under George W. Bush experienced a housing bubble that was built on using the deregulated banking system to extend home loans to less well-off people.[142] Alongside this expansion of the mortgage market American lenders permitted homeowners to re-mortgage for purchases from home improvements to cars, or to consolidate debt. The debt-fuelled bubble created risky investment choices which led to defaults and eventually caused the collapse of the investment bank Lehman Brothers on 16 September

---

[140] Merijn Oudenampsen, *The Rise of the New Dutch Right: An Intellectual History of the Rightward Shift in Dutch Politics* (London: Taylor & Francis, 2020), 9.

[141] Samuel P. Huntington, *Who Are We? The Challenges to America's National Identity* (London: Simon & Schuster, 2004).

[142] Gerstle, *Neoliberal Order*, 210–218.

2008. Lehman's collapse led to further banking insolvencies that required propping up by central banks and governments. The extent of the integration of global financial systems meant that the financial crisis spread rapidly to Europe and beyond, causing a rapid fall in house prices and increasing unemployment.[143] Following the economic crash, politicians in many nations blamed public spending instead of irresponsible banking practices. They instigated programmes of austerity, cutting public-sector funding and ensuring that wages remained low. In the USA applications for immigration from Mexico fell during 2008 for the first time since 1970. A clampdown by authorities on undocumented immigration that targeted employers led to a reduction in estimates of irregular immigrant numbers from around 12 million to around 11.1 million in 2009.[144] Across all continents populist movements that opposed immigration and favoured elements of isolationism increased their support.

The 2010 revolutions of the Arab Spring and subsequent reactionary pushback increased the numbers of asylum seekers in Europe. These migrants might previously have found low-paying or manual jobs. However, with depressed economies and austerity policies in place governments had less need for them and limited immigration. Whereas previous arrivals in Ceuta and Melilla had been processed and sent to Spain, where they might secure low-paying work, they were now to be detained in camps. The migration routes were being curtailed.[145]

Migrants and their children bore the brunt of the War on Terror and economic downturn of the 2010s. In France visible symbols of religiosity and other cultures remained contentious, with schoolgirls who wore veils threatened with exclusion from school in 2004, before the wearing of headscarves was banned from schools. In 2011 certain types of covering were banned in public, with a similar ban introduced in the Netherlands amid rising anti-Islamic rhetoric. The issue of identity became more animated during the War on Terror. Sharif Gemie found that many of those who wore a veil in the early twenty-first century did so not because of an expression of religiosity but as an expression of North African identity, which runs alongside their French identity.[146] For others, however, the veil was often not an expression of difference but a symbol of their integration into French society and ability to participate while wearing the religious dress. The meanings of women's religious headscarves were nuanced but the issue was often reduced to one of difference and exclusion by the mainstream press and opponents of migration.

---

[143] Adam Tooze, *Crashed: How a Decade of Financial Crises Changed the World* (London: Penguin, 2019).

[144] Jerry M. Rosenburg, *The Concise Encyclopaedia of the Great Recession 2007–2012* (Plymouth: Scarecrow Press, 2012) 339–340.

[145] Gatrell, *Unsettling*, 367.

[146] Sharif Gemie, *French Muslims: New Voices in Contemporary France* (Cardiff: University of Wales Press, 2010), 39.

The economic instability of the 2010s combined with migration caused by the War on Terror, the Arab revolutions of the 2010s and the subsequent spread of Islamic State across much of Iraq and Syria allowed anti-migrant sentiment to grow in many Western nations. Popular newspapers printed scare stories about boatloads of migrants in the Mediterranean. The British *Daily Mail* sensationalised the issue, talking about 'soaring numbers'.[147] The newspaper vilified a 'Muslim migrant boat captain' who they claimed 'threw six Christians to their deaths', raising the issue of religious conflict alongside migration.[148] Vitriol was amplified in comments from readers, which included 'Put them on a boat and send them back', 'AND MORE TO COME THANKS TO THE HANDWRINGERS' and 'Why bother with a trial'. The comment space allowed public voices (assuming they came from the public) to be aired that had previously been out of tune with mainstream politics. The idea of a migrant crisis has further exacerbated the rise of far-right parties in much of Europe including Italy, Hungary, Sweden and Greece. In the United Kingdom rhetoric on migration from the Middle East and North Africa became a feature of the 2016 referendum on leaving the EU, with the UK Independence Party producing a poster in June shortly before the vote. The poster showed Middle Eastern refugees in a queue with the tag-line 'Breaking Point' and aimed to mobilise a vote against all immigration whether inside or outside of the EU.

Some nations had politicians who were more sympathetic to the migrants' plight. In 2015, in response to increasing refugee numbers, Germany accepted around one million refugees, while Sweden greatly increased its numbers. The negative coverage from other countries compounded the problem, which became commonly referred to as a crisis, something which Neeraj Kaushal suggests is part of the racialised rhetoric that surrounds the issue of immigration. Kaushal shows that only 3 per cent of the global population live outside their country of birth, the same percentage as in 1990.[149] She also points out that the tabloid image of migrants arriving by boat or smuggled inside lorries represented a very small proportion of migrants; the vast majority were middle class and moved using legitimate channels. The sensationalism of the anti-migrant press and politicians exaggerated the issue and focussed on a small proportion of the total immigrant population, vilifying those most in need of support.

The far right did not need to win power; instead these politicians pressured centre-right parties to adopt their policies. The Hungarian *Fidesz* party,

---

[147] 'A Record 218,000 Migrants', *Daily Mail*, 2 Nov 2015.

[148] *Mailonline*, 21 Sept 2016, https://www.dailymail.co.uk/news/article-3799681/Muslim-migrant-boat-captain-threw-six-Christians-deaths-vessel-religion-goes-trial-murder.html, last accessed 6 June 2024.

[149] Neeraj Kaushal, *Blaming Immigrants: Nationalism and the Economies of Global Movement* (New York: Columbia University Press, 2019), 4.

initially a liberal party which campaigned to end communism, echoed the policies of the neo-fascist *Jobbik* in an attempt to outflank them. When *Fidesz* won a majority in 2010 Prime Minister Victor Orbán implemented authoritarian policies and made statements against Islam and the Roma community, inducing hatred against migrant communities. When refugees and non-EU migrants arrived in any number in Hungary they were quickly deported to third countries or threatened with jail.[150] In neighbouring Austria the far-right Freedom Party's entry into the parliamentary coalition of 2017 led to the centre-right Austrian People's Party copying their anti-immigration policies, often aping their xenophobic language.[151] The belief in an immigration crisis was greater in countries which feel threatened by a culture different to their own. By 2019 Turkey had admitted 2.7 million refugees from Syria's civil war, equivalent to 3.5 per cent of Turkey's population. The nations shared some common history, meaning that many Turkish people see humanitarianism towards Syrians as important. The EU nations by contrast had accepted around one million, equivalent to 0.2 per cent of their population, yet it is within Europe that hostility to these refugees is strongest.[152] Hostility towards migration is greatest in nations which accepted fewest refugees. It is perhaps the ethnic and religious homogeneity of these nations (which became especially apparent following World War Two) that drove anti-migrant sentiment.

This Europe-wide anti-immigration political atmosphere began to impact those who were long settled. In 2018 Paulette Wilson, a 61-year-old cook, was written to by the British Home Office saying that she had 'no leave to enter or remain' in the UK. She was soon imprisoned at the Yarl's Wood detention centre, pending her deportation to Jamaica. She had lived in the UK since 1968 and had no surviving relatives in Jamaica.[153] Wilson was one of a growing number of post-war immigrants, known as the Windrush Generation, now threatened with deportation. While the group had become settled and assimilated, their citizenship was now under threat and several were deported. Many of them had never formalised their British citizenship or taken a passport because they had not travelled out of Britain (having often not had the money to go on holiday); but now they could no longer be guaranteed re-entry to Britain if they travelled abroad. To compound the issue, the government had destroyed the paperwork related to their landing, removing the proof that they had migrated six decades earlier. The exposure of this scandal by Amelia Gentleman led to great embarrassment for the government who were forced to back down and began to retrospectively grant British citizenship to

---

[150] Paul Lendvai, *Orbán: Hungary's Strongman* (Oxford: OUP, 2018), 175.

[151] Anita Bodlos & Carolina Plescia, 'The 2017 Austrian Snap Election: A Shift Rightward', *West European Politics*, 41.6 (2018), 1354–1363.

[152] Kaushal, *Blaming Immigrants*, 21.

[153] Amelia Gentleman, *The Windrush Betrayal: Exposing the Hostile Environment* (London: Guardian Faber, 2019).

some, but not all, of the Windrush Generation. The scandal forced the Home Secretary, Amber Rudd, to resign, with the government apologising to the Anglo-Caribbean community for the distress caused. However, the incident showed that, seven decades after the post-war migration began, long-settled communities could become an easy political target for an anti-immigration government.

The 2010s increasingly saw politics dominated by anti-migration feeling. The UK's referendum on EU membership in 2016 saw illegal campaigning practices,[154] and the political murder of Labour MP Jo Cox by a Leave supporter. Throughout her short time in Parliament she had sought to bring different parts of the community together and create a shared sense of identity. In her maiden speech in Parliament she said, 'Whilst we celebrate our diversity, the thing that surprises me time and time again, as I travel around the constituency, is that we are far more united and have far more in common than that which divides us.'[155] Her speech had celebrated the diversity that had been brought by migration since World War Two. She sought to unite those of different backgrounds by building commonalities and celebrating the differences. Cox was a Remain supporter and campaigner for asylum seekers' rights, but her murder did not stem support for the divisive Brexit policy. In France the *Front National* gained support with Marine Le Pen inheriting her father's leadership role in the party and getting to the presidential run-off in 2017 and 2022. Italy's coalition government with far-right Matteo Salvini as interior minister adopted a hard line and prevented the docking of ships containing migrants at its ports from 2018. The USA saw a right-wing backlash to the election of its first black president Barack Obama in 2008. The racialised and anti-migrant rhetoric was capitalised upon by Donald Trump who won in 2016. One of his policies was to build a wall to keep Mexican migrants out of America for which he claimed he would make the Mexican government pay. The ongoing impact of the economic downturn and rise of populism meant that migrants were depicted as enemies of many Western states and became targets of stringent laws.

At Trump's presidential campaign launch he attacked Mexican immigrants, stating that 'they're bringing drugs, they're bringing crime, they're rapists'.[156] Such fiery rhetoric won him support among those Americans who felt left behind by economic changes since the 1980s. Trump's campaign targeted

---

[154] 'Investigation: Vote Leave Ltd, Mr Darren Grimes, BeLeave and Veterans for Britain', https://www.electoralcommission.org.uk/who-we-are-and-what-we-do/our-enforcement-work/investigations/investigation-vote-leave-ltd-mr-darren-grimes-beleave-and-veterans-britain, Accessed 25 July 2022.

[155] Jo Cox, MP for Batley and Spen, Maiden Speech to UK Parliament, 3 June 2015, UK Parliament website, https://www.parliament.uk/business/news/news-by-year/2016/june/jo-cox-maiden-speech-in-the-house-of-commons/, accessed 8 July 2024.

[156] Donald Trump, 'Presidential Announcement Speech', 16 June 2015, cited Terry Smith, *Whitelash: Unmasking White Grievance at the Ballot Box* (Cambridge: Cambridge University Press, 2020), 10.

votes in post-industrial states; stopping immigration from Mexico and Islamic nations was one of his key policies. This strategy won him the presidency in the electoral college, despite losing the popular vote. Ten per cent of Mexicans lived in the United States and yet Mexico's living standards were improving while its birth rate decreased, which had begun to lower the rate of emigration. Mexico itself had become a destination for migrants from Central America.[157] But American media made Mexican immigrants targets. When combined with perceived changes in national identity and ethnic make-up in major cities, Mexican immigration prompted fears of deeper cultural changes in areas that often have lower migration rates. Urbanites were perceived to have gained economically during the Age of Globalism and the Great Recession, leading to them being labelled as 'elites' who were upwardly mobile, liberal in outlook and happy to live and work alongside immigrants. Anti-migrant rhetoric had seemingly won the day in both Europe and America.

Migration has been one of the defining features of the global era. The creation of hybrid cultures and preservation of traditions among migrants in the second half of the twentieth century led to the celebration, or at least a grudging acceptance, of these cultures. When economic times hardened, however, immigrants and their families became the target for frustration. Anger, which sometimes boiled over into violence towards migrants, has predominantly occurred in places which have experienced the least immigration and which see a threat to homogeneous cultures. The ability of communities to adapt and resist violence has helped to create hybrid cultures drawing together people of different heritages, despite the extreme rhetoric and violence that increased in the second decade of the twenty-first century as it had done at various times in the previous six decades. Immigration has certainly created numerous cultural encounters from the end of World War Two: from the encounters of different German speakers, the Jewish diaspora and exiled Europeans to formerly colonised people, Central and South Americans, Asians, Africans and people from the Middle East who have all made temporary or permanent homes in other nations. The responses have sometimes been to reject the incomers and sometimes to offer an embrace with assimilation, acceptance and hybridity.

Discussion Questions

How far can global migration in the post-war era be said to have enabled encounters between people of different cultures?

What is the relationship between migration and globalisation?

Why have people in some areas responded negatively towards immigration, especially in comparison to some of the more metropolitan areas in the same countries?

How have politicians used immigration and anti-immigration policies to their advantage?

---

[157] Kaushal, *Blaming Immigrants*, 14.

CHAPTER 3

Tourism as a Cultural Encounter

For most people in the world's richest nations, tourism is their main form of mobility. It is one of the world's leading industries and many national economies rely on its income. Tourism can be a sightseeing city break, a holiday in an all-inclusive resort or a journey lasting months or years taking in several continents. The modern holiday came of age in the post-war world when disposable incomes increased and improved air technology enabled more cross-border travel. By the twenty-first century the inability to afford a week-long holiday away from home (not necessarily abroad) was seen as an indicator of poverty in wealthy countries.[1] The popularity of tourism became apparent in 2020: the year we stayed at home. The global tourist industry collapsed as the Covid-19 pandemic closed borders and depressed global tourist revenues by an estimated four and a half trillion dollars.[2] The sudden decline revealed how tourism had created a mobile global population. Tourism also helped to spread Covid-19. In Europe early 'super-spreading' began in Austrian ski

---

[1] Cf. Geranda Notten and Keetie Roelen, 'A New Tool for Monitoring (Child) Poverty: Measures of Cumulative Deprivation', *Child Indicators Research*, 5.2 (2012), 335–355.

[2] World Travel and Tourism Council 'Economic Impact Reports', https://wttc.org/Research/Economic-Impact#:~:text=The%20Travel%20%26%20Tourism%20sector%20suffered,the%20global%20economy%20in%202020, Accessed 24 Jan 2022.

resorts,[3] with returnees bringing the virus to their home nations: an unwanted memento that had disastrous consequences.

This chapter explores the growth of tourism and its post-war boom as part of the expansion of global economies before questioning how far this type of mobility can be called an encounter and outlining some of its negative impacts. Ultimately the ability of tourism to provide an encounter is limited due to the staging of national customs, linguistic barriers and the limited spaces allowed for contacts between visitors and local people. The lure of foreign income from tourists has led many governments to open their borders to temporary flows of people. The economic benefits of tourism, however, are mixed. Companies and some individuals have become wealthy but others, in poorer communities, are sidelined and miss out on tourism income while losing access to their local areas. Travel can spur an interest in learning new languages and about unfamiliar cultures; it can break down or sometimes reinforce long held stereotypes, but its ability to do these things and provide a cultural encounter is questioned.

Tourism Before World War Two

While the post-war period saw the unprecedented growth of tourism, travel was not new. In the seventeenth and eighteenth centuries upper-class youths (usually, but not always, men) undertook 'the Grand Tour'. Their journeys through the unfamiliar countries of Europe could last several years. The encounter was supposed to provide education and prepare young men for a career in public life. These trips often featured regular bouts of drinking, gambling and the pursuit of sexual satisfaction. During the nineteenth century the nature of travel changed with the emergence of the 'holiday' spent away from the home. In this century travel developed alongside the revolutionary technology of the railway. The first tours offered by several travel companies, most famously Thomas Cook, were domestic rail packages. Cook began to organise trips taking British workers to other cities and attractions in 1846, before beginning to organise railway sojourns to Europe from 1855.

The nineteenth century saw the rise of the holiday resort. The popularity of English spa towns had grown from the mid-seventeenth century. The initial attraction was to 'take the cure': to bathe in or drink the sulphurous water. As a trip to one of Britain's remaining spas like Harrogate will reveal, this often tasted like the gases inside one's own stomach. From the eighteenth century, spa towns like Bath, Scarborough and Buxton began to

---

[3] Carlos Correa-Martinez et al. 'A Pandemic in Times of Global Tourism: Superspreading and Exportation of Covid-19 cases from a Ski Area in Austria', *Journal of Clinical Microbiology*, 58.6 (2020), DOI: https://doi.org/10.1128/JCM.00588-20.

cater for leisure.⁴ Alongside the health infrastructure, developers built ballrooms, pleasure gardens and paths for walks. The English spa town became a proto-holiday resort.

The popularity of spas spread throughout Europe. During the nineteenth century French spa towns were developed for visitors, especially in the latter half of the century with the railway offering easier transportation and a getaway from the industrialisation of the cities. Nearly a million people per year were visiting French spas by 1900.⁵ Perhaps most famous was Vichy, which became one of Europe's most celebrated spas, attracting thousands of well-heeled French visitors throughout the nineteenth and early twentieth centuries. German spa towns also expanded with Baden-Baden becoming the most famous. With state support aiding their growth they soon began to outshine their English counterparts.⁶ Other nations built similar including Russia, which developed numerous sanatoria that remained popular to the end of the twentieth century. Spas were a getaway for the affluent, but they remained some way from the modern holiday.

As industrial life became established in the mid-nineteenth century, leisure became regularised. Alongside standardised work time factory owners eventually introduced closure weeks, which were a trade-off for factory discipline. These common holiday periods often led to workmates or towns taking excursions together. Coastal resorts had begun to develop when people began to bathe in the ocean around existing ports from the mid-1730s.⁷ As Alain Corbin shows, a cultural shift took place through the late eighteenth and early nineteenth centuries whereby people stopped fearing the sea and instead viewed it as a more inviting entity with health-giving properties.⁸ Following this reimagining, attractions such as inns, theatres and libraries opened, aiming to supplement the idea of leisure for health.

As the railway unlocked the seaside to working-class visitors, northern English coastal towns like Blackpool and Scarborough (which also had a spa), and Coney Island for American workers, gained amusements including piers. These seafront platforms hosted funfairs, swimming pools and dance halls to

---

⁴ Jon Stobart, 'In Search of a Leisure Hierarchy: English Spa Towns and their Place in the Eighteenth Century Urban System', in Peter Borsay and Ruth-Elizabeth Mohman (eds), *New Directions in Urban History: Aspects of European Art, Tourism and Leisure Since the Enlightenment* (New York: Waxmann, 2000) 19–36.

⁵ Douglas P. Mackaman, 'Competing Visions of Urban Grandeur: Planning and Developing Nineteenth-Century Spa Towns in France', in Borsay and Mohman (eds), *New Directions in Urban History*, 41-

⁶ William Bacon, 'The Rise of the German and the Demise of the English spa industry: A critical analysis of business success and failure', *Leisure Studies*, 16.3 (1997), 173–187.

⁷ Allan Brodie, 'Towns of "Health and Mirth": The First Seaside Resorts, 1730–1769', in Peter Borsay and John K. Walton (eds), *Resorts and Ports: European Seaside Towns Since 1700* (Bristol: Channel View, 2011), 18.

⁸ Alain Corbin, *The Lure of the Sea: The Discovery of the Seaside in the Western World, 1750–1840* (Berkeley: University of California Press, 1994).

entertain the workers. Such attractions transformed seaside towns. Blackpool's famous tower opened in 1894.[9] It was inspired by Paris's Eiffel Tower and housed a circus and ballrooms. The late nineteenth-century seaside, however, was not wholly the domain of the working classes: among more well-heeled visitors was Friedrich Engels, the industrialist and co-author of *The Communist Manifesto*, who frequented the Wirral's resort of New Brighton.[10] Towns like this, Eastbourne and Bournemouth often catered for more middle-class visitors than places like Blackpool, which focused on industrial workers. European nations too saw the development of resorts based around bathing in the warmer summer seas. Italy's coast had long been a draw for grand tourists, who visited sites like the Venice Lido; now other Adriatic resorts like Rimini developed following increased domestic demand.[11] These nineteenth-century developments began the changes in holidaying that would later develop into mass tourism.

Improvements in transport systems helped people to find new ways of getting away from it all. In the early twentieth century a road network developed across North America, which offered new means to get to the coast or countryside. British workers tended to take trips in the Charabanc, an open-topped motorised coach, often organised by their place of work. Britain and several other nations had clubs offering cycling or camping holidays. The train, however, remained the main means of travel until the interwar years, when the road became more dominant in the USA and Britain.[12] Those with higher incomes were, from the end of the nineteenth century, able to holiday abroad, but it was not until the interwar years that commercial air travel became a possibility. A number of headline-catching flights such as the American army's circumnavigation of the earth in 1924 seemed to shrink the world.[13] Airplanes and the short-lived Zeppelin services carried passengers between countries and even continents. Flights, however, remained expensive, inaccessible and slow; on the few transcontinental routes operated by flying boats, the route took several days and required frequent stops for refuelling.[14] During the late 1920s and 1930s companies like Pan American Airways received diplomatic support and won Post Office contracts. This support acted as an unofficial subsidy, helping them to open new flight routes especially linking the USA to Central and Southern America and forging transatlantic and transpacific routes. These

[9] Fred Gray, *Designing the Seaside: Architecture, Society and Nature* (London: Reaktion, 2006), 51.

[10] Tristram Hunt, *The Frock-Coated Communist: The Life and Times of the Original Champagne Socialist* (London: Penguin, 2010), 270.

[11] Patrizia Battilani & Francesca Fauri, 'The Rise of a Service-based Economy and its Transformation: Seaside Tourism and the Case of Rimini', *Journal of Tourism History*, 1.1 (2009), 27–48.

[12] Gray, *Designing the Seaside*, 52.

[13] Jenifer Van Vleck, *Empire of the Air: Aviation and the American Ascendency* (Cambridge, MA: Harvard University Press, 2013), 38.

[14] Eric G. E. Zuelow, *A History of Modern Tourism* (London: Palgrave, 2016), 131–2.

routes aided American companies' expansion in the region while paving the way for the growth of passenger air travel.[15]

The Growth of Tourism in the Post-war Period

In 1945 many nations of Europe and Asia lay in ruins. The United States, however, was physically undamaged by the war and President Harry Truman sought to ensure that the liberal trading system would re-emerge, with his nation as the leading power. The granting of Marshall Aid to Western European nations boosted the continental economies with credits that could be exchanged for goods and services. Alongside these stimuli, tourism was believed to be a sector which could help the global economic system to grow. The historian Christopher Endy argues that the promotion of American tourism to Europe was intended as a bulwark against communism.[16] For Endy tourism boosted these economies by acting as an export. It also became a Cold War tool to educate Americans by introducing them to the perceived higher levels of cultural refinement in nations like France and Italy. One of the key reasons for the promotion of tourism, therefore, was the belief that it would aid the transfer of ideas across borders and the creation of more cosmopolitan hybrid identities. Mass tourism, however, did not truly emerge until flight became cheaply available.

During World War Two aviation technology had improved massively; longer journeys were initially enabled by the introduction of pressurised cabins. 1952 saw the appearance of the first jet airliner, the British de Havilland Comet, whose operations were initially short-lived due to several disasters prior to the redesign of the craft. While air travel was growing, prices remained protected and customers tended to be wealthy. Flight remained lavish, exciting and expensive. Many airlines were still nationalised and governments saw these as 'flagships' to be protected. New tour operators emerged amid these technological advances. One of these was Horizon Holidays, started in Britain by Vladimir Raitz. Horizon began offering air package holidays in 1950, creating a new kind of concept. Initially Raitz sold flights to Corsica, which included camping and all food and drink for 32 pounds 10 pence (898 pounds in 2023 inflation adjusted).[17] In order to undercut the standard airfare price Raitz sold his holidays via a club. These stays were initially limited by lack of hotel accommodation, but the air package holiday had been born.

In the early 1950s Pan American had struggled to raise the numbers of journeys by air above those taken by steamship and tried to make air travel more

---

[15] Van Vleck, *Empire of the Air*, 41.

[16] Christopher Endy, *Cold War Holidays: American Tourism in France* (London: University of North Carolina Press, 2004).

[17] Dave Richardson, *Let's Go: A History of Package Holidays and Escorted Tours* (Stroud: Amberley, 2016), 14–15.

accessible. They did this by increasing passenger capacity; some of the luxurious elements like coat racks and galleys were removed from cabins, making an early step towards the creation of 'cattle class'.[18] The Jet Age took off with the inauguration of the Boeing 707 in 1958. The new aircraft allowed for increased passenger numbers and shorter flight times, with cheaper packages soon following. Through the 1960s cheaper short-haul flights and better technology led to the expansion of package companies across Europe. The holiday craze gave countries with dubious governments the opportunity to earn much needed foreign currency. Dictatorships in Spain, Greece and Portugal had the kind of commodity that could not be bottled: plentiful sunshine. This opportunity to get away from home proved a huge draw for Germans and young newly affluent working-class Britons who were as eager to escape from the monotony of work as they had been in the nineteenth century. Now they did not need to go to Warnemünde or Blackpool to get away from it all, although many still did.

Spain's dictator Francisco Franco simultaneously viewed tourism as an opportunity and a threat. Spain was isolated after World War Two because of its support for the Axis powers: it was excluded from the United Nations and received no Marshall Aid. Recovery from its brutal civil war, which ended in 1939, was sluggish despite Spain's formal abstention from World War Two. The beginning of the Cold War from 1947 offered Franco's government the opportunity to re-engage with the nations of the Western bloc as an anti-communist nation. The enthusiasm for tourists from the Spanish government, combined with the Cold War, led to a rebuilding of the Spanish-American diplomatic relationship in 1950. As the rest of Europe began its post-war recovery Franco attracted foreign income by encouraging inbound tourism. Horizon began offering tours in Menorca in 1952 but found accommodation inadequate: there was only one hotel and Raitz found the same when he began offering packages in Benidorm.[19] Nevertheless the infrastructure of tourism was soon created, with Benidorm among a number of Spanish towns and villages to have been denigrated because of apparent over-development. By the 1960s Spain had transformed itself from a nation which attracted few foreign visitors into a major European tourism destination.[20] By opening tourism routes the regime was able to improve its international relations because they presented a more friendly face that was no longer the fascist ally of Hitler and Mussolini.

---

[18] Van Vleck, *Empire of the Air*, 214.

[19] Richardson, *Let's Go*, 15.

[20] Neal Moses Rosendorf, 'Be El Caudillo's Guest: The Franco Regime's Quest for Rehabilitation and Dollars After World War II via the Promotion of US Tourism to Spain', *Diplomatic History*, 30. 3 (2006), 376.

Yet tourists contradicted the conservative values of Franco's dictatorship.[21] The Spanish state established a series of youth hostels, which were limited to single-sex accommodation for people under the age of 21. As Spain's youth hostel organisation sought to make connections outside its borders by forming reciprocal arrangements via the International Youth Hostel Federation (IYHF), they were met with requests to make youth hostels independent of the state, drop the age limit for foreigners and permit mixed accommodation.[22] The government reluctantly agreed to these requests and opened an era of cross-border youth travel both in and out of Spain. The influx of young foreigners mixing with Spaniards was problematic for the highly conservative dictatorship.

Tourism certainly increased the flow of people and capital to Spain but a question remains over the extent of the exchange of ideas. Historians such as Sasha Pack suggest that Spanish tourism provided the regime with the veneer of legitimacy and respectability, allowing it to modernise and create a more urban consumer society. It was this modernisation that Pack argues helped to pave the way for Spain's integration into the European community (if not its formal institutions) and its eventual conversion to democracy. In part this was facilitated by encounters between people from different cultures allowing Spanish people to adopt some of the more liberal practices of the visiting foreigners, in turn leading the regime to lessen its severity. Pack notes how media in the USA and other European nations depicted Spain as different, often encouraged by the regime's self-representation. Pack compares these representations to Edward Said's concept of *Orientalism*.[23] Said wrote that Western-created knowledge of the 'Orient' helped Europeans to assert their power over the colonies by depicting these areas as simultaneously barbarous and exotic. Advertisements often presented an older vision of Spain, including its occupation by the Moors. Tourism led to the performance of traditions that had lapsed or never existed.[24] Bull fighting or *corridas*, which was one of Franco's favoured forms of Spanish identity, became one such example. As tourism increased so did the number of bull fights, with entrepreneurs selling the custom to tourists and spreading it to towns, often along the coast, with no previous tradition of holding the fights.[25] However, Pack argues that throughout the 1960s and 1970s this myth of Spanish difference was eroded, in part resulting from locals' exposure to the more liberal cultural norms of

---

[21] Sasha D. Pack, *Tourism and Dictatorship: Europe's Peaceful Invasion of Franco's Spain* (New York: Springer 2006), 11.

[22] Richard Ivan Jobs, *Backpack Ambassadors: How Youth Integrated Europe* (Chicago: University of Chicago Press, 2017), 24.

[23] Edward W. Said, *Orientalism* (New York: Pantheon Books, 1978).

[24] Pack, *Tourism and Dictatorship*, 2–3.

[25] Carrie B. Douglas, *Bulls, Bullfighting and Spanish Identity* (Tuscan: University of Arizona Press, 1997), 28–9.

tourists. The political elite were eventually left with little choice but to accept a democratic transition.

Justin Crumbaugh, however, argues that it is simplistic to suggest that tourism led the regime towards democracy. Rather, he argues, Franco's government used tourism to legitimise its rule by producing propaganda in magazines, and popular films carrying the message that tourism had modernised Spain and brought foreign currency. The regime continued to present itself as different to other nations to maintain its distinct identity.[26] Thus, he argues, the dictatorship shed its fascist trappings and replaced them with a less politicised embrace of consumer capitalism with a view to strengthening the regime's control. This double-facing strategy was also seen in matters of 'morality'. Sexual encounters between Spaniards and tourists were officially frowned upon. Yet certain Spanish films such as *Un Beso En El Puerto* (1966, A Kiss in the Port) celebrated the stereotype of the macho Spanish man wooing foreign women, although seldom were Spanish women shown in relationships with foreign men. As Catholic and more conservative figures in the government fought back against 'inappropriate' behaviour, the desire to bring in foreign currency meant that certain values, deemed abhorrent by the regime, had to be tolerated.

More recently Richard Jobs has argued robustly that tourism to Spain helped to build a more hybridised European identity. He argues that encounters with European tourists exposed young Spaniards to more cosmopolitan influences and that they began to see themselves as part of a greater Europe. Jobs argues that tourism brought 'European' values to Spain and helped their government to counter the diplomatic isolation of the early post-war years, ultimately paving the way for later democratisation.[27] In part this was advanced through the 'bodily emancipation' that many tourists exhibited, and which challenged conservative morals. Often the liberal behaviour of tourists challenged the authoritarian legal system. The law formally forbade public displays of bare arms and legs, but these were common: several tourists were arrested by the Guardia Civil for their inappropriate dress.[28] The government permitted the wearing of bathing costumes on beaches but prohibited them in town centres. Certainly, Spain's government presented a more liberal yet distinctly 'Spanish' face to tourists, while hoping to shore up their rule. The impact of mixing with tourists, who often held more cosmopolitan values, is harder to judge: Spain's transition to liberal democracy after Franco's death suggests that a large section of the population had had enough of dictatorship, but the role of tourism in preparing the way is less clear.

---

[26] Justin Crumbaugh, *Destination Dictatorship: The Spectacle of Spain's Tourism Boom and the Reinvention of Difference* (New York: SUNY Press, 2009).

[27] Jobs, *Backpack Ambassadors*, 25.

[28] Pack, *Tourism and Dictatorship*, 144.

Throughout the 1960s and 1970s the beach holiday to Spain and other parts of Europe boomed. At times tourism development was deemed detrimental to communities, with major hotel and apartment building programmes taking place on Mallorca and mainland areas including Benidorm and the Costa del Sol. The 1970s saw Greece and its islands remarketed as sunshine destinations that were less developed and therefore supposedly 'undiscovered'. This campaign changed from Greece's previous designation as a place for cultural tourism, with both types remaining popular into the twenty-first century. The dubious political systems did not deter holiday makers. British holiday firms sought to take advantage of the popularity of these and other countries with lots of sun by buying larger and faster jet airlines like Boeing's 707 and 737. Their increased efficiency and price wars between tour companies meant introducing more flying hours to keep prices down, leading to an ever-increasing number of tourists. Sometimes these arrived to find half-built or overbooked accommodation. Several resort representatives recall sending passengers who had arrived in mainland Spain to the Canaries because hotel accommodation did not exist.[29]

Similarly, throughout Northern Europe tourism expanded as wartime devastation turned to steady economic growth. In West Germany tourism became tied to the economic and diplomatic rebuilding process. It was hoped that foreigners travelling to Germany and Germans going abroad would help to integrate the nation into a growing European community. The division of Germany into zones of occupation meant that opportunities to spread ideas of a pan-European identity through travel were mainly limited to Western Europe.[30] However, the promotion of travel to West Germany meant that during the 1950s the FRG received the highest visitor numbers of any European nation and had the highest number of its citizens going abroad. Often, as Jobs shows, the most mobile were young and enthusiastic Germans keen to join a European community. The sense of a common European identity allowed young Germans to develop an alternative collective identity that diverged from the destructive nationalist ideology that had dominated European politics in the 1930s.

The development of tourism as part of economic recovery plans required new infrastructure. The building of hotel chains enriched many businessmen from Conrad Hilton to Donald Trump and sometimes enabled political power to be facilitated through this ownership of leisure facilities. Elsewhere an effective system of money exchange needed to be developed. While early travellers carried cash and feared robbery, mass tourism was enabled by safe money transfer. Banks and money exchange companies frequently worked with national governments to expand tourism. This is particularly true of Spain, where American Express executives foresaw the role of tourism after

---

[29] Richardson, *Let's Go*, 36–7, 42.
[30] Jobs, *Backpack Ambassadors*, 26.

World War Two as part of Europe's reconstruction efforts.[31] American Express offered currency exchange and had begun a travel booking service in 1915. In the post-war era they earned American government support for overseas expansion by promoting their service as a quick way to get dollars into the hands of Europeans. American Express shared advertising costs with the Spanish government as they attempted to expand their business. New tourist infrastructure followed the rebuilding of diplomatic relations and in March 1951 American Express opened their first Spanish office in Madrid. Their money transfer and travellers' cheques paved the way for tourism to become extremely lucrative to local economies.

By the mid-1950s American governments believed that air travel and the tourism industry were important in promoting liberal ideology as superior to communism. By 'opening' air routes before the Soviets, American governments hoped to use their affluent population as cultural 'diplomats' who would spread Western ideas. However, as more Americans travelled abroad the State Department began to worry about the potentially counter-productive 'arrogance' displayed by some tourists, who demanded to be served American food or chipped away parts of ancient monuments.[32] Even worse, governments of America's NATO allies, such as France, began to complain that the transatlantic market had been rigged in favour of American operators, with Pan American purchasing its rivals to become the largest operator.

The State Department also supported the creation of national carriers to prevent the Soviets from dominating the air industries of newly independent nations. They nursed infant national airlines in Asia, Africa and the Middle East, sometimes using American airlines as proxies. From 1948 and throughout the 1950s advisers from the Civil Aeronautics Administration trained crew while funding helped to develop new carriers, initially in Turkey and Pakistan. It was hoped that American technological advancement could help to expand business links and influence through a programme of modernisation, in what were often recently decolonised nations. In 1955 the American government used its Technical Assistance Programme to fund Pan American's purchase of a 49 per cent stake in Ariana Afghan Airlines. The joint venture between the American and Afghan governments allowed the Central Asian nation to showcase its independence and the extent of its development.[33] The opening of flight routes helped to nurture the Afghan tourist industry.[34] However, the 'modernising' mandate of the Pan American team often meant

---

[31] Rosendorf, 'Be El Caudillo's Guest', 380.

[32] Van Vleck, *Empire of the Air*, 201, 226.

[33] Jenifer van Vleck 'An airline at the crossroads of the world: Ariana Afghan Airlines, modernization, and the global Cold War', *History and Technology*, 25.1 (2009), 3–24.

[34] Holly Edwards, '"You need not take a camel": The Archive of the Afghan Tourist Organisation', in *Photo Archives and the Idea of the Nation*, edited by Costanza Caraffa and Tiziana Serena (Berlin: de Gruyter, 2015), 265–278.

introducing Western values such as Ariana's stewardesses discarding the traditional *purdah* and the *chadri* in favour of a more secular uniform.[35] In response religious leaders criticised the airlines' adherence to globalised values. Thus, the expansion of international flight routes was in part a consequence of the Cold War and America's globalisation of its liberal system, both economic and social. However, the Afghan government was adept at playing the Americans against the Soviets, accepting funding for civil aviation from both parties and appearing non-committal, leading the Americans to doubt the value of such programmes and cease future funding.

Regardless of potential conflicts of values, flagship airlines soon became symbols of nationhood. Uniforms incorporating national dress, and national dishes served in-flight helped newly independent countries to display symbols of nationhood on the international stage.[36] Often this was for the benefit of foreigners. Singapore Airlines, established in 1972, employed Ian Batey, a British creative, to design their stewardess uniforms, making their famous 'Singapore Girl' a Western creation that appealed to foreigners. The uniform of the national *sarong kebaya* was worn by women who were selected for their slim body shape and encouraged by airline bosses to maintain their figure. The airline insisted on creating the best level of welcome based on a sense of 'Asian hospitality' that appealed to Western tourists and businessmen, with speech therapy used to soften accents. Academics including Weiqiang Lin have termed this representation of Singapore a form of 'self-orientalism'.[37] In a similar manner to Spain's re-staging of bull fighting, the airline shaped its identity according to how it believed foreigners viewed Singaporeans.

The protections for national airlines prevented package tour operators from price-cutting. In 1977 Freddy Laker, a businessman who had built up his airline during the 1948 Berlin airlift, began his Skytrain air service. He had spent five years battling the American authorities who had supported the view of the established airlines that it was better to fly fewer passengers at higher prices.[38] This precursor to the modern-day budget airline offered a one-way transatlantic flight for 59 dollars. They could only be booked on the day and many customers lacked the return fare. In its first year the carrier became a success. However, Skytrain's cheap fares led to price wars which, along with Laker's rapid expansion, left the carrier at the mercy of the economy. The 1982 recession soon left Laker with no other choice but to fold his company. The first attempt at budget flight may have ended in failure but the idea would take off in the early twenty-first century. For Western Europe and the USA, the post-war period saw a growth in leisure travel, but citizens from these areas

---

[35] Van Vleck 'Ariana Afghan Airlines, 15–16.

[36] Zuelow., *Modern Tourism*, 157.

[37] Weiqiang Lin, '"Cabin Pressure": Designing Affective Atmosphere in Airline Travel', *Transactions: Institute of British Geographers*, 40.2 (2015), 287–99.

[38] Hugh Somerville, 'Freddie Laker: First Giant of Low Cost Air Travel', in Richard Butler & Roslyn Russell (eds), *Giants of Tourism* (Wallingford: CABI, 2010), 118.

were not the only ones desiring a holiday: the socialist nations hoped to prove to their citizens that their way of life was the best.

The Eastern Bloc

The new mobility also spread in the Eastern Bloc. In the USSR throughout the 1940s and 1950s, rest at a sanatorium contended with sightseeing tourism and active holidays, which historian Diane Koenker likens to a scout camp. Holidays in the sanatoria were initially more plentiful and were theoretically available to certain types of people. Immediately after the war, 'shock-workers' and war invalids were prioritised as the USSR sought to rebuild its system of health spas and rest homes.[39] It took some time, however, for supply to keep up with the promise: in the late 1940s Soviet tourists could expect little in the way of comfort, with poor service, crowded dormitories and repetitive poor-quality meals. The reality became especially obvious during the 1946–47 famine when grounds were used to grow vegetables to feed the staff and visitors rather than as pleasure gardens. Gradually through the 1950s, but especially after Stalin's death in 1953, the resorts began to improve: they offered more comfort, better food and entertainments like cinema and music, alongside the emphasis on recovering visitors' health. By the 1960s, as Koenker argues, Soviet tourism had become like that of the West with the middle class (in the form of the intelligentsia) being most likely to be able to enjoy a holiday,[40] before becoming more available during the 1970s.

In the post-Stalin era 'health' resorts such as Sochi were built along the Black Sea coast, and in the Balkan countries including Bulgaria and Romania. These usually followed the Soviet model with the resorts aiming to create a transnational leisure space that could benefit the people of all socialist nations.[41] Many towns like Sochi and the Latvian coastal town of Jurmala already boasted sanatoria and they offered a getaway from industrialised centres. New holiday housing and architecture meant that the Soviets could promote their resorts to other socialists and visitors from outside the Iron Curtain. Tourism also became popular within Eastern nations with Soviet resorts on the Black Sea, Yalta, Georgia and the Crimea becoming particularly popular, mainly among party members and those in high-status jobs. These resorts often followed the spa town model and were formed as 'sanatoria'; health remained the order of the day. Yet demand for official breaks always outstripped supply and many Soviets chose to holiday unofficially. Such was the lure of Jurmala that residents rented out rooms and some even built

---

[39] Diane Koenker, *Club Red: Vacation Travel and the Soviet Dream* (Ithaca, NY: Cornell University Press, 2013), 4–6.

[40] Koenker, *Club Red*, 136, 262–4.

[41] Johanna Conterio, '"Our Black Sea Coast": The Sovietisation of the Black Sea Littoral Under Khrushchev and the Problem of Overdevelopment', *Kritika: Explorations n Russian and Eurasian History*, 19.2 (2018), 327–61.

extra to make money. Tourists sometimes claimed to be relatives of the homeowners to get around the official regulations.[42] Throughout the 1960s and 1970s Soviet holidays diversified and independent tourism, often in campsites, became more acceptable and accounted for a larger proportion of the holidays taken, but always lagged behind the sanatoria.

From 1955 Soviet tourists, usually specially selected citizens or workplace and trade union associations, were able to travel abroad in tour groups. These groups predominantly visited the Eastern Bloc nations, but some went to China, Mongolia, Vietnam (from the 1970s) or the non-aligned countries including India, while a limited number were able to visit the West, but the tendency for holidaymakers to abscond reduced this cross-Curtain travel. Certain Soviet people were able to experience aspects of how other nations lived and the standards afforded to tourists overseas, which their own nation often lacked – at least until 1969 when the Soviets began to treat tourism as an industry and to incorporate the lessons learned from visiting foreign tourist industries.[43]

The communist nations hoped to use tourism to build ideas of fraternity and a common communist identity. Notable tourist itineraries included Soviet tour groups to Czechoslovakia and vice versa. Part of the aim of these journeys was to expose Czechoslovakians to Soviet people in the hope that it would build socialist solidarity and weaken nationalist sentiment. The result, however, was that some Soviets realised that other Eastern nations had better living conditions than their own. Furthermore, many of the Czechoslovakian tour guides sought to blur the official narrative by showcasing their more liberal heritage. Some openly questioned the advancement of the USSR and its communist system. These critical voices became louder during the liberalisation programmes under Alexander Dubček, known as the Prague Spring, and following the suppression by the Soviets in 1968, when many Czechoslovakians expressed antipathy towards the Soviets.[44] Czechoslovakian tourists to the USSR often demanded to be shown the real story and tended to look down on their poorer counterparts to the East. By making these journeys they continued to advocate the ideas of the Prague Spring. In this way tourism often became a contested site where official and unofficial narratives of history and politics clashed.

Some Western holidaymakers were able to cross the Iron Curtain. The death of Stalin prompted a change in approach to the Cold War from the new Soviet leadership. They sought foreign currency and hoped to use

---

[42] Simo Laakonen and Karina Vasilevska, 'From a Baltic Village to a Leading Health Resort: Reminiscences of the Social History of Jurmala, Lativa', in Borsay and Walton eds, *Resorts and Ports: European Seaside Towns Since 1700*, (Bristol: Channel View, 2011), 101; Koenker, *Club Red*, 194.

[43] Koenker, *Club Red*, 240–1.

[44] Rachel Applebaum, 'A Test of Friendship: Soviet-Czechoslovak Tourism and the Prague Spring', in Diane Koenker and Anne Gorsuch, *The Socialist Sixties: Crossing Borders in the Second World* (Bloomington, IN: Indiana University Press, 2013), 213–232.

Western tourism as cultural diplomacy with inbound visits promoting a positive image of their nation and people.[45] This meant that holidays to the Eastern Bloc countries and particularly to the USSR became more available. In 1959 the British embassy in Moscow reported that around 4,000 British people and 10,000 Americans were known to have travelled to the USSR, and this was just the start.[46] They suggested that the main obstacle to greater tourist numbers was 'lower standards of comfort'. Advertisements promising adventure attracted visitors to the USSR; many of these were wealthy adventure-seeking individuals, similar to those who undertook the Grand Tour a century or so earlier. One of these, Francis Dashwood, was a Baronet and descendant of Sir Francis Dashwood who had undertaken an eighteenth-century Grand Tour.[47] Cross-Curtain holidays became less uncommon, with the Soviet Union attracting 1.2 million foreign visitors in 1965.[48] The Iron Curtain was for much of the Cold War not the solid barrier it was often depicted as; indeed Michael David-Fox has described it as a semi-permeable membrane with mobility between the blocs for certain people.[49]

Major tourist companies attempted to grow their businesses in the USSR. In 1972 the British holiday firm Thomson introduced a £29 weekend package to Moscow.[50] Their first offering to around 5,000 tourists soon expanded into longer winter stays that included Leningrad, Kiev and Siberia. They finally ended the operations after the Chernobyl nuclear disaster of 1986 caused them to bring a group of tourists home early. The Western tourist trade with USSR was ultimately limited. The falsely high exchange rate meant that foreign visitors' spending money did not go very far. When factors such as limits on removing currency from a nation as part of the Bretton Woods system, which included capital controls until 1979,[51] were taken into account, the chances of getting value for money were limited, yet holidays to other nations behind the Iron Curtain still appealed.

Several other communist countries, especially Yugoslavia, whose government had split from the Eastern Bloc in 1948, attracted Western Europeans (Fig. 3.1). It had a tradition of international tourism dating to the

[45] Sune Bechmann Pederson, 'Eastbound Tourism in the Cold War: The History of the Swedish Communist Travel Agency Folkturist', *Journal of Tourism History*, (2018), 10.2, 130–145.

[46] TNA/FO371/152017/NS1632/1 Moscow Embassy to Foreign Office, 7 Jan 1960.

[47] 'Tanfield's Diary', *Daily Mail*, 17 March 1956.

[48] '1967 International Tourist Year', *UNESCO Courier*, December 1966, 8.

[49] Michael David-Fox, 'The Iron Curtain as Semi-permeable Membrane: Origins and Demise of the Stalinist Superiority Complex', in Patrick Babiracki and Kenyon Zimmer eds. *Cold War Crossings: International Travel and Exchange across the Soviet Bloc 1940s-1960s* (College Station, TX: A & M University Press, 2014), 14–39.

[50] Richardson, *Let's Go*, 43.

[51] Kojo Koram, *Uncommon Wealth: Britain and the Aftermath of Empire* (London: John Murray, 2022), 104–108.

nineteenth century, before the country's formation, its Adriatic coastline proving as much of a draw as it does for present-day Croatia. In the early 1950s the Yugoslav authorities urged foreign tourists to 'Come and see the truth',[52] but it retained its reputation of basic comfort with a distinct lack of amenities and lower standards of cleanliness.[53] As the country underwent a process of rapid industrialisation and urbanisation, President Tito sought to increase both foreign and domestic tourism with the modernisation of seaside resorts, restoration of its Roman monuments and the beautiful Plitvice national park. The communist state was often seen as a cheaper alternative to Italy, with whom the Croats had a shared heritage. By 1964 the number of foreign arrivals was experiencing something of an explosion, with 59.7 million overnight stays in the peak of 1986, a 23 per cent increase on the previous year.[54]

By the 1980s several Eastern Bloc countries, Romania, Bulgaria and Hungary, sought to exploit the burgeoning tourist trade to attract foreign currency, often with Western companies offering package deals.[55] From 1964, the British company Lord Brothers operated holidays in Bulgaria. Businessman John Bloom, who helped to negotiate the deal, claimed to have been given heavily subsidised prices because the resorts built for domestic holidaymakers were often empty, because Bulgarians had no money.[56] This venture was soon expanded as other tour operators sent Western holidaymakers to Bulgaria up to and beyond the collapse of communism. By 1970 Bulgaria was serviced by fifteen nations' airlines, attracting up to 2.5 million foreign visitors per year.[57] Tourists from the Eastern Bloc as well as Westerners visited these resorts, increasing the opportunities for people from either side of the Iron Curtain to mix and learn about other cultures through casual meetings if they could get over the language barriers and be sure to be free from the oversight of Communist Party observers. The communist nations drew Western European visitors because they offered a low-cost resort or touring holiday in a distinctly different culture. More adventurous tourists, however, sought to go even further afield to 'discover' supposedly untouched areas of the world.

---

[52] Karin Taylor and Hannes Grandits, 'Tourism and the Making of Socialist Yugoslavia', in Hanes Grandits and Karin Taylor (eds), *Yugoslavia's Sunny Side: A History of Tourism in Socialism (1950s to 1980s)*, (Budapest: CEU Press, 2010), 5.

[53] J. K Walton, 'Preface: Some Contexts for Yugoslav Tourism History', in Grandits and Taylor (eds), *Yugoslavia's Sunny Side*, xvii.

[54] '1967: International Tourist Year', *UNESCO Courier*, Dec 1966, 8; Taylor and Grandits, 'Tourism and the Making of Socialist Yugoslavia', in Grandits and Taylor (eds), *Yugoslavia's Sunny Side*, 11.

[55] For figures see Peter J. Buckley & Stephen F. Witt., 'The International Tourism Market in Eastern Europe', *The Services Industries Journal*, 7.1 (1987), 92.

[56] Richardson, *Let's Go*, 68.

[57] Johanna Conterio, '"Black Sea Coast"', 326.

Fig. 3.1 'On the Adriatic', poster for Yugoslavian tourism, 1950s

Beyond Europe

Longer-haul holidays attracted those seeking something different and numbers increased from the 1990s. Kuoni offered luxurious long-distance travel from most of Europe during the post-war era. It took a while, however, for other travel companies to probe this market. From the late 1960s companies such as Oasis offered Westerners coach tours across Asia and India (the original magical mystery tour). But by the 1980s political turmoil in states like Iran and Afghanistan prevented overland tours from entering those countries. Instead new companies offered similar land trips across South America with arrival by long-haul flight. In China, Deng Xiaoping's economic changes from 1976 included attempts to attract cultural tourists other than the delegation tour offered to communist 'fellow-travellers'. Previously isolated communist China became a holiday destination. Through the 1980s Kuoni expanded the long-haul market by offering cheaper hotel packages. They purchased excess passenger capacity, often on the national airlines of developing nations, which tended to operate for prestige, rather than to meet demand. The development of Egyptian purpose-built resorts like Sharm El-Sheikh offered tourists an all-inclusive break that shielded them from 'real life' in Egypt. Elsewhere the British company Airtours began to offer packages to Florida, Barbados and Hawaii from the late 1980s and added Thailand, Kenya and Australia to their retinue, making these places become familiar destinations for Western tourists.[58]

Holidays in South Asia and beyond became more common for Western tourists. The continued expansion of the consumer classes made these destinations increasingly viable for travel businesses. Thailand's popularity grew throughout the 1990s, peaking about the time of the release of the film *The Beach* in 2000.[59] The film's protagonists search for an 'unspoiled' island beach with an idyllic travelling community that soon becomes beset by isolation, betrayal and the violence of local drug gangs. It reflects on the ruination of wildernesses that the tourism of this community can bring and the false perceptions of paradise in the minds of many Western travellers. The Asian tourist boom continued with Vietnam's reinvention as a destination for both holidays and business. Its Đổi Mới (renovation) programme announced in 1986 and Tourism Development Plan of 1991 began a stuttering increase in inbound Asian and Western tourism, as government regulations relaxed. Its tourist appeal often echoes that 'curiosity' aspect to witness an area that the press and literature have depicted as 'exotic', which also drew travellers to the USSR.[60] Where once Americans invaded this country as an act of war, from the late 1990s they visited to appreciate its rich culture and heritage. However, as in other nations, the environmental impact of development and tourism cast a shadow. Tourists were drawn to the beauty of UNESCO World Heritage site Hạ Long Bay. But tourist development meant land reclamation for high rises and the stripping of nature's flood barrier and protector of marine life: the mangrove. The coal industry, over-fishing and the dumping of human waste from tourist boats meant that the area suffered extreme damage. Bill Hayton comments that the devastation is so great that 'As a visitor attraction Hạ Long Bay survives, but as a natural environment, it is dying'.[61] Tourism, while certainly not the whole problem, has been a contributory factor to ecological disaster.

Elsewhere places like Dubai, Singapore and Hong Kong offered stopover facilities but have grown to become end destinations. By making itself a shopping hub from the 1970s and building an image of hospitality and cleanliness, Singapore increased the time long-distance travellers spent there. Dubai likewise built up its reputation for shopping and attractive hotels from

---

[58] Richardson, *Let's Go*, 92, 84.

[59] *The Beach*, dir. Danny Boyle, (20th Century Fox, 2000).

[60] Wantanee Suntikul, Richard Butler and David Airey, 'Changing Accessibility to Vietnam: The Influence of a Government in Transition', in *Asian Tourism: Growth and Change* by Janet Cochrane (London Routledge, 2007), 71, 75.

[61] Bill Hayton., *Vietnam: Rising Dragon* (London: Yale University Press, 2010), 162.

the 1990s.[62] The potential effects of abstinence in Muslim countries have often been lessened by allowing Westerners to drink alcohol in enclaves, which are reminiscent of the extraterritoriality of colonial incursions into China and Japan in the nineteenth century. This sanitised version of a cultural encounter suggests that many nations are willing to overlook the breaking of traditions to accommodate tourists.

Much of this chapter has explored tourism made by Americans and Europeans. But tourism also flowed from Asian nations and other continents to the Western nations. The rise in wealth among the middle classes and emergence of many East Asian nations as economic powerhouses within a globalised world has given many from that region the impetus to travel abroad. From the 1970s Asian tourism to Western nations became more common, first in organised groups, but from the twenty-first century an increasing number of Asians travelled to the West independently or for study. The wave of tourists and travellers were initially Japanese, whose outbound tourism grew during the 1980s. Chinese outbound tourism has also grown, and David Harrison predicts that it is set to dominate tourism markets into the mid-twenty-first century.[63] The Chinese government's permissive approach to outbound tourism was seen as a way of promoting soft power to aid China's integration into the international community. Increasing numbers of Chinese, Malaysians, Thais and Vietnamese have travelled either to other Asian nations or the West during the twenty-first century. Scholars have compared Asian experiences to those of Western tourists and see an imagined West that Asian travellers aim to reach. Many hoped to experience a cosmopolitan form of Western cultural heritage and language acquisition.[64] It is this mixing of cultures that many travellers, especially those on longer-term stays, hope to gain from inter-continental travel.

The growth of mass tourism in the post-war period can be attributed to four main causes. The first of these is advances in infrastructure. Air travel, roads, railways, telephony and hotel networks were all vitally important to the growth of tourism. Second, the Cold War caused the establishment of new tourist routes as the USA sought a way to recapitalise countries in need of reconstruction. American governments also sought to bring often unpalatable regimes and previously neutral nations into its sphere of influence by offering enticements to make the relationship acceptable to Western populations. From 1953 the USSR responded in kind and attempted to increase its foreign currency reserves as well as creating cultural diplomacy between the nations of West and East, and between the nations of its own sphere of influence. Both sides attempted to showcase their best features to visitors. Third

[62] Guilherne Lohmann, Sascha Albers, Benjamin Koch and Kathryn Pavlovich, 'From Hub to Tourist Destination – An Explorative study of Singapore and Dubai's aviation-based transformation', *Journal of Air Transport Management*, 15 (2009), 205–211.

[63] David Harrison, 'Looking East but Learning from the West: Mass Tourism and Emerging Nations', *Asian Journal of Tourism Research*, 1.2 (2016), 1–36.

[64] Huong T. Bui, Hugh Wilkins, & Young-Sook Lee, 'The "Imagined West" of young independent travellers from Asia', *Annals of Leisure Research*, (2013), 16.2, 130–148.

was the global increase in consumption. From the 1950s, as disposable income increased, a holiday abroad became more accessible. The fourth aspect that perhaps underpins the expansion of tourism is profit-chasing and building foreign currency supplies. Tourism is one of the largest economic sectors in the world; it is facilitated by a criss-crossing network of often multinational capitalist enterprises. Simply put, the desire of business owners to make more money has caused them to offer pre-packaged or less loosely structured travel opportunities to those who want to bask in the sun or have an adventure.

The expansion of globalised tourism has reversed the isolation of some of the world's more remote communities; none more so than in the Himalaya. Before the twentieth century the main visitors to this region, which spans five nations, were Indians undertaking pilgrimage. In the Age of Imperialism the great mountain ranges embodied mankind's yearning for conquest. Mountaineering became popular in mid-Victorian Britain as part of the imperial project. Once the Alpine peaks were scaled, mountaineers turned their attention beyond Europe to other ranges including the Himalaya.[65] Several ill-fated attempts to scale the seemingly unclimbable Mount Everest led to disasters in the early twentieth century. But on 29 May 1953 the Sherpa Tenzing Norgay and the New Zealander Edmund Hillary, who were part of the British Mount Everest Expedition, organised by John Hunt, reached the summit.

The mountaineering craze took off as Nepal's King Tribhuvan was determined to modernise the country. He invited a Russian acquaintance, Boris Lisanevich, to move to Kathmandu where, in 1951, he opened the luxurious Hotel Royal. Foreign adventurers and climbers made a base there, with locals often wondering why they bothered.[66] With the liberalisation of the visa regime in 1955, Himalayan tourism became more of a possibility. Over time, trekkers and those seeking to follow in the footsteps of Hillary and Tenzing made the camp sites a regular feature of the climbing season. Hillary continued to engage with the people of Nepal, building schools, and in 1964 found a site for Lukla airport, which has become the main entry point for thousands of tourists and mountaineers.[67] More formalised tourism increased when the former British naval attaché to Nepal, Colonel J. Roberts, started a trekking company in 1965.[68] While the intentions of foreigners were often altruistic, including the provision of education and healthcare, they have ensured that a once undisturbed community was changed by the summer influx of climbers and Western projects. Over time the region became a magnet for Westerners seeking spirituality and to undertake transcendental meditation, including the Beatles who in 1968 visited the foothills of Uttarakhand in India. The lower

---

[65] Peter Hansen, 'Albert Smith, the Alpine Club and the invention of mountaineering in Mid-Victorian Britain', *Journal of British Studies*, 34.3 (1995), 300–324.

[66] Ed Douglas, *Himalaya: A Human History* (London: Vintage, 2020), 469–71.

[67] Edmund Hillary, *View from the Summit* (London: BCA, 1999), 230–2.

[68] Paul Beedie 'Adventure Tourism' in Simon Hudson (ed.), *Sport and Adventure Tourism* (London: Taylor & Francis, 2002), 218.

altitude parts of the region experienced something of an influx of backpackers through the 1960s to 1990s. Since the 1980s India, Pakistan and China have recognised the tourist potential of the region and opened their borders to the Himalayan range. The numbers of climbers and trekkers in the Everest region of Nepal rose from a few dozen in the 1970s to over 60,000 in 2019.[69] The regional authorities have adapted to this influx by building lodges and roads; trekking routes have become formalised while many Nepalese have moved to the higher areas to capitalise on the influx of visitors. The practice of pilgrimage to Sikh, Buddhist and Hindu shrines increased from the 1970s as roads and other infrastructure made even the more remote high Himalaya accessible.[70] The Tibetan city of Lhasa, situated on the north side of the Himalaya, has welcomed tourists from China and further afield, with authorities building shopping arcades to attract more people. A number of governments in the region have become financially dependent on money from visitors. Nepal of the 2020s relies on the income from licences sold to wealthy foreign climbers. The impact of tourism has meant the landscape has been transformed through lodge building, firewood burning, including rare alpine junipers and dwarf rhododendrons, and disposal of waste (human and debris). By the twenty-first century, these tourism-derived issues, as well as other forms of modernisation such as agriculture and industry, were threatening to contribute to the degradation of this delicate ecosystem. Tourism in some of earth's great wildernesses has grown in the wake of exploration and the desire of some Westerners to experience another way of life.

Problematising Travel

Some modern package tourists barely leave their hotels, except for a few occasions, eating and drinking all their meals buffet style in the hotel restaurant and spending most of their time around the pool, competing (sometimes fighting) with other tourists to secure a sunbed. There is little here that many would regard as a cultural encounter. The idea that tourism has led to the transplanting of one's own customs into a different environment has often led to a form of snobbishness. Some holidaymakers distinguish between those they regard as travellers and tourists. Those who label themselves 'travellers' are often more middle class and stay aloof from the habits of the all-inclusive holidaymaker. This type assumes that only the 'traveller' has a valid experience, which includes learning about a new culture.

Those who label themselves 'travellers' believe they are more cultured. They visit different parts of the country that are deemed less commercialised, visiting

[69] Alton C Byers and Milan Shresta,'Conservation and Restoration of Alpine Ecosystems in the Himalaya', in *Tourism and Development in the Himalaya: Social, Environmental and Economic Forces* edited by Gyan P. Nyaunpane and Dallen J. Timothy (London: Taylor and Francis, 2022), 58.

[70] Gyan P. Nyaunpane and Dallen J. Timothy, 'Introduction: Tourism and Development in the Himalaya' in their *Tourism and Development in the Himalaya*, 8.

heritage sites and indulging in local culture and food customs. Their trips can last much longer than the two-week holiday, perhaps months or even years, often visiting many countries or continents. In many ways they are following the path first trodden by those aristocratic youths who undertook the Grand Tour. As affluence has spread, the children of middle-class parents have been able to undertake this journey as a rite of passage, often before or after university. This type of tourism, however, can give a false impression of forming a cultural encounter, and its impact is often questioned.

Traditionally scholars have been sceptical of tourism; Daniel Boorstin perceives mass tourism as a 'pseudo-event' where tourists are insulated from the real experience. He argues that no encounter takes place, with an effective *cordon sanitaire* placed around tourists. Hotels recreate the comfort standards of the USA so that Americans effectively never leave home. Yet, while tourists spend their time in Westernised hotels they still expect novelty and the exotic. Often they are shepherded around certain sites by tourism professionals, where they are presented with a performance or imitation of local culture. Sometimes this is local craft work where Boorstin claims that the tourist expects 'more strangeness and more familiarity than the work naturally offers'.[71] The locals, therefore, reproduce their culture in a sanitised and stereotypical way that shields the tourist from their new surroundings.

Dean MacCannell argues that tourists seeking authenticity at cultural sites may be met with pre-packaged versions of national culture.[72] He discusses how sites are marketed and sacralised through a range of media. They are also often physically enhanced to emphasise their importance to visitors. Statues may be put on a pedestal, spotlights might emphasise important buildings, the site may be mechanically reproduced to create souvenirs, or viewing spaces added for traditional crafts and industries to allow tourists to encounter something perceived as authentic.[73] The viewing of customs and traditions at specified tourist sites is a form of secularised pilgrimage. This 'sacralisation' might be formal, such as the blue plaques that indicate sites of significant heritage in the UK, or part of a cultural process, for instance the development of the Eiffel Tower as an icon through its reproduction in photographs, souvenirs, films and television. Other scholars have suggested that tourists are aware of the shortcomings of their journeys but still delight in the experience. Maxine Feifer argues that these 'post-tourists', who might visit 'dreamworlds' like Disneyworld, do so as escapism.[74] Others might visit cities like Bruges in Belgium, which has become shaped along ideas of tourist expectations, but

---

[71] Daniel J. Boorstin, *The Image: A Guide to Pseudo Events in America* (New York: Harper, 1961), 79.

[72] Dean MacCannell, *The Tourist: A new Theory of the Leisure Class* (New York: Schoen, 1989 [1976]), 12.

[73] MacCannell, *The Tourist*, 40–50.

[74] Maxine Feifer, *Going Places: The Ways of the Tourist from Imperial Rome to the Present Days* (London: Macmillan, 1985).

they do so to absorb the associations of romance with the city and to indulge those external staples of Belgian culture – beer, fries, waffles and chocolates – that are perhaps seen as too unhealthy to consume regularly at home. The authenticity in tourism may be elusive and changing; the awareness of this by some has led to pastiche versions of cultures being consumed for fun.

John Urry's seminal book *The Tourist Gaze* focuses on the way in which tourists see places. Tourists are socially conditioned to build an image of cultural and sometimes racial stereotypes from their own culture and ideological make-up, hence different tourists will experience the same place differently. For Urry,

> Gazing at particular sights is conditioned by personal experiences and memories and framed by rules and styles, as well as by circulating images and text of this and other places. Such 'frames' are critical resources, techniques, cultural lenses that potentially enable tourists to see the physical forms and material spaces before their eyes as 'interesting, good or beautiful'. They are not the property of mere sight. And without these lenses the beautiful order found in nature or the built world would be very different.[75]

Urry therefore argues that the tourist's impression of culture is preconceived: it has been shaped by television, postcards, adverts and 'tourism professionals' like bloggers, travel writers and guides. They are directed by their expectations to certain sites: a first-time visitor to London will invariably head to Big Ben, St Paul's Cathedral and Buckingham Palace, spending several hours in queues and paying their entrance fees, or they might buy a package or city card that includes all the sites. The vast majority would see only London's more prosperous and attractive districts, being shielded from the more deprived areas. In doing so they reinforce an image of British tradition involving royalty, deference to Parliament and quirky hangovers from centuries past. All this amounts to the consumption of a place through the tourist's pre-conception.

For Urry these expectations, reproduced by tourism professionals, amount to a 'tourist gaze': the direction of tourist viewpoints and consumption of pre-packaged and distorted views of national cultures. Visitors to Paris will experience it as romantic because they have been conditioned to perceive it as such. Often the sense of the nation is 'performed': for instance, local folk music is played by buskers such as the violins and tamboura played in Croatia, or the music of the Beatles that is invariably heard at the tourist sights of Liverpool. Ritual dances became associated with places, like Hula in Hawaii and Samba in Brazil. Urry suggests that many of these customs are repackaged for foreign visitors, as discussed earlier with the spread of bullfighting in Spain. These traditions which are projected outwards become the image of the

---

[75] John Urry, *The Tourist Gaze* (London: Sage, 1990), 15.

country or city. Thus, tourism shapes domestic cultures and visitors associate those traditions with that place.

Some scholars such as Jobs, however, are more positive about tourism. Jobs sees trips made by the young as a vital part of the European project, enabling Europeans to build an imagined community beyond their borders. Those aged under 25 were the most mobile by the end of the twentieth century.[76] This age group have tended to spend longer travelling and seeing it as part of their personal development. Institutions like the European Union valued intra-European travel and promoted cross-border mobility. This recent re-interpretation of the tourist experience runs counter to a long period of scepticism about the industry.

Critics of tourism often question how far tourists encounter different cultures and some deem tourism (along with other forms of globalisation) a form of cultural imperialism.[77] This classification would imply the expansion of a society's interests to the detriment of host cultures, with their values and economies changing as a result. Tourism, according to this model, is little better than a cash crop. The role of foreign airlines, tour companies, banks and hotels in expanding tourism suggests that there is an economic imperative for the 'imperial' nation, which effectively exerts its power, especially over developing countries. These companies and the tourists who follow their routes change local values and attitudes. Foreign guests are catered for and treated by tourism staff with a greater reverence than is afforded to locals. In the early post-war years delegations of French hoteliers travelled to the USA to learn about the levels of comfort expected by American tourists. These French professionals formed one of several European delegations who sought to learn from the American industry and modernise their own to cater for transatlantic travellers.[78] Subsequent changes included how breakfast was to be taken, optimal room temperatures, provision of small bars of soap, and building shops in lobbies.[79] However, while these innovations were often transplanted into European settings, industry bosses were keen to not merely replicate the American model but to preserve their own distinctive cultures, for instance preventing shops from imposing on attractive lobbies. Throughout this era the shaping of the tourist experience allowed travellers to have fun and experience levels of comfort that might have surprised many locals.

The comfort of the resort sometimes contrasts with the surroundings; governments and the tourist industry shield holidaymakers from areas outside the tourist zone. In the Dominican Republic poverty-stricken neighbourhoods

---

[76] Jobs, *Backpack Ambassadors*.

[77] Cf. Alison Broinowski, 'Culture and Tourism', *Media International Australia*, 1995, 22–26.

[78] Zuelow, *Modern Tourism*, 153.

[79] Brian McKenzie, 'Creating a Tourist's Paradise: The Marshall Plan and France, 1948 to 1952', *French Politics, Culture & Society*, 21.1 (2003), 40.

often exist next to tourism zones. From the late 1960s the country 's government actively promoted the tourist industry, creating a Ministry of Tourism in 1967. This development was made with the encouragement of the World Bank who saw tourism as a means of economic diversification away from reliance on sugar exports.[80] Tax breaks for multinational firms facilitated the development of new resorts around coastal areas such as Luperón or the former sugar-refining town of Boca Chica. During the 1970s and 1980s the nation's tourist industry expanded and tourist numbers surpassed a million in 1987. Land was compulsorily purchased or expropriated to build specially designated tourism zones, often displacing local populations. Impoverished former agricultural workers were attracted to the outskirts of tourism zones. The displaced population consequently increased as more were drawn to the edges of the tourist zones by the promise of foreign wealth.

The impact of tourism on local populations has also exacerbated gender and wealth divides. Women in the Dominican industry have historically been paid less than the national average and have often been excluded (informally or formally) from supervisory and customer-facing roles where the opportunity for gratuities exists.[81] Others have been drawn into sex work with tourist networks targeting specific areas of the nation. However, some studies find that tourism increased household income overall for those employed in the sector (often in the informal sector).[82] Most resorts are classed as 'enclave tourism'. Tourists in these centres stay in isolated resorts often on all-inclusive packages having little contact with the outside. Multinational corporations monopolise tourism, leaving a local semi-legal parallel economy on the edges of tourist zones that the authorities clamp down on, fearing it will damage the reputation of the Dominican Republic. The tourist boom had questionable economic impacts for many but undoubtedly improved the lives of certain groups.

The Dominican government aimed to keep local populations separated from the tourists wherever possible. In Luperón local elites benefitted from investment in the beach resorts but the working classes remained limited to low-paying jobs serving the tourists. Into the 2020s local communities, especially those with darker skin, were overlooked for tourism positions, with the best roles going to those from the capital. Many workers were laid off outside the peak season. Small-scale industries such as farming and fishing re-oriented to supply the tourist industry, with middlemen making profits while locals struggled.[83] When the UK company Airtours started a contract with Luperón

---

[80] Stephen Gregory, *The Devil Behind the Mirror: Globalization and Politics in the Dominican Republic* (Berkeley, CA: University of California Press, 2014), 54.

[81] Amalia Cabezas, 'Tropical Blues: Tourism and Social Exclusion in the Dominican Republic', *Latin American Perspectives*, 35.3 (2008), 29.

[82] Yolanda León, 'The Impact of Tourism on Rural Livelihoods in the Dominican Republic's Coastal Areas', *Journal of Development Studies*, (2007), 43.2, 340–359.

[83] Tilman Freitag, 'Enclave Tourism Development: For Whom the Benefits Roll?', *Annals of Tourism Research*, (1994), 21.3, 538–554, 545.

Beach Resort hotel in 1989 many British tourists left the hotel's bars and shops in search of cheaper food, drink and souvenirs in town. The hotel owners refused to renew the Airtours contract and over time more hotels limited tourism to fully inclusive to maximise their profits, reducing contacts with the outside communities. Other resorts were designed with bridges between hotels and privatised beaches, ensuring that tourists avoided public space. Private guards and warnings of street crime created an impression of a lawless country beyond the resort.[84] By the early twenty-first century special tourist police operated in many resorts, such as Boca Chica. Part of their duties involved preventing the parallel businesses run by locals profiting from the tourist industry. In this atmosphere the chance of a cultural encounter is perhaps little to none. The anthropologist Stephen Gregory claims that,

> Cultural hybridity (a consequence, in part, of international tourism) is targeted as a threat to the seamless atmosphere of tourism and as a principle of social exclusion. This unruly hybridity risks disrupting the binary oppositions undergirding the industry's symbolic economy – between "guests" and "hosts", between subjects and objects of consumption, and between cosmopolitan modernity and the static charm of a fantasized native culture. It was precisely this subversive hybridity, a symbolic as much as an economic threat, that the hotel industry and tourism authorities worked to exclude.[85]

Enclave tourism limits the opportunity of the tourist to have a cultural encounter and to challenge their pre-determined vision of the culture of the host nation. Future profits are defended, meaning that areas close to resorts are represented as dangerous – if they are mentioned at all. Tourists and locals maintain a mutual wariness, reducing the opportunity for people to mix and engage with each other's culture. The imagined idyll that the tourist authorities promote detaches the tourist from the local community.

In other countries new cities have been created with the specific purpose of drawing in tourists and getting them to spend money. Most notable in this case are Dubai and Las Vegas. At the start of the twentieth century both had tiny populations: 10,000 for Dubai and only nineteen in Las Vegas.[86] During the twentieth century Las Vegas built up a reputation for fun, earning the nickname 'Sin City' for its casinos, high-profile shows and links to organised crime. Throughout the 1980s and 1990s mega-resorts were built including accommodation, casinos, entertainment complexes and cinemas. These themed hotels often featured copies of great cultural sites including Hotel Luxor, which opened in 1983 boasting a miniature Egyptian pyramid and Sphinx; and the Venetian, housing a replica of Venice. These themed zones allow tourists, often from different countries, to mix with each

---

[84] Gregory, *Devil Behind the Mirror*, 92.

[85] Gregory, *Devil Behind the Mirror*, 94.

[86] Tim Simpson, 'Tourist Utopias: Las Vegas, Dubai Macau', *Asia Research Institute Working Paper*, 177 (2012), 3.

other while rarely encountering the local population. That is not to say that no cultural encounter occurs. These sites, which make no claims to authenticity, are frequented by an international class of tourists that mixes solely with itself and tourism workers.

Such resorts have been labelled as 'hyper-reality' because of their creation solely to draw in tourism, often ignoring the issues of populations or the absence of a previous authentic experience.[87] Tim Simpson prefers the term 'tourist utopias' after the idea of going to the 'other place', a dreamworld for visitors, for which many have paid a huge social price (for instance bonded labour practices in Dubai). In cities like Dubai and Macau development followed a similar path of serving the needs of tourists. Each city has become a 'space of exception' where the laws of the country, for instance on gambling or taxation, are waived for these tourist enclaves. These resorts are perhaps some of the clearest examples of hybridity available to tourists: influences drawn from numerous countries are brought together to produce a separate culture, which is encountered by a global class of tourists. Tourism itself may create a form of cultural hybridity with ideas and practices crossing borders to cater for expectations. In turn an international tourist class that shares similar ideas about place and tourism itself travels and often meets in these locations. This restriction to meeting a globalised hyper-mobile class of people may fall some way short of encountering local cultures that many anticipated. Tourism can provide an encounter, but it is rarely the same kind that was expected.

The End of Mass Tourism?

By 2019 global tourist numbers had reached 1.4bn.[88] The scale of the industry has caused many to question its benefits. Tourism has long been seen to cause over-development and many locals have felt a need to fight back against tourist incursions. In the communist era, planners noted that the building of resorts in the Black Sea area had, in some cases, caused land erosion, contamination of drinking water, traffic, noise pollution, overcrowded beaches and loss of vegetation.[89] The spoiling of treasured seaside views by concrete apartment blocks and hotels has caused many to bemoan the presence of holidaymakers. Visitors to popular Spanish cities like Barcelona may be greeted with the graffitied slogan 'Tourist go home'. This opposition is driven by the increasing conversion of housing stock to tourist lets, particularly on

---

[87] Christian Steiner, 'From Heritage to Hyper-reality? Tourism destination development in the Middle East Between Petra and the Palm', *Journal of Tourism and Cultural Change*, 8. 4 (2010), 240–253.

[88] 'International Tourist Arrivals Reach 1.4 billion Two Years Ahead of Forecasts', *United Nations World Tourism Organisation*, 21 Jan 2019 http://www2.unwto.org/press-release/2019-01-21/international-tourist-arrivals-reach-14-billion-two-years-ahead-forecasts, Accessed 30 May 2019.

[89] Johanna Conterio, '"Black Sea Coast"', 354.

websites like Airbnb. This results in locals feeling driven out of their communities and like second-class citizens in their own cities. Tourism also has a noted impact on the landscape, with transport fuel and construction producing carbon emissions and activities such as jet-skiing adversely impacting on the landscape.

Global terrorism has also impacted tourism. Stringent flight restrictions were introduced in the wake of the attacks on the World Trade Centre on 11 September 2001. Their appearance, alongside budget airlines, eroded the remnants of a romanticised 'golden' era of flight. When these fears were combined with the effects of flight on the environment, public attitudes around flying began to change. Moreover, holiday resorts and tourists became the direct target of attackers. The bombings of Western nightclubs in Bali in 2002 killed 202, mainly foreign people, and in the 2015 massacre at the Tunisian Port El Kantaoui resort 38 tourists were murdered. The idea of a foreign paradise that allowed tourists to escape from their everyday lives was increasingly fraught with danger. Yet holidays continued, often in other resorts deemed safer, until the pandemic of 2020 brought a shuddering halt to virtually all mobility.

Tourism is both a cause and effect of an increasingly globalised world. The ability to travel long distances has been enabled by the development of transport and flight in particular. When visiting other nations many people like to immerse themselves in that culture and believe that they are encountering something different or exotic. However, a lot of tourists prefer the idea of home, even when they are abroad, often causing those in foreign nations to change offerings of food and customs to accommodate visitors. Scholars question the ability of all tourists, including those seeking to embrace something different, to form an encounter, with nations presenting a certain form of culture to visitors that is in line with their preconceived ideas. This repackaging of culture means that place is often 'consumed' rather than encountered. The separation of locals and tourists means that hybrid cultures find little space to develop through tourism.

For many governments and national economies, the benefits of tourism are seen to outweigh the impact on local communities. Tourism acts as an export, bringing in foreign earned currency. Some nations such as the USA have promoted tourism, both in and outbound, as a means of spreading liberal social and economic values and opening new markets. For these nations tourism has promoted a positive image of their nation. The role of the industry in shaping tourist visits, often to preferred sites and zones, has perhaps reduced the opportunities for foreign visitors to encounter a sense of a true culture. But tourism can lead travellers to empathise with those in other nations. For some it can spur the learning of languages and a fascination with learning about other cultures. The presentation of a preferred national narrative or founding story to tourists can satisfy some yearning for knowledge, prompting some to learn more, to return and to know better.

Discussion Questions

How far can an authentic encounter with other cultures be formed through tourism?

How has tourism helped to promote understanding between different nationalities and cultures?

What have been the adverse effects of mass tourism?

What is the relationship between globalisation and tourism?

How far are global encounters formed through tourism mediated by governments and/or businesses?

CHAPTER 4

Globalising Activism

Political campaigns became progressively international in scale during the Age of Globalism. As ideas crossed borders political activists increasingly perceived themselves as part of a global community. Transnational activism was not new. The French Revolution of 1789 became internationalised as its ideas spread around Europe and South America. During the nineteenth century the socialist movement proliferated and several international 'working men's' and communist associations sought to co-ordinate the global spread of this ideology. Similarly, the Fascist movement of the 1930s had global aspirations with both Italian and German Fascists funding and supporting similar nationalist movements in other nations.[1] Other less party-political movements also had long international heritages: the women's peace movement sought to globalise its work throughout the twentieth century with the Women's International League for Peace and Freedom holding a conference at the Hague in April 1915 that sought to bring an end to World War One. The period after World War Two, however, witnessed changes to the nature and scale of transnational activism.

Increases in the speed of transmission of media, communications technology and mobility allowed groups to better empathise with people in other nations and to apply pressure on multiple governments, increasing their impact. This chapter considers three such movements, anti-apartheid, the women's movement and environmentalism, exploring how, during the latter part of the twentieth century, these groups became globalised and

---

[1] Arnd Bauerkämper and Grzegorz Rossolinski-Liebe (eds), *Fascism Without Borders: Transnational Connections and Cooperation between movements and regimes in Europe, 1918–1945* (Oxford: Berghahn, 2017).

© The Author(s), under exclusive license to Springer Nature Switzerland AG 2024
N. J. Barnett, *Cultural Encounters in the Age of Globalism*,
https://doi.org/10.1007/978-3-031-68797-6_4

applied pressure to governments around the world. Previous ideological movements like international communism had concerned a political system and sought to transform the way people lived their lives. In the post-war era new global movements emerged which often focussed on single issues and many became tied into the development of identity politics. Indeed Margaret Keck and Kathryn Sikkink see the 1960s as fermenting the emergence of transnational advocacy networks around human rights and environmentalism, among others.[2] That decade, which became famous for headline-grabbing protest movements, saw the emergence of coalitions that could consist of activists, non-governmental organisations (NGOs), large social movements, media, churches, trade unions, consumer groups, intellectuals, intergovernmental organisations and sometimes parts of the government. Several of these organisations formed around aspects of universal human rights that characterised the international agenda of the post-war world. The globalisation of ideas such as anti-racism, feminism and environmentalism led activists to campaign for people and causes in other nations and to view the world as more interconnected.

International Anti-apartheid Activism

One of the major international solidarity campaigns of the late twentieth century saw global activists campaign against the apartheid laws of South Africa. The South African Federation had been a dominion of the British Empire since 1909. The mid-twentieth century saw this nation take a turn towards increasingly racist politics at a time when racial equality and human rights were becoming global political issues (although racial inequality was still embedded in law in the USA). After winning the 1948 election the National Party introduced new laws which reinforced the pre-existing racist nature of the South African state and precipitated the systemic removal of black voting and citizenship rights. New laws divided the population into four racial groups that were labelled white, coloured, Indian and African, with whites as the largest group (due to the division of the African grouping into ten nations). By 1950 marriages and sexual relations between the 'races' were illegal. Changes to educational provision meant ten times as much per capita was spent on white children as black children. The majority of black South Africans were relocated into rural 'homelands', which often consisted of poor-quality land where they were kept at or below subsistence levels (Fig. 4.1).[3] The introduction of the Pass Laws in 1952 banned black South Africans from visiting towns and cities for more than 72 hours without a permit. These laws resulted in

---

[2] Margaret Keck and Kathryn Sikkink, *Activists Beyond Borders: Advocacy Networks in International Politics* (New York: Cornell University Press, 1998), 3.

[3] Leonard Thompson, *The History of South Africa* (New Haven, CT: Yale University Press, 2001), 190–196.

thousands being arrested and ultimately led to a tragic outcome that prompted the growth of an international anti-apartheid movement.

The Pass Laws met with opposition in South Africa with the African National Congress (ANC), which had existed since 1912 but took a more radical turn during the 1940s, the most vocal group. In 1952, alongside the South African Indian Congress, the ANC launched Defiance: a united non-white civil disobedience campaign to resist the apartheid laws.[4] The government responded by arresting key activists, including Nelson Mandela, using anti-communist laws. Their persecution of ANC members increased throughout the decade.[5] The Pan-Africanist Congress (PAC), an exclusively black organisation, launched a separate campaign against the Pass Laws on 21 March 1960. Activists gathered at police stations hoping to overwhelm the state's ability to process those who had broken this law. At Sharpeville a crowd of 10,000 gathered to show the limitations of the state's power. The police opened fire killing 69 people; many were shot in the back.

The Sharpeville massacre reached immediate prominence in international news, drawing condemnation and outrage. Black activists in America saw Sharpeville as a clarion call linking their struggle for racial equality and apartheid as a transnational campaign. The South African jazz singer Miriam

Fig. 4.1 Racial Segregation: Apartheid in South Africa

---

[4] Thompson, *South Africa*, 208.

[5] Elleke Boehmer, *Nelson Mandela: A Very Short Introduction* (Oxford: Oxford University Press, 2008), 40.

Makeba, who lived in exile in the USA, performed at a memorial in Harlem to those gunned down. She angrily denounced the South African government, helping to build a sense of international solidarity for black rights.[6] These transnational links had developed over several decades. The sociologist W.E.B. Du Bois had formed the ideas of pan-Africanism in the early twentieth century and supported anti-colonial movements in the post-war years. The singer and activist Paul Robeson and campaigner Max Yergan had formed support groups in the interwar years and in 1941 they formed the Council on African Affairs which campaigned for African liberation from colonialism. The organisation was attacked by the US state under the McCarthyite purges and they disbanded in 1955.[7] Anti-apartheid was a matter for global civil rights and governments on both side of the Atlantic were keen to hinder the movement.

In the post-Sharpeville clamp-down the South African government declared a state of emergency, arrested thousands of black South Africans and banned the ANC and PAC. The ANC continued to operate illegally, often organising from other African nations. It expanded its campaign against apartheid; it planned protests, strikes and transport boycotts to coincide with South Africa becoming a republic on 31 May 1961. The ANC and the PAC co-ordinated with pan-Africanists across the continent, many of whom were engaged in their own struggle for independence from European colonialists. In early 1962 Mandela undertook a tour of pan-African conferences, met with Algerian and Moroccan armed liberation movements and in London met with Labour and Liberal MPs.[8] Upon returning to South Africa he was arrested and charged with inciting a strike and leaving the country without a valid passport. On 7 November 1962, having conducted his own defence, he was sentenced to five years in prison. In July 1963 the police raided an ANC compound called Liliesleaf Farm and found documents which were used to prosecute nine leading members of the organisation, including Mandela, with sabotage and conspiracy. The lengthy trial resulted in a sentence of life imprisonment for eight of the accused, who began their incarceration in 1964. Their imprisonment was mainly spent in grim and isolated conditions on Robben Island. The trial, however, had allowed the ANC to state their political views including their belief in socialist redistribution and Mandela stressed his support for the democratic Westminster-style parliamentary system, in which all could participate regardless of the colour of their skin. The state's attack gave the ANC an international platform.

Throughout the twentieth century the South African police used lethal violence to suppress discontent. Yet international news rarely covered this

---

[6] Nicholas Grant, *Winning Our Freedoms Together: African Americans & Apartheid, 1945–1960* (Chapel Hill, NC: University of North Carolina Press, 2017), 65.

[7] Rob Skinner, *The Foundations of Anti-Apartheid: Liberal Humanitarians and Transnational Activists in Britain and the United States, c.1919–64* (Basingstoke: Palgrave, 2010), 61.

[8] Boehmer, *Nelson Mandela*, 47.

brutality.⁹ While calls for a consumer boycott against South Africa had emerged previously it was the worldwide reporting of the Sharpeville massacre in 1960 that turned apartheid into a mainstream concern. In the UK and USA, the Anti-Apartheid Movement grew as alliances formed between existing groups of civil society such as churches and trade unions to build an international network of groups supporting the struggle of black South Africans. For Håkan Thörn these campaigns built a transnational sense of solidarity, similar to the imagined communities which many academics hold to be the founding basis of nationhood. Thörn sees this international coordination as the formation of a 'transnational civil society', and similar movements emerged in ecology and feminism. Thörn argues that the international media condemned Sharpeville so strongly because of the pressure that was beginning to be applied by the international Anti-Apartheid Movement. This network ensured that the massacre made headlines rather than slip away with little focus as previous atrocities against black people had, including three months earlier at Windhoek, where eleven protesters had been murdered by police.¹⁰ The Anti-Apartheid Movement hoped to appeal to national governments to create boycotts of South African goods but also to deny the nation the opportunity to apply its 'soft power'.

Support for the ANC in the United Kingdom had emerged almost immediately when apartheid was imposed. Part of the movement was led by Caribbean migrants. In 1951 a Barbadian seaman, Milton King, was assaulted and killed by police in Cape Town. The subsequent light treatment of the culprits prompted protests throughout the Caribbean with many who were influenced by pan-Africanist ideas empathising with the plight of black South Africans.¹¹ When they arrived in Britain, Caribbean migrants and South Africans worked alongside the pre-existing black community and formed groups which fought racism in the UK and campaigned against apartheid. These included the West Indian Standing Committee, the Black Parents Movement and other groups which were influenced by American anti-racism groups. Black Britons organised against apartheid but often shunned the white-dominated groups. The more mainstream Anti-Apartheid Movement formed in 1956 (it was originally called the Committee of African Organisations). It was predominantly led by and consisted of white anti-apartheid campaigners and throughout its existence struggled with its relative lack of black representation.

American civil rights campaigners continued to tie their struggle to opposing apartheid. The civil rights leader Martin Luther King Jr. took up

---

⁹ Tom Lodge, *Sharpeville: An Apartheid Massacre and its Consequences* (Oxford: Oxford University Press, 2011), 25–6.

¹⁰ Hakan Thörn, *Anti-Apartheid and the Emergence of a Global Civil Society* (Basingstoke: Palgrave Macmillan, 2006), 200; Benedict Anderson, *Imagined Communities* (London: Verso, 1983), 18.

¹¹ Elizabeth M. Williams, *The Politics of Race in Britain and South Africa: Black British Solidarity and the Anti-apartheid Struggle* (London: Tauris, 2017), 12.

the case of black South Africans and urged the British and American governments to issue sanctions. He used his acceptance speech of the Nobel Peace Prize in 1964 to label the South African regime the 'most brutal expression of man's inhumanity to man'.[12] Throughout the next year King made speeches about the need for the USA to refuse to do business with the racial state of South Africa. His use of the civil rights movement to fight for the rights of black Africans was part of a broader turn of black rights groups towards pan- Africanism. The activist Malcolm X undertook a tour of Africa in 1964 showing that the struggles in America and Africa were part of the same search for justice for all people of African descent. He sought to make the campaign for equality in the USA an internationalised African American campaign.[13] The interconnected campaigns also took on a Cold War political aspect with campaigners often associating fighting discrimination with anti-imperialism (including that by America). Western governments, as historian Nicholas Grant has shown, used anti-communism to discredit or legally hamper the campaigners.[14] From the 1960s to the late 1970s, under the influence of pan-Africanists, campaigns focussed not just on conditions in South Africa but promoted a broader idea of liberation across the continent.

While the international campaigns grew, Mandela and his comrades suffered in prison, often undertaking hard labour. The fame of the prisoners drew international attention. The campaign for racial equality continued, but for the prisoners, survival was the immediate priority. Mandela wrote 'I was now on the side-lines, but I knew that I would not give up the fight ... We regarded the struggle in prison as a microcosm of the struggle as a whole. We would fight inside as we had outside.'[15] His international profile meant that he and the other men's treatment became the subject of the South African state's attempt to present themselves as humane upholders of law and order. The government encouraged occasional visits by Western journalists and politicians in an attempt to show that the prisoners were being treated humanely. These visits helped campaigners to maintain the international awareness of Mandela and his comrades' imprisonment and allowed the inmates to complain about their conditions. By the 1970s authorities permitted the prisoners to write two letters per month. The prisoners used this rare contact with the outside world to maintain the international profile of their struggle. Outside South Africa the ANC decided to focus their campaign on Mandela's imprisonment.[16] Thus the ANC and AAM collaborated to raise the international profile of Mandela and attempt to isolate the National Party government.

---

[12] Francis Njubi Nesbitt, *Race for Sanctions: African Americans Against Apartheid, 1946–1994* (Bloomington, IN: Indiana University Press, 2004), 62.

[13] Nesbitt, *Sanctions*, 58.

[14] Grant, *Freedoms Together*.

[15] Nelson Mandela, *Long Walk to Freedom: Autobiography of Nelson Mandela* (London: Little Brown, 1994), 451.

[16] Mandela, *Long Walk*, 590.

The campaign for a boycott of South African goods helped to draw attention to the international Anti-Apartheid Movement. The first calls for an international boycott came in 1958 from the All Africa People's Conference. In 1960 the British Anti-Apartheid Movement announced the first boycott of South African goods. Its message was boosted by anger at the Sharpeville massacre. The boycott fitted well with the age of globalisation. The protesters' aims were to apply economic pressure, but they also felt that boycotts were a good technique for consciousness raising. The intention of this campaign was to apply bottom-up pressure on governments to use either the UN or EEC to apply sanctions.[17] The boycott had limited impact because few South African companies operated in America. Instead, from the 1960s, activists opted for a strategy of divestment, which meant encouraging international companies to end all business in South Africa. The pan-African nature of anti-apartheid was visible in this campaign, with the American Committee on Africa and University Christian Movement encouraging people to withdraw their investments from banks, including Chase Manhattan who had loaned money to business in South Africa.[18] In 1969 black churchmen representing the US Pentecostal Episcopal Church informed executives of Chase that they intended to withdraw two million dollars if the bank did not change its strategy. Campaigners hoped that the global investment chains of multinational companies could be broken by transnational civil societies who believed in a universal value of anti-racism.

The success of the boycott movement has perhaps been overstated. In part this was due to Thabo Mbeki, Mandela's successor as president 1999–2008, making a post-apartheid attempt to create a global role for South Africa which played on this anti-apartheid tradition. While foreign companies did officially leave the apartheid nation, they often allowed South African companies to buy their assets or licenced production via third parties. Yehonatan Alsheh goes as far as to suggest that the sanctions enabled the South African government to convince the white population that opponents of apartheid threatened their way of life and that the white monopoly on power must stay.[19] However, the involvement of international organisations helped the movement become more visible and made it difficult for the South African government and companies to operate in globalised markets.

The consumer boycotts of goods rarely impacted on trade compared to action taken by the UN General Assembly or the EEC. International campaigners pressured transnational organisations to take up their fight. The UN became increasingly important and African nations were particularly adept at using its levers to pass resolutions. In 1973 the UN declared apartheid a

---

[17] Thörn, *Anti-Apartheid*, 61.

[18] Nesbitt, *Sanctions*, 55.

[19] Yehonatan Alsheh, 'Sanctions Against South Africa: Myths, Debates and Consequences' in *Boycotts Past and Present: From the American Revolution to the Campaign to Boycott Israel,* edited by David Feldman (London: Palgrave Macmillan, 2019), 175–196.

crime against humanity. It enacted a ban on the arms trade with South Africa in 1977. In 1978 it created a Special Committee Against Apartheid, regularly hearing from anti-apartheid activists, allowing them to give evidence and sponsoring their activities. Later the UN declared 1982 its International Year for Mobilisation Against Apartheid. These resolutions and events were usually organised by African nations. Action via the UN, however, was also limited: when resolutions were proposed at the Security Council level, such as to enact sanctions, they would usually be vetoed by the USA, UK or France.[20] Up to the late 1980s governments of right and left in these nations maintained close ties with South Africa because of the anti-communist domination of the National Party and its access to materials like gold. Even when they did accept sanctions, from 1985 onwards, this was largely down to pressure from the international community, and the EEC in the case of Britain. Throughout the 1970s and 1980s British and American firms exploited loopholes in the weapons sanctions to sell arms to South Africa. Yet activists showed that they could apply pressure via supranational organisations.

It was only in the early 1980s that American companies began to end their investment. On 17 March 1985 a crowd gathered in Uitenhage to hold a funeral procession for six people shot by police the previous week. Police ordered the dispersal of the mourners, who refused, and then opened fire killing 35 people. Reports of this massacre led to further outcry against the South African government and galvanised the divestment campaigns. On 1 August Chase Manhattan Bank announced that it would no longer loan money to South African companies or individuals, after protests by its investors. This was one of several successful actions directed against corporations that had some impact in the final decade of apartheid. In 1986 the US Congress finally passed the Comprehensive Anti-Apartheid Act, voiding the veto of President Reagan meaning that effective action to limit business came from within the USA.

Throughout the period the global AAM also maintained a cultural and sporting boycott following the ANC's appeal in 1958. Sports like rugby union and cricket had been globalised by British imperialism and were played in many Commonwealth nations including South Africa. Now, however, they became contested battlegrounds as activists and sporting authorities campaigned against apartheid. From 1949 New Zealand campaigners fought against South African requests to exclude Māoris from rugby union tours, continuing throughout the 1950s and early 1960s.[21] By the late 1960s the New Zealand authorities refused to authorise tours that banned Māori participation, leading to the cancellation of the 1967 rugby tour. In response to this success, campaigners led by the activist Trevor Richards formed Halt All Racist Tours (HART), which protested against any tour that involved South

---

[20] Thörn, *Anti-Apartheid*, 65.

[21] Trevor Richards, *Dancing on Our Bones: New Zealand, South Africa, Rugby and Racism* (Wellington: Bridget Williams Books, 1999), 15–18.

Africa so long as it remained a racial state. Other bodies focussed directly on apartheid; the International Olympic Committee banned South Africa from the Olympics in 1964 and the UN endorsed the sporting boycott in 1968. It was hoped that international condemnation would exacerbate the effect of pressure from within South Africa and force change. The British Commonwealth strengthened the pressure to oppose cultural and sporting ties with South Africa with the Gleneagles Agreement of 1977. This understanding formally committed all nations of the Commonwealth to 'combat the evil of apartheid by withholding any form of support for, and by taking every practical step to discourage contact or competition by their nationals with sporting organisations, teams or sportsmen from South Africa'.[22] As the Commonwealth became a post-colonial institution the independent nations united to oppose the racism that remained state policy in South Africa. Yet from the 1950s to 1980s other rugby-playing nations, notably the British Lions team, undertook official tours of South Africa, even after the Gleneagles Agreement.

South African teams still arranged tours of other nations, which met with opposition. The 1967 South African rugby union tour of the UK drew mass protests and marked the start of a sustained sporting boycott. The opening match at Oxford University was cancelled because protesters used weedkiller to spell out 'Oxford Rejects Apartheid' on the pitch. This match marked the start of a series of protests, with activists employing direct-action tactics including handcuffing themselves to goalposts and the steering wheel of the Springboks' coach.[23] The 1969–70 rugby union tour of Britain met with protests or disruption at all 24 games. This move became one of the earliest campaigns designed to isolate South Africa from cultural engagement with the world. The position of rugby as a game associated with Britain's empire made the statement one of anti-imperialism as well as anti-apartheid. It unified Commonwealth activists against the National Party government.

The politicisation of tours by South African teams extended to cricket. Basil D'Oliveira was a South African who had been classified as 'coloured' and moved to Britain in order to build a career as a professional cricketer. In 1968 he was omitted from the England team to tour South Africa following lobbying from the latter's government. Later D'Oliveira was called up as a replacement for the injured Tom Cartwright. The ensuing controversy included the South African government trying to bribe D'Oliveira to stay away and its Prime Minister, B. J. Vorster, publicly claiming that his selection was politically motivated.[24] As a result the Marylebone Cricket Club (MCC), which represented the English team, cancelled the tour.

---

[22] The Gleneagles Agreement on Sporting Contacts with South Africa, June 1977, published https://production-new-commonwealth-files.s3.eu-west-2.amazonaws.com/s3fs-public/documents/GleneaglesAgreement.pdf?VersionId=GMK06u9YdM5q2M3yKNhUZMP87fNelaMd, Accessed 23 June 2022.

[23] Peter May, *The Rebel Tours: Cricket's Crisis of Consciousness* (Cheltenham: Sportsbooks, 2009), 12.

[24] May, *Rebel Tours*, 7.

Activists saw participation in tours in South Africa as supporting the regime. In protest at the proposed South African cricket team's tour of England in 1970, campaigners launched the 'Stop the Seventy' campaign. Their direct-action tactics included breaking into county cricket grounds and spraying weedkiller on the pitch.[25] With a general election approaching, Britain's Labour government wanted to avoid mass protests and pressurised the MCC to cancel the tour. The controversy was closely followed by the International Cricket Conference announcing an international boycott of South African cricket teams.

As the international anti-apartheid campaign gathered momentum, the South African government sought ways to maintain its international profile. It attempted to break the boycotts and encouraged rebel sports tours. Despite many international sporting authorities banning tours of South Africa, some athletes were willing to break the boycott. In 1982 a rebel English cricket tour included stars like Graham Gooch and Geoffrey Boycott. The MCC reacted with staunch measures against participants, banning them from playing for England. After his subsequent three-year ban Gooch depicted himself as a victim, writing 'perhaps now I know how a prisoner feels, standing in the dock convinced of his own innocence but hearing the judge pass sentence, sending him to jail'.[26] His 'sentence' came while Nelson Mandela was imprisoned for his political activity and demonstrated the lack of repentance among many of these sportsmen. Further rebel cricket tours by Sri Lanka (1982), West Indies (1982–83 and 1983–84) and Australia (1985–86 and 1986–87), along with similar rebel rugby tours, threatened the solidity of the boycott movement. Several cricketers were once again banned from playing for England after a rebel tour led by the former English captain Mike Gatting.[27] The international campaign against the racial state by no means drew universal support, with several sportsmen willing to maintain ties with South Africa following inducements from the National Government.

The cultural boycott extended to music from the late 1950s. Musicians were requested not to play concerts in South Africa. However, many American artists including Frank Sinatra and The Beach Boys and British stars including Queen, Cilla Black and Status Quo ignored the boycott.[28] In 1981 an American group called Artists United Against Apartheid formed to further publicise the actions. Their 1985 song *(Ain't Gonna Play) Sun City* aimed to strengthen the boycott. By now international anti-apartheid campaigners were focussing their publicity around Nelson Mandela and his fight for freedom. The British musician Jerry Dammers, formerly of The

---

[25] Colin Shindler, *Barbed Wire and Cucumber Sandwiches: The Controversial South African Tour of 1970* (London: Pitch Publishing, 2020).

[26] Graham Gooch, *Out of the Wilderness* (London: Grafton, 1986), 63.

[27] May, *Rebel Tours*.

[28] Thörn, *Anti-Apartheid*, 63.

Specials, and Dali Tambo, the son of ANC President Oliver, founded a UK-based group called Artists Against Apartheid. Their song *Nelson Mandela* (1984) with its demand to 'Free Nelson Mandela' became a clarion call for anti-apartheid activists around the world. Peter Hain, one of the key organisers of the anti-apartheid campaign and later a British cabinet minister, said '"(Free) *Nelson Mandela*" was absolutely crucial in Mandela's breakthrough and in him becoming a global figure. It brought his brand and his identity into people's living rooms.'[29] The song's popularity spurred artists to organise concerts that they hoped would prompt political actions against the apartheid state from recalcitrant governments like those of Margaret Thatcher and Ronald Reagan in the UK and USA. During this time Thatcher opposed sanctions and campaigners believed that pressure from below was the only way to force governments to act.

On 11 June 1988 a massive concert was held at Wembley Arena to commemorate Mandela's 70th birthday. It was broadcast globally to millions of viewers who tuned in to see popular artists such as Whitney Houston and Dire Straits perform and to demand that Mandela be freed. An ironic twist saw a performance by Eric Clapton, whose comments had led to the establishment of Rock Against Racism, from which the musicians' Mandela campaign had emerged (see Chapter 2).

This televised concert was such a success that it was repeated in April 1990, this time with a special guest: the newly freed Nelson Mandela walked out in front of the packed Wembley Stadium. He thanked the crowd for their support and urged them to continue to push for the abolition of apartheid.

Mandela had been freed from prison on 11 February 1990. While a romanticised interpretation of worldwide activism sees the concerts organised in his support as playing a major role, the most effective pressure came from within South Africa. Peter Hain states that 'The reason that South Africa negotiated Mandela's freedom was to save the country and save themselves because the country was becoming ungovernable.'[30] Throughout the 1970s black South Africans had been killed by the police for protesting, including an attack on a student protest against unequal education in June 1976, and the murder of activist Steve Biko in 1977. In 1983 the National Party attempted to reform the constitution by offering some parliamentary representation to other racial groups, but these changes locked in a white majority. The response to the new constitution, which was deemed to further entrench apartheid, was regular protests, often including violence against symbols of the state. By 1985 the government had declared a state of emergency in much of the country. The police response was one of detention, torture and murder of campaigners.[31]

---

[29] Quoted in Daniel Rachel, *Walls Come Tumbling Down: The Music and Politics of Rock against Racism, 2 Tone and Red Wedge*, (London: Picador, 2016), 519–521.

[30] Rachel, *Walls*, 528.

[31] Nancy Clark and William Worger, *South Africa: The Rise and Fall of Apartheid* (London: Taylor and Francis, 2016), 108.

As international businesses pulled out their investment, partially in response to divestment campaigns, South Africa's economy became increasingly destabilised. South African authorities negotiated with Mandela over his release from 1986 (while wholesale repression continued). But the activists did help to raise international awareness of the apartheid regime and demonstrated to the South African government that there was a worldwide system of friendship from which they were excluded.

Despite the release of Mandela, the state of near civil war continued. It was not until April 1994 that the South African government arranged elections, with the franchise including South Africans of all ethnic groups. Most of the apartheid laws had by now been repealed in an attempt by the government to hold onto power. Pressure from inside South Africa, supported by global networks formed of activist groups, multinational organisations and businesses, had caused the National Party to instigate change. The ANC won a majority and formed a government of national unity, which continued to dismantle the racial state. The ending of apartheid allowed for mainly peaceful change between ethnic groups in South Africa as the 'Rainbow Nation' re-entered the world stage. However systemic poverty and calls for retribution limited the scope of this encounter. While South Africa entered a period of recovery and reconstruction it will still take several generations to undo the effects of legalised racism under the apartheid state. International activists from around the world created a global civil society in support of the ANC. They pressured national governments and international organisations, sometimes bringing sanctions against South Africa. Their actions and solidarity with others and their 'imagined community' of activists helped to publicise the actions of the National Party government and meant that the name of Nelson Mandela became associated with the push for the overthrow of apartheid.

Women's Liberation

A similar global civil society formed around women's rights in the postwar era. Sometimes, however, differing global conditions created influences on movements that caused their diverse sections to pull in different directions. From the mid-twentieth century onwards women's movements became increasingly interconnected and globalised. Activists from around the world used the mechanisms of global institutions like the UN to better connect with other women and to push for change on a global scale.

Organised campaigns for women's political rights began in the late nineteenth century and earned the franchise for women in most democracies by the end of World War Two. There were attempts to globalise women's struggles in the early twentieth century with the foundation of the International Council of Women in 1888 and the International Women's Suffrage Alliance (later renamed International Alliance of Women) in 1904. But organisation on a local and national scale was the predominant way women co-ordinated activities before World War Two. After 1945 women's struggles for equality in the workplace, the right to control over their reproductive functions and against sexual violence continued. This period, which saw its biggest expressions in the 1960s and 1970s, has often been labelled the second wave of feminism and saw attempts to challenge discriminatory laws and change the mentalities of the—usually—men in power. By the 1990s the movement was more focussed on the individual rights of women and especially critical of the gendered division of labour. It subsequently became tied into other battles over identity, and the concept of intersectionality allowed the movement to incorporate issues of race and class.

In America and Western Europe narratives about the growth of second-wave feminism from the late 1960s have presented women from these regions as the activists who pushed for equal rights for women in the home and workplace, and control over their bodies. Histories of feminism have suggested that a political movement grew out of this Western intellectual tradition that began with Simone de Beauvoir's book *The Second Sex* in 1949 and was reinforced in Betty Friedan's *The Feminine Mystique* (1963).[32] De Beauvoir and Friedan focussed on the social construction of gender roles that led to women taking a subservient position in society and the need to change domesticity by achieving equality in the home. Through the 1960s many women activists influenced by these texts began to organise as a response to being marginalised by men in the New Left movements. Women's groups also began to campaign to change the role of women in society and push for workplace equality.

The movement which emerged around these ideas campaigned on issues like equal pay, the removal of legalised discrimination in the workplace and ending of violence against women. Women's groups had campaigned for equal pay in Britain since the 1930s. World War Two helped some employers to realise the value of women's labour but they still tended to prioritise men. Britain's wartime government established a Royal Commission on Equal Pay, which reported in 1946. The report, however, relied on pre-war assumptions and effectively sidelined the issue. Trade unions only paid lip service to equal pay, often prioritising the men's settlement, a tendency that continued even after increasing participation by women in unions from the mid-1960s.[33] A number of middle-class women's groups continued the campaign for equal pay during the 1950s and early 1960s. One of their members was the film-maker Jill Craigie. Her 1951 film *To Be A Woman*[34] challenged the idea that women's sphere was the home. It showed the reality that women did work, but often for unfair pay and with limited opportunities for advancement. Craigie's film made clear the moral duty to pay women equally and end prejudice in

[32] Simone de Beauvoir, *Le Deuxième Sexe: Les Faits et les Mythes* (Paris: Gallimard, 1949); Betty Friedan, *The Feminine Mystique* (New York: Norton, 1963; cf. Patu & Antje Schrupp, *A Brief History of Feminism*, Trans. Sophie Lewis (Cambridge, MA: MIT Press, 2017), 43–45; June Hannam, *Feminism* (London: Taylor and Francis, 2011).

[33] Dolly Smith Wilson, 'Gender: Change and Continuity', *A Companion to Contemporary Britain 1939–2000* (London, Wiley: 2005), 245–262.

[34] Jill Craigie, *To Be a Woman*, (Outlook Films, 1951).

the workplace. Politicians in many countries eventually came round to the idea of equal pay. Following a lengthy strike by women sewing machinists at Ford plants in Dagenham and Halewood Britain's Labour government implemented an Equal Pay Act in 1970. The USA had done so in 1963. The reality, however, was often different and employers exploited loopholes, meaning that gender pay gaps continued.

In other areas the movement adopted direct-action tactics, which are often seen as bringing the concerns of radical feminists into the mainstream. In 1968, the activist and scholar Robin Morgan organised a protest against the Miss America beauty pageant in Atlanta. The competition embodied the sexism that feminists wanted to challenge and their protest targeted the standards of beauty to which women were expected to conform. The protesters symbolically threw several 'feminine' items, including bras, into a dustbin; these were not set alight, despite the myth which surrounds the movement.[35] Inside women held up banners demanding 'Women's Liberation'. The tactic grabbed media attention and inspired women in other nations to attempt similar action. In 1970 British protesters invaded the stage of the Miss World contest in London, throwing flour bombs at the host Bob Hope. This event was dramatised in the 2020 film *Misbehaviour*, which follows the journey of the activist Sally Alexander into joining a radical feminist group and undertaking this direct action.[36] During the late 1960s these ideas about women's rights and campaigning styles crossed borders and influenced similar groups in other Western nations.

As the movement grew, its intellectual publications expanded; the Australian feminist Germaine Greer published *The Female Eunuch* in 1970.[37] Greer writes that the traditional family suppresses women, especially because of unequal levels of domestic servitude, with women pushed into subordinate sexual relationships. In many Western nations legalised discrimination against women persisted and societies often failed to accept women's independence. In 1972 the American magazine *Ms* was founded by a collective of feminists including Gloria Steinem. That year the magazine published an issue in which women openly discussed abortion, which remained illegal in much of the USA. The same year another feminist magazine, *Spare Rib*, began publication in Britain. These regular publications enabled the women's liberation movement to build larger transnational networks. As the movement progressed, two distinct wings emerged that worked in tandem but sometimes disagreed. Liberal feminism focussed on achieving equality under the law and in society, while radical feminism advocated segregation from male-dominated institutions and society as the only way to overcome oppression by men. Popular

---

[35] Beth Kreydatus, 'Confronting the "Bra-Burners": Teaching Radical Feminism With a Case Study', *The History Teacher* (2008), 41.4, 490.

[36] Finn Mackay, *Radical Feminism: Feminist Activism in Movement* (Basingstoke: Macmillan, 2015), 48; Philippa Lowthorpe, *Misbehaviour* (Walt Disney: 2020).

[37] Germaine Greer, *The Female Eunuch* (London: MacGibbon & Kee, 1970).

culture has celebrated and romanticised the Western women's movement in the American series *Mrs America* (2020), which dramatised the life of Friedan and Steinem among other prominent, including anti-feminist, conservatives.[38] The movement has thus become embedded in Western memory, with its major figures being celebrated as women's fight for equality has continued in the twenty-first century.

Those labelled second-wave feminists focussed on male violence against women and one campaign was the 'Reclaim the Night' marches. Sociologist Finn Mackay explains that the origins of this movement were at the International Tribunal on Crimes Against Women conference in Brussels in March 1976. On the last day of the conference the women processed through the city bearing candles to voice their anger at violence against women. A few months later women in Rome protested against increasing numbers of rapes in the city, bearing signs with the slogan 'Reclaim the Night'. In April 1977 the first co-ordinated Reclaim the Night protests took place across West German cities. Women dressed as witches carried flaming torches as they marched through the streets throwing flour and dye at men.[39] From 1975 Britain saw a spate of murders of women by Peter Sutcliffe, nicknamed the Yorkshire Ripper; police advised women to stay off the streets after dark, prompting feminists to demand a curfew for men instead. In November 1977 women organised the first British Reclaim the Night marches across eleven British cities including Leeds, Manchester and London. Women in multiple nations began to use the symbols of Reclaim the Night to start their own movements to protest violence against women. Across the West the women's movement was increasingly integrated and worked together as something approaching a global civil society.

While global solidarity became increasingly important for the women's movement it would be inaccurate to view it as a single unified group, despite its interconnections across nations. Campaigners of the global majority South tended to tie women's rights to changing the global economic situation. Women's movements from around the world came together at conferences organised by the UN in Mexico City in 1975, Copenhagen in 1980, Nairobi in 1985 and Beijing in 1995, but at other times the aims of these organisations were more divergent. Historiography and activist scholarship have often been divided. Scholars such as Nanette Funk depict the Western liberal feminist movement in a positive light, suggesting it led a globalised push for women's equality.[40] Other scholars, however, have accused Western activists of portraying those of Eastern Europe or the developing world as merely victims

---

[38] Anna Boden, *Mrs America* (Shiny Penney Productions, 2020).

[39] Mackay, *Radical Feminism*, 1.

[40] Nanette Funk, 'A Very Tangled Knot: Official state socialist women's organisations, women's agency and feminism in Eastern European state socialism', *European Journal of Women's Studies*, 21.4 (2014), 344–360.

and without their own agency to campaign for women's rights.[41] Their work, among others, shows that the women's movement has always been transnational. There were, however, differences in outlook from groups of activists around the world.

Activists in the Eastern Bloc developed their own form of feminism, and Francesca de Haan shows that women were more than mere victims of the state-socialist regimes. The Women's International Democratic Federation (WIDF) formed in Paris in 1945 and became a mobilising organisation for women in Eastern Europe who used it to push for women's rights globally. During the McCarthyite purges of suspected American communists the WIDF was labelled as a communist-supporting organisation by the House Un-American Activities Committee (HUAC). WIDF activities were essentially shut down with the threat of sanctions against its American members, who in turn suppressed evidence of their membership. De Haan suggests that three decades after the collapse of the Berlin Wall, this Cold War mentality has persisted in the minds of scholars who have ignored or essentialised women's activism in Eastern Europe, reducing members of women's movements to mere communist dupes who were insincere about improving women's rights.[42] De Haan and other researchers have examined how 'second-world' women were often the instigators of globalised women's activism, including agitating for the UN's International Women's Year. Magdalena Grabowska expands on the group's activism by examining how a group of Polish women organised via WIDF in the 1960s. They used the institution to move beyond being a pro-Soviet front and to work for women's rights on a global scale.[43] These activists did not form a non-state group. Instead, by working within the Polish state's framework they travelled to international women's congresses organised by WIDF from the late 1940s, before many Western states proscribed this federation, and fed these ideas back into the formal policy of the state. By engaging with Western and non-Western activists the Polish women were able to influence the direction of emerging transnational women's activism.

When attending international conferences, activists from communist nations stressed that women in socialist countries were more equal in terms of pay, something which Grabowska sees as influencing Western campaigns during the 1960s. By the 1960s, however, the WIDF spoke with a unified

---

[41] Francisca de Haan, 'Continuing Cold War Paradigms in Western Historiography of Transnational organisations: The case of the Women's International Democratic Federation', *Women's History Review*, 19.4 (2010), 547–573; Magdalena Grabowska, 'Beyond the "Development" Paradigm: State Socialist Women's Activism, Transnationalism and the "Long Sixties"', in *Women's Activism and "Second Wave" Feminism: Transnational Histories*, edited by Barbara Maloney and Jennifer Nelson (London: Bloomsbury, 2017), 147–172; Elisabeth Armstrong, 'Before Bandung: The Anti-Imperialist Movement in Asia and the Women's International Democratic Federation', *Signs: Journal of Women and Culture in Society*, 41.2 (2016), 305–331.

[42] De Haan, 'Cold War Paradigms', 547–573.

[43] Grabowska, 'Beyond the "Development" Paradigm', 147–172.

voice about how women's equality could only be achieved within a state-socialist system, leaving less room for independent action like that of the Polish women. The main areas that the group now sought to influence were the newly decolonised states, hoping to bring them in line with Eastern Bloc views. Scholarship into these institutions has continued to grow, despite claims from academics such as Funk that any organisation engaging with state socialism was more of a hindrance than a help.[44]

WIDF attempted to spread its influence in Africa and Asia. In conjunction with African and Asian transnational women's groups it organised conferences in Beijing (1949), Columbo (1958) and Cairo (1961). While Elisabeth Armstrong questions how far WIDF was able to create a single 'third-world feminism', she presents these conferences as part of the developing attempt to challenge 'feminist imperialism' and to demonstrate the agency of women in the developing world.[45] The elucidation of a third-world feminist agenda at these conferences helped to decentre global feminism away from the Western nations, with some activists criticising the attitudes of Western feminists. Several Asian, Arab and African groups looked to build links across the colonised and newly decolonised nations with many, such as the All-Indian Women's Commission and the Mahila Atma Raksha Samiti (Women's Self Defence Organisation) from Bengal, forming around a mass-based feminism built among peasant women. Many of these groups sent delegates to the WIDF congress, where their common goals included social reform for women in education and health, equal rights and participation in public life, and anti-colonialist economic restructuring. Among them was Lise Oculi, an Algerian who hoped to challenge the predominant ideas of feminism being centred on Europe and to demonstrate women's struggles against colonial oppression. Oculi was one of a number of non-Western feminists who were building transnational women's rights networks independently of the Western organisations and tied women's rights into the anti-colonial struggle.

The success of the transnational women's movement continued and WIDF persuaded the UN to declare 1975 its International Women's Year, with the first World Conference on Women held in Mexico City. The *UNESCO Courier* published two special issues on the subject. It highlighted the progress that women had made in obtaining voting rights worldwide but also examined issues resulting from unequal pay, access to education and domestic responsibilities. Articles explained the problems that women faced in African nations where they were shown to have responsibility for the 'man-child on her back' meaning that they must 'help her man to stand on his own two feet and discover his role in a relationship of equal responsibility'.[46] Similar articles on

---

[44] Cf. Funk, 'Tangled Knot', 344–360.

[45] Armstrong, 'Before Bandung', 305–331.

[46] Thelma Awori, 'For African Women Equal Rights are not Enough', *UNESCO Courier*, March 1975, 21–25.

Asian and South American nations showed the true global scale of the intentions of the UN. This year was one of the key moments in the globalisation of women's rights campaigns, kick-starting what some historians see as the UN Decade for Women.[47]

The legacy of International Women's Year is contested. Historians from the former communist bloc and developing world are critical of the way that its success has frequently been portrayed as being created by Western feminists.[48] Kristen Ghodsee sees the Cold War rivalry as something that benefitted women's groups because governments in both spheres competed to show that they were best placed to deliver equality. She shows how the American government, despite its initial reluctance to support a women's conference, agreed to sponsor the event in Mexico to avoid it being held in a communist nation.[49] The official status of the Mexico conference was initially suspect because it had emerged from WIDF. The pressure applied by non-Western movements at the UN forced the Western governments to support the conference despite their initial opposition.

Around 8000 delegates attended the Mexico conference. Some radical feminists criticised the event because of their perception of the UN as a male-dominated institution.[50] Greer was dismissive of the participation of delegates such as Imelda Marcos, the wife of the Philippine dictator Ferdinand Marcos, and Ashraf Pahlavi, the sister of the Iranian Shah. Greer wrote, 'We had all been duped into attending a debacle, where women who had come to prominence through their relationships with men were employed by those men to further their policies at the expense of the women of the World.'[51] For these radical feminists the equality on offer at the Mexico conference appeared merely to be integration into the male-dominated institutions. Similarly, women from the developing world were worried about the likelihood of American and European feminists dominating the UN conference and the parallel NGO Tribune. Many Asian women activists were suspicious of the word feminism because of the way Western campaigners had been stereotyped as radically individualistic, anti-men and anti-family; they questioned how far

---

[47] J. Zisner, 'From Mexico to Copenhagen to Nairobi: The United Nations Decade for Women, 1975–1985', *Journal of World History*, 13.1 (2002), 139–68.

[48] Kristen Ghodsee, *Second World Second Sex: Socialist Women's Activism and Global Solidarity during the Cold War* (London: Duke University Press, 2019), 2–3.

[49] Ghodsee, *Second World Second Sex*, 7.

[50] Chaira Bonfiglioli, 'The First UN World Conference on Women (1975) as a Cold War Encounter: Recovering Anti-Imperialist Non-Aligned and Socialist Genealogies', *Filozofija Drustovo*, XXVII (3), 2016, 526.

[51] Germaine Greer, *The Madwoman's Underclothes: Essays and Occasional Writings* (New York: Atlantic Monthly Press, 1986), cited Bonfiglioli, 'The First UN World Conference', 526.

feminist principles could be applied in the Asian context.[52] For them it was important that women's movements developed independently in each nation in distinction from Western feminists. Some Western feminists, such as Charlotte Bunch, acted on their awareness of this issue: she opted not to attend for fear of American feminists dominating proceedings.[53] The difference in priorities reflected geopolitical and economic structures: women in the developing world wanted to link their activism to anti-imperialist struggles and global economic equality.

The parallel Tribune conference of NGOs was attended by 6000 delegates. The Tribune allowed women from the less developed nations to air their grievances. Many non-Western activists were angry that Western feminists held most of the prominent positions, such as Betty Friedan assuming the spokesperson role. Delegates from the communist bloc and developing nations saw the need for the women's movement to be tied to international events and to campaign for economic equality, the same issues that men discussed on the international stage. Western feminists, on the other hand, preferred to focus on legal equality.[54] Friedan acknowledged the importance of non-Western women's activism and toned down the idea of feminism as a 'revolution against men', which many of the non-Western activists felt the American feminists desired.[55] However, Latin American delegates remained angry that poverty reduction was a lesser concern for many Western activists. While differences between certain women's organisations existed, the process of discussion allowed these views to be heard and global civil society to mature.[56]

The differences in perspective between Western and non-Western women's activism sometimes remained, despite the emerging global solidarity. Mary Daly's 1978 book *Gyn/Ecology* condemned rituals of oppression in developing countries such as suttee (the practice of widow-burning) in India, foot binding in China and female genital mutilation.[57] Critics of Daly have taken issue with her presentation of Western women activists as the saviours of all women, while stereotyping those outside the West as victims of male domination who lacked their own voices. Priya Jha sees Daly and other Western feminists as

---

[52] Mina Roces, 'Asian Feminisms: Women's movements from the Asian perspective', in *Women's Movements in Asia: Feminism and Transnational Activism*, edited by Mina Roces and Louise Edwards (London: Taylor and Francis, 2010), 2.

[53] Jocelyn Olcott, *International Women's Year: The Greatest Consciousness Raising Event in History* (Oxford: Oxford University Press, 2017), 115–118.

[54] Ghodsee, *Second World Second Sex*.

[55] Olcott, *International Women's Year*, 125.

[56] Helen McCarthy, 'The Diplomatic History of Global Women's Rights: The British Foreign Office and International Women's Year, 1975', *Journal of Contemporary History*, 50.4 (2015), 850.

[57] Mary Daly, *Gyn/Ecology: The Meta Ethics of Radical Feminism* (Boston, MA: Beacon Press, 1978).

continuing the practices of colonisation.[58] Transnational women's activism was a series of interconnected movements, which were decentred, with leadership emerging around the world. The paternalist assumption that Western cultures were the best placed to deliver women's equality was criticised by global majority South activists. Historians of communist bloc and third-world feminism have continued to emphasise this division, which was tied to Cold War assumptions. Many see the 'second-world' and 'third-world' feminism as placing women's struggles behind state ideology. Women's activists from these regions, argues Kristen Ghodsee, never prioritised recognition over redistribution because they saw little point in arguing for equal pay in a system where all lived in poverty or for equal rights between men and women in a system of racial inequality.[59]

As criticisms from the developing world were aired, many Western feminists took the opportunity to strengthen the global feminist alliance. In 1984 the American activist and political theorist Robin Morgan co-founded an NGO promoting global feminism and published a collection of essays, *Sisterhood is Global*. In the book Morgan aimed to bring together the different objectives of divergent feminists, showcasing the work of activists from around the world while highlighting global inequalities that women suffered including illiteracy, pay disparity, overwork, lack of reproductive control, violence and poverty. Morgan wrote about her intention to unify global women's movements explaining that, '*Women constitute not an oppressed minority, but a majority—of almost all national populations, and of the entire human species*. As that species approaches critical mass and the capacity to eradicate all life on the planet, more than ever before in recorded history that majority of humanity is now mobilising.'[60] For Morgan and the contributors, feminism was something that had begun in each individual culture; the future of the women's movement was in building cross-border connections that advanced feminist ideas. Migration, exile and educational campaigns all played a role in allowing these ideas to spread and to build a global sense of solidarity among women.

The 1990s saw renewed vigour in the globalised feminist movement. Through the 1980s women's conferences at the UN were linked to development and focussed on the impact of poverty on women while demanding economic changes and improvements in women's education. Regional networks strengthened their linkages agitating for these changes and brought together activists, NGOs and policy makers to shape new policies. In 1995 a conference in Beijing commemorated the UN International Women's Year twenty years earlier. It drew around 3000 delegates with 30,000 attending the

---

[58] Priya Jha, '"Making a Point By Choice: Maternal Imperialism, Second Wave Feminism and Transnational Epistemologies', in Barbara Maloney and Jennifer Nelson (eds), *Women's Activism and "Second Wave" Feminism: Transnational Histories* (London: Bloomsbury, 2017), 173–5.

[59] Ghodsee, *Second World Second Sex*, 27.

[60] Robin Morgan (ed.), *Sisterhood is Global: The International Women's Movement Anthology* (Open Road Media, 2016 [1984]), [emphasis hers].

parallel NGO conference. The NGO conference tackled the issue of poverty among women and attributed the issue to globalisation, which had diverted wealth and resources from South to North.[61] Wang Zheng and Ying Zhang have shown how the conference raised the profile of Chinese feminists and helped them launch NGOs that operated outside the control of the Communist Party.[62] Despite legal gains in terms of stopping many discriminatory laws, however, the global women's movement had many victories still to win.

The form of feminism that emerged in the late twentieth century built on the trend for increasing connections between movements for women, combined with earlier tendencies to engage with related movements such as racial equality. This intersectionality was first described by the law professor Kimberlé Crenshaw, who felt that as a black woman she was treated worse than both white women and black men.[63] Consequently the overlapping black and female identities made her feel as though she was at an intersection or crossroads, with traffic—in the form of discrimination—rushing at her from all sides. In response the other organisations striving for equality for marginalised groups have begun to pool their activism and to fight for multiple causes that are mutually beneficial to the participants. This intersectionality became one of the key concepts of the global feminist network into the twenty-first century.

Environmentalism

Few readers will be unaware of the effects of global climate change and the disasters caused by increasingly frequent extreme weather events. This awareness is testament to the effectiveness of an international campaign by activists, scientists and journalists that has sometimes led to global political action. Environmentalism has been seen by Keck and Sikkink as different in form to other campaigns, being instead a framework in which 'a variety of claims about resource use, property rights, and power may be reconfigured'. Environmentalism, therefore, incorporates numerous campaigning organisations with different and complementary goals. Keck and Sikkink believe that in part this is because the Earth lacks the human face that other campaigns have been able to create.[64] Figures like Chico Mendes, David Attenborough and Greta Thunberg have at various times received huge publicity, but none have yet become the face of the campaign to protect Earth in the way that Nelson Mandela embodied the anti-apartheid struggle. Nevertheless, disparate

---

[61] Devaki Jain, *Women, Development and the UN: A Sixty Year Quest for Equality and Justice* (Bloomington: Indiana University Press, 2005), 102–134, 144.

[62] Wang Zheng and Ying Zhang, 'Global Concepts, Local Practices: Chinese Feminism Since the Fourth UN Conference on Women', *Feminist Studies*, 36.1 (2010), 40–70.

[63] Kimberlé Crenshaw, 'Demarginalizing the Intersection of Race and Sex: A Black Feminist Critique of Antidiscrimination Doctrine, Feminist Theory and Antiracist Politics', *University of Chicago Legal Forum*, (1989) 1.8.

[64] Keck and Sikkink, Activists Beyond Borders, 121.

campaign groups have turned concern for the future of the Earth into one of the key political issues of the twenty-first century.

The first nature campaigns emerged in the late nineteenth century in response to industrialisation and its visual effects, like the bellows of smoke that blanketed many cities. Logging became a concern because of erosion and decimation of the forests, and many European countries introduced replantation programmes.[65] Ultimately, however, attempts to limit pollution fell flat, with the burning of coal often becoming an indicator of prosperity and comfort. The spread of capitalism relied on ever-increasing uses of natural resources. Several localised groups emerged that were dedicated to defending the natural environment. In the USA the Sierra Club was formed in 1892 to protect America's wildernesses. In 1895 three Austrians founded the *Naturfreunde* (Friends of Nature), which promoted access to the natural world. The same year in Britain the National Trust was founded to preserve natural beauty and heritage. These groups focussed on access to nature and protection of the natural environment. Some governments and local authorities designated areas as national parks, including USA's Yosemite Valley in 1864 and Australia's Royal National Park in 1879. Small steps were taken to internationalise these local movements: in 1909 a conference addressing the protection of the countryside took place in Paris with speakers from six European countries. Even at this stage there was some understanding that the challenges facing the environment expanded beyond borders.

The interwar years saw increased economic developments as industrialisation spread around the world. The Soviet Union's first five-year plan under Stalin demanded 'the great transformation of nature', meaning deforestation and increasing the amount of land under tillage.[66] This expansion of industry into undeveloped areas echoed that of the Western nations during the previous century and shows how humankind shaped nature to accommodate its industrialisation. Despite the use of terror under Stalin some Soviet scientists organised to defend nature. The All-Russian Society for the Protection of Nature (VOOP) was founded in 1924. It held conferences and published a magazine and papers that called for the protection of Russia's wildernesses, forests and the animals living within them against the planned industrial revolution. They were far from a mass movement, but they did have around 15,000 members by the 1930s and had limited foreign contacts. The totalitarian nature of the Soviet state limited the scope for environmental campaigns, but some scientists persisted in their endeavours.

The post-war era saw Western governments prioritise an aspect of political economy that in retrospect appears to be incompatible with environmentalism: the emergence of affluence and consumerism. Sustained increases in consumer spending, often brought about through reliance on credit, was

---

[65] David Peterson del Mar, *Environmentalism* (Harlow: Longman, 2006), 33.
[66] Peterson del Mar, *Environmentalism*, 39.

seen as the outcome of the ideology of 'freedom'. Under consumer capitalism an increasing proportion of the world's population were encouraged to accumulate more items of comfort, including cars, without thinking of the external costs like pollution and the devastation caused by resource extraction. The globalisation of supply chains allowed the environmental impacts, and often horrific working conditions, to be displaced onto developing nations. Ramachandra Guha labels the period before the early 1960s as the 'age of ecological innocence'.[67] Guha argues that the belief in the benefits of an ever-expanding economy created by the development of science and industry meant the world ignored its consequences. Every product that was made from chemicals created toxic waste and the safe disposal of products, which often had inbuilt obsolescence, was rarely considered. Many of the products that became celebrated from the 1960s onwards required the use of synthetic plastics, one of the worst pollutants. These low-cost and versatile materials were invented in the late nineteenth and early twentieth centuries but found increased use in mass-produced goods after World War Two. Many are made from oil and do not decompose naturally; they are sent to landfill and seep into the oceans where they break down into microplastics, entering the food chain via water courses and sea-life. Mass consumption wrought a hugely damaging impact on the environment, of which many people were wilfully unaware.

It often took industrial disasters to prompt public outcry and for authorities to act. There were few limits on industrial activity and Western industries quickly recovered from World War Two, expanding to satisfy consumerist desires. Since the late nineteenth century London had experienced thick 'pea-souper' fogs which were associated with coal smoke. Public health concerns had long been raised about links between smog and respiratory diseases. In 1952 a thick fog enveloped Britain's capital and mixed with industrial smoke. The ensuing smog caused the deaths of 4000 people and heightened concerns about the effects of pollution on human health. Similar air pollution disasters occurred in Donora, Pennsylvania in 1948 and Poza Rica, Mexico in 1950, and saw the emergence of the Yokkaichi asthma in Japan from the late 1950s, an illness whose origins have been attributed to the rebuilding of its petrochemical industry. The London killer smog, however, allowed groups against pollution including the Coal Smoke Abatement Society (founded 1898) to have their voices heard, with media coverage focussing on the impact of pollution. The deaths and burgeoning campaign against industrial smoke prompted government action and in 1956 the Clean Air Act was passed to lessen factory

---

[67] Ramachandra Guha, *Environmentalism: A Global History* (Harlow: Longman, 2000), 64–6.

pollution. In this instance public health was the driving factor.[68] Conservationists, however, were beginning to be able to see that environmental degradation could be turned into an official concern.

The effects of nuclear weapons tests also began to concern scientists and journalists. When thermonuclear weapons began to be tested in 1952 newspapers printed scare stories about fears that the weapons might vaporise the atmosphere or destroy the Earth.[69] While these scientific scare stories were sensationalised by newspapers, they allowed readers to see the interconnectedness of the world. On 1 March 1954 the USA detonated its Castle Bravo shot on Bikini Atoll; it was the first explosion of a hydrogen bomb. Public consciousness around the world was awakened to the danger of this new generation of nuclear weapons. Several Marshall Islanders suffered radiation-related sicknesses and the crew of a Japanese fishing vessel called the *Lucky Dragon* became contaminated, despite being outside the official exclusion zone. The radiation eventually killed one of the sailors. The incident heightened fears around the effects of radiation. These new devices were depicted as living destructive beings and many people felt that they threatened the Earth. As Jodie Burkett has shown, news of the power of nuclear weapons and their destructiveness in often distant areas brought about a change in thinking throughout the 1960s, which enabled people to ponder the needs of the planet and the dangers of manmade destruction. The early anti-nuclear movement helped to incubate modern environmentalism.[70]

During the 1960s awareness of environmental degradation and the impact of chemicals became a major concern. In 1962 Rachel Carson, an American biologist, published *Silent Spring*. Carson wrote about a future in which wildlife had been eliminated because of excessive pesticide use, leaving the skies song-less. The book was an exposé of industrial-scale farming, which had caused a rise in single-crop yields relying on the heavy use of pesticides. These pesticides were poisoning wildlife and human beings. She wrote,

> [F]or the first time in the history of the world, every human being is now subjected to contact with dangerous chemicals, from the moment of conception until death. In the less than two decades of their use, the synthetic pesticides have been so thoroughly distributed throughout the animate and inanimate world that they occur virtually everywhere ... For these chemicals are now stored in the bodies of the vast majority of human beings, regardless of age.[71]

---

[68] Mark Jackson, 'Cleansing the air and promoting health: The politics of pollution in postwar Britain', in *Medicine, the Market and the Mass Media*, edited by Virginia Berridge and Kelly Laughlin (London: Routledge, 2005), 206–226.

[69] Adrian Bingham, '"The Monster"?: The British Press and Nuclear Culture, 1945-early 1960s', *British Society for the History of Science*, 45.4 (2013), 609–624.

[70] Jodie Burkett, 'The Campaign for Nuclear Disarmament and Changing Attitudes Towards the Earth in the Nuclear Age', *British Journal for the History Science*, 45.4 (2012), 625–639.

[71] Rachael Carson, *Silent Spring* (Boston, MA: Houghton Miffin, 1962), 31.

Worse, Carson found that the chemicals were failing to serve their purpose and detailed the emergence of pesticide resistance among insects, alongside devastation to animals relying on contaminated soil and toxic water courses. For Carson the conquest of nature by humankind was creating a new kind of environment where the theory of evolution was demonstrating its effectiveness: weaker insects had been destroyed by chemicals leaving 'only the strong and fit', which were immune to chemical control and growing in number.[72] Carson's almost apocalyptic observation made readers question the impact of industrial farming on the natural environment. Her book helped to awaken the nascent environmental movement.

Silent Spring was received warmly, with American President John F. Kennedy among those who were horrified by its warnings about environmental catastrophe.[73] Prior to the book's UK publication in 1963 the Duke of Edinburgh handed out advance copies. Awareness of environmental degradation grew and the book motivated a campaign by members of the House of Lords to have 1970 declared as the European Conservation Year. By the 1970s the USA and several European countries had taken measures to limit pesticide use. Several were banned including DDT, a chemical that Carson linked to cancer, which disappeared from the USA in 1972. *Silent Spring* helped to raise awareness of the damage to the environment and the threat to animal, plant and human life. However, as evidence about the danger of pesticides emerged, consecutive British governments dragged their feet on control measures before eventually banning DDT in 1984. Even then numerous other harmful pesticides remained legal. While *Silent Spring* raised awareness about the need to defend the environment, government responses were mixed and only led to limited action.

As environmental concerns increased, corporations used public relations to try to shape popular narratives arounds the effects of industry. Petro-chemical companies sought to deflect attention from the environmental impacts of their operations. In 1965 the oil company Shell released a short film called *Shellorama*.[74] This film aimed to show the past destruction of the environment that industry had caused. It also reassured viewers that Shell and many similar companies were now working to protect the environment from further damage. Their measures included masking onshore oil rigs behind coverings that looked like foliage and lobbying governments to ensure that there was more road space, so that cars would not run idle. The film was an early example of greenwashing, whereby transnational corporations defend their profits while issuing subtle propaganda to deter legislative action.

Nevertheless, a number of headline-grabbing ecological disasters in the 1960s increased awareness about the impact of industrial production on the environment. On 18 March 1967 the *Torrey Canyon* super-tanker ran aground

---

[72] Carson, *Silent Spring*, 229.
[73] Guha, *Environmentalism*, 72.
[74] Richard Cawston, *Shellorama* (Shell Film Unit, 1965).

off the coast of Cornwall. The ship shed much of its cargo of 1,118,000 tonnes of oil into the sea, becoming the world's largest oil spillage. Televised images showed the harm to sea birds, with locals and the army attempting to clean up oil from the shorelines in England and France. The authorities tried several methods to disperse the oil including the use of corrosive detergents, which were also used to clean beaches, before eventually bombing the oil slick in an attempt to ignite it. Meanwhile, Americans became similarly shocked by another massive spill off Santa Barbara in January 1969. The sense of disaster was exacerbated when on 22 June that year the heavily polluted Cuyahoga River in Cleveland briefly caught fire, sparking media fears about the environmental damage caused by American industry.

Participation in activism in the United States increased as more people began to accept the arguments about the environment. Membership of the Sierra Club had steadily increased throughout the 1960s, but now it boomed and supporters were encouraged to write to their representatives protesting against the destruction of the natural environment. Bills to protect 2 per cent of America's wilderness (1964) and ensure that rivers flowed in their natural state (1968) were passed following this campaign. Sections of the public appeared ready to listen, especially with such visible damage. As the 1970s approached the American government made some concessions to campaigners and created the Environmental Protection Agency, leading to renewed efforts to clean up waterways.[75]

The 1960s marked a shift in consciousness in the way that activists thought about the environment. The Earth was increasingly perceived as a single connected entity. Previously environmentalists tended to focus on a single aspect of conservation or geographical area. The connection between localities became more apparent as the Age of Globalism began to be realised. Photographs of the Earth from the Apollo Eight space mission in 1968 marked the first time that the planet had been seen in its entirety from space, stimulating new environmental and scientific thinking (Fig. 4.2). Whereas previously scientists and campaigners thought in terms of conservation and nature preservation, now activists began to envisage Earth as a whole and saw that a problem for one part could be a problem for all. The ultimate expression of single-planet thinking came from ecologist James Lovelock, whose book *Gaia* framed the Earth as a single living organism.[76] While Lovelock did not fully realise the dangers of climate change, something that he has subsequently warned about, the idea of the Earth as a single organism that was adversely affected by human activity grew and was taken up by activists around the world

---

[75] David Stradling & Richard Stradling, *Where the River Burned: Carl Stokes and the Struggle to Save Cleveland* (Cornell University Press, 2015).

[76] James Lovelock, *Gaia: A New Look at the Earth* (Oxford: Oxford University Press, 1979).

Fig. 4.2 Earthrise. *Source*: NASA/Bill Anders

during the 1980s and 1990s.[77] No longer could human desires be placed above the protection of the planet. Environmentalism led to an international cultural encounter with ideas transcending nations and becoming global.

Throughout the 1960s and 1970s environmental movements developed in many Western nations. Often, however, these were national movements campaigning for global objectives rather than being truly transnational. More globally minded activists began to popularise the slogan 'Think Globally, Act Locally'. This mantra allowed activists to challenge their own government, but progress was often slow. Britain's movement often consisted of upper- and middle-class groups campaigning against infringements into the countryside by industrial corporations. In Germany, France and the Netherlands the movements had made little impact by the 1970s, neither did they in Southern Europe. But further north in Sweden the *Silent Spring* moment invigorated campaigns against pollution, particularly against mercury in the pulp industry, and a more comprehensive Environmental Protection Law was passed in 1968. Australia also had greater environmental awareness with laws protecting water and air from pollution in each state and protection of the wilder areas including the Great Barrier Reef, which was made a marine park in 1975. But these national efforts were mainly focussed on preservation of areas and limited protection from activities like mining.

Many communist countries had their own environmental movements. Rapid industrialisation programmes and intensification of agriculture had degraded the atmosphere and used up natural resources with the same and

---

[77] James Lovelock, *The Revenge of Gaia: Why the Earth Is Fighting Back—and How We Can Still Save Humanity* (London: Allen Lane, 2006).

sometimes even more destructive consequences than in the West. Environmentalists had to cleave semi-autonomous space away from the Soviet state to campaign.[78] Indeed Douglas Weiner has shown that such movements began before Stalin's rise to power and continued to agitate for the defence of nature, often going against the grandiose economic plans of the state. Naturalists and geographers organised under various groups including VOOP, the Moscow Society of Naturalists (MOIP), Young Naturalists and later the All-Russia Society for the Protection of Nature and the Greening of Population Centres (VOSOPiONOP). These mainly scientist-activists were followed by their students who established Student Brigades for Nature Protection at many universities. Nature protection organisations opposed many large-scale projects such as river diversion and deforestation caused by logging. They were often opposed to the regime's centralised economic policy. Nikita Khrushchev particularly sought to reduce the area designated as nature preserves, prompting letter-writing campaigns from the nature community. These campaigns did open some discussion on the management of forests and logging, although lax enforcement of protections and wastage during transportation (usually by floating logs down a river) meant that replanting efforts were often ineffective.[79]

In 1958 the Soviet government announced its intention to build new hydro-electric plants and factories on Lake Baikal, a huge Siberian inland sea. The industrialisation would reduce its volume and pollute the freshwater sea. In response the largest-scale Soviet environmental campaign to date emerged. The group's main tactic was writing letters to Soviet politicians and newspapers. While the campaign was ultimately unsuccessful, Nicholas Breyfogle argues that activists brought Soviet environmental issues to the mainstream and opened a conversation about the impact of industrialisation.[80] The Soviet government was often able to sideline controversial voices or restrict their audience to the scientific community. Occasionally, however, environmentalists mustered public opinion against official policy such as in defence of Lake Baikal. They were sometimes able to form overseas contacts, although this was often through the communist-supporting 'friendship societies' of Western countries. Their participation in international discussions on nature protection and the environment was limited. In common with the WIDF campaigners mentioned above, these activists had to operate within officially sanctioned state campaigns. Their ability to conduct activism was limited until unofficial groups began to organise independently, prompting harassment from the state.

---

[78] Douglas R. Weiner, *A Little Corner of Freedom: Russian Nature Protection from Stalin to Gorbachev* (Berkeley, CA: University of California Press, 1999).

[79] Paul Josephson et al., *An Environmental History of Russia* (Cambridge: Cambridge University Press, 2013), 58–61.

[80] Nicholas Breyfogle, 'At the Watershed: 1958 and the beginnings of Lake Baikal Environmentalism', *The Slavonic and East European Review*, 93.1 (2015), 147–180.

The explosion in the Chernobyl nuclear reactor on 26 April 1986 spread radioactive fallout across much of Europe. In the USSR a cloud of radioactive dust spread across Belarus and Ukraine. It poisoned human and wildlife, causing the evacuation of 100,000 people, many of whom later suffered from radiation poisoning and cancers caused by the exposure. It poisoned the trees of the Red Forest in Ukraine. The area remains off limits because of the high levels of radioactivity. The devastation helped to spur environmental campaigns by dissident groups in the Eastern Bloc. The Soviet Union, which banned non-governmental campaigns, saw substantial environmental protests after the Chernobyl disaster, with new movements emerging across the union. The openness of the era brought in by Mikhail Gorbachev's *glasnost* policy from 1986 meant that these non-official groups became more tolerated. In 1987 and 1988 a series of protests occurred, including in September 1988, when Lithuanians expressed their objections to a similar nuclear reactor at the Ignalina power plant.[81] Many civil society groups became associated with the national liberation movements that hastened the end of the USSR, but they were motivated by the protection of nature and emboldened by the Chernobyl disaster. The destruction of nature resulting from rapid industrialisation became a key component of the push for reform. From 1985 the Greenway network brought together campaigners from Poland, Yugoslavia, Hungary and Czechoslovakia and it spread into the USSR and East Germany by 1989. The Chernobyl meltdown helped to raise protests against the nuclear industry that later became part of the anti-Soviet organisations.

Similarly in China the state, as the creator of policy, introduced limited environmental measures, restricting the space for independent action. Official environmental measures were often tied to improving the lives of the population and increasing agricultural productivity. Measures to eliminate 'the four pests' (rats, sparrows, flies and mosquitos) from 1957 were different to actions using industrialised pesticides but nonetheless altered the food chain. Sparrows were soon dropped from the pest category after it was noticed that their decline led to an increase in the numbers of insects and that their elimination was therefore counterproductive. By the 1980s the government tied environmental measures to development and public health, and this 'official environmentalism' became one of the key areas of action. The government took measures to conserve water and reduce soil erosion. These actions, however, while good for the environment, were primarily about increasing the lifespan of the Chinese population.

Unofficial environmental activism was often a response to large-scale industrial projects. International campaigns played their part in increasing environmental measures for the Chinese government. From 1972 the UN began to play a leading role, with its Environment Programme hoping to convince governments to act. For Bao Maohong, the United Nations Conference on the Human Environment held in Stockholm in 1972 became a watershed

---

[81] Josephson et al., *Environmental History of Russia*, 280–282.

moment in the official acceptance of the need to introduce environmental measures.[82] Under the leadership of Deng Xiaoping the official line gradually began to incorporate the idea that pollution was not just an inevitable outcome of capitalism—but of industrialisation itself. Thus the Chinese state appeared willing to compromise.

However, during the 1980s and beyond, China defended its right to industrialise and catch up with the processes that had taken centuries in the West. In the twenty-first century its building of coal-fired power stations made efforts by many of the Western nations to decarbonise (which themselves were often half-hearted) insignificant. While consecutive Chinese leaders have made pronouncements on the need for environmental measures and taken some action, including green taxes and environmental charges, words have rarely been followed by deeds. China is, therefore, similar to developed nations whose leaders have often spoken platitudes but failed to implement effective measures. Citizens of China have, therefore, sometimes taken environmental measures outside government control.

Chinese environmental activists have found limited scope to act outside the remit of their government. Emboldened by China's first environmental law of 1979 and the accompanying permissiveness to environmental activism, citizens felt justified in protesting against soil erosion and pollution of the air and water. While these protests usually aimed to help people live better lives rather than protect the environment, the means may be said to have justified the ends. Rural activists pressed collective lawsuits on local authorities and firms, sometimes taking direct action including sabotage against heavy polluters. In one case during the 1990s, villagers of Dachuan in Gansu province targeted a fertiliser factory that was polluting drinking water. While initial protests led to the building of a clean water pipeline the river remained polluted and in 1996 a bridge collapsed because of the increased flow of water. In response, villagers commenced direct action including setting up hoses to spray polluted water over the factory, causing the owners to rebuild the bridge and ensure a clean water supply.[83] By the end of the twentieth century Chinese campaign groups became more organised: the Friends of Nature, a semi-official group, formed in 1994, and The Global Village of Beijing was founded in 1995 aiming to educate people on sustainable living and development. These groups became established in part because of engagement with foreign organisations and have helped a more organised version of Chinese environmentalism to grow.

The Chinese state sought to control non-governmental activism. On 13 April 2007 Wu Lihong, an activist against the pollution of Lake Tai, was

---

[82] Bao Maohong, 'Environmentalism and Environmental Movements in China since 1949' [translated by Yubin Shen], in *A Companion to Global Environmental History*, edited by J. R. McNeil and Erin Maudlin (London: Blackwell, 2012), 474–492,480.

[83] Jun Jing, 'Environmental Protests in Rural China', in *Chinese Society: Change, Conflict and Resistance*, edited by Elizabeth Perry (Abingdon: Routledge, 2003), 211.

arrested by police. Since 1998 he had lobbied authorities about the pollution caused by increases in the number of factories, but investigations covered up the issue. Wu was imprisoned for extorting local companies by threatening to expose their pollution and the contamination continued.[84] NGOs such as Friends of Nature are forced to operate with government agency sponsorship to attain legal status. This means that they tend to operate in a semi-official manner, reducing their ability to freely act against the state. The ability of Chinese citizens to act independently of government has, therefore, been curtailed by the state through persecution and co-option of the groups.

In many nations collective action via the UN and pressure by domestic campaigners was required to awaken politicians to the impending catastrophe. NGOs were vital in campaigning locally and internationally pressuring governments into taking action. Friends of the Earth was founded in America in 1969 when David Brower was expelled from the American Sierra Club over his stance against nuclear power.[85] In 1971 the American group joined with the French, British and Swedish branches to form Friends of the Earth International. It quickly became a transnational organisation and covered a wide range of environmental issues including nuclear power, toxic waste and animal protection. A large part of the organisation's resources were dedicated to bringing lawsuits in defence of the environment. But individual local branches still took part in protests and direct action, although breaking the law was strongly discouraged. These protests took varied forms such as the early campaigns against the fur industry and when, in 1971, the British chapter dumped 2000 empty bottles outside the London HQ of Cadbury Schweppes, who had refused to recycle them. The tactics were often designed to draw media attention. As the organisation grew, it focussed its attention on changing the attitude of individual governments. By the 1980s the organisation linked chapters in 30 countries, growing to 56 by 1996. These interconnected chapters took their own actions with minimal interference from the centre. The pressure from activists soon turned into a multinational effort to limit the impact of humans on the environment.

The environmental movement was connected to and inspired by the growing anti-nuclear movement. The tactics of civil disobedience, which were inspired by Gandhi and had been used by the peace movement, spread across both. In 1958 anti-nuclear campaigners attempted to sail their boat *Golden Rule* into the American testing zone in the Pacific, but they were apprehended and arrested, although their journey was continued by another group who were able to attract publicity but not disrupt the tests. In 1971, following the example of *Golden Rule*, an anti-nuclear group called Don't Make A Wave sailed a fishing vessel that was renamed *The Greenpeace* to Amchitka Island,

---

[84] Robert B. Marks, *China: An Environmental History* (London: Rowman & Littlefield, 2017), 367.

[85] Tom Turner, *David Brower: The Making of the Environmental Movement* (Berkeley, CA: University of California Press, 2015).

Alaska where they hoped to stop an American nuclear test. Changes to the government's plan and bad weather prevented the activists reaching the exclusion zone on time. Instead the crew stopped at a number of Canadian towns where they raised awareness of their anti-nuclear and environmental activism. The movement known as Greenpeace was born.

Initially Greenpeace aimed to inspire people to change their life. The historian Frank Zelko depicts Greenpeace as being inspired by the counter-cultural movement of the 1960s and wanting 'nothing less than a radical change in Western culture'.[86] From 1975 they focussed firmly on environmental issues with the protection of sea mammals as their foremost campaign. By the end of the 1980s the organisation could count its members in the thousands and, like the Campaign for Nuclear Disarmament before it, received publicity and funding via the Glastonbury Festival, further tying it into the legacy of 1960s counterculture. As the organisation became more internationalised it became more corporate in nature, turning away from the overtly 'hippy' connection, although never quite abandoning its spiritual routes with names like *Rainbow Warrior* given to its fleet of boats into the twenty-first century. Greenpeace, along with Friends of the Earth, helped to keep environmental issues in the mainstream news during the 1980s and 1990s by campaigning and taking direct action on issues such as the logging of the rainforest, whaling, acid rain and climate change. These largely Western-based organisations have progressed thinking and led to activism reaching beyond the advanced nations. However, leadership on environmentalism is far from the preserve of Western-based activists.

Environmental activism gained a global reach with campaigns emerging throughout the developing world. Brazilian activists have built one of the most prominent environmental movements, based on disrupting not just the actions of industrialists but addressing the inequality that they reinforce. During the 1960s the attempts to industrialise the Amazonian basin barely disguised the poverty of the population in this area. Squatter communities began to organise against actions that degraded the environment, such as the torching of the rain forest and pollution. Sao Paolo and Rio de Janeiro are among some of the world's most heavily polluted environments and shanty-town communities there have been at the forefront of protest since the twentieth century. The highly literate Brazilian population took on board many of the warnings by the intellectuals, with *Silent Spring* translated into Portuguese in its first year of publication and chapters added about Brazil. While it was once thought that Brazilian environmentalism lagged behind the more developed nations, recent examinations of its ecological movement have shown that throughout

---

[86] Frank Zelko, *Make it a Green Peace: The Rise of a Countercultural Environmentalism* (Oxford: OUP, 2013), 5.

the second half of the twentieth century it developed in parallel with Western movements.[87]

Jose Augusto Padua splits environmentalism into two forms: middle-class environmental activism and the 'environmentalism of the poor'. Padua suggests that the environmentalism of the poor was a form of proto-environmentalism in which Brazilian intellectuals expressed fears over environmental degradation from the end of the eighteenth century and which continued throughout the nineteenth, while perhaps lacking the modern-day scientific terminology and interconnected thinking of the environmental debates and movements that developed from the 1970s.[88] Environmentalism has emerged throughout the developing world, with groups outside the middle classes undertaking activism. For instance, the Penan, a tribe in Malaysia, have campaigned since the 1990s to prevent deforestation of their tribal land. Guha suggests that these instances where poorer communities from the global South acted to protect the environment disproves the common belief that environmental activism is the preserve of affluent middle-class communities.

The environmentalism of the poor refers to the rural conflicts that have resulted from environmental degradation, mainly in the southern hemisphere, including Africa, India and South America.[89] The extraction of natural resources often drove the poor to defend nature against the corporations and the state. In 1995 nine Nigerian activists from the Ogoni tribe were executed by the military dictatorship because they protested against the extraction of oil by Shell while the local population went without basic amenities like schools.[90] These campaigns often pitted local groups against some of the largest multinational corporations, for instance the Ogale people of the Niger Delta took on Shell over the pollution of their waterways. But this is not just a case of local power versus globalisation. Developing-world environmentalists have been able to build international alliances: the Ogale formed a network with campaigners against oil drilling in the Ecuadorian Amazon area and lobbied at the 1997 Kyoto Climate Change Conference to limit extraction in certain areas. While more middle-class activists utilised broad networks to petition governments, those engaged in the environmentalism of the poor sought to demonstrate directly against degradation caused by infrastructure projects. Those advocating the environmentalism of the poor focussed on the effects

---

[87] Kathryn Hochstetler and Margaret Keck, *Greening Brazil: Environmental Activism in State and Society* (Durham, NC: Duke University Press, 2007).

[88] Jose Augusto Padua, 'Environmentalism in Brazil: A Historical Perspective', in *A Companion to Global Environmental History*, edited by J. R. McNeil and Erin Maudlin (London: Blackwell, 2012), 455–9.

[89] Joan Martinez-Alier, 'The Environmentalism of the Poor: Its origins and Spread', in *A Companion to Global Environmental History*, edited by J. R. McNeil and Erin Maudlin (London: Blackwell, 2012), 513.

[90] Guha, *Environmentalism* (Harlow: Longman, 2000), 99–102.

on their communities—displacement from the land and campaigns against large-scale farming operations.

The figurehead of this movement was Chico Mendes, a Brazilian, who led a campaign to defend forest communities against commercial operations that destroyed landscapes by extracting Brazil nuts or rubber, or by industrial-scale farming. He became the leading figure in an international campaign against tropical deforestation.[91] Mendes' participation gave this campaign a global face rather than activism appearing to come solely from concerned Westerners. Mendes became a worldwide symbol of impoverished people's environmental activism, but his assassination in 1988 turned him into a martyr. By the 1980s these two forms—middle-class Western and localised activism—began to align on certain campaigns. They formed groups such as the Movement of People Affected by Dams (*Movimento dos Atingidos por Barragens*, 1985) which works to highlight how apparently 'clean' energy projects can destroy natural and human habitats, and the Movement of Landless Rural Workers (*Movimento dos Trabalhadores Sem Terra*, 1984) which organises squatting campaigns and occupations of unused agricultural land. By the end of the 1980s the new civilian government of Brazil had begun to implement environmental protection measures and the 1988 constitution ordained the protection of huge areas of rainforest.

Other environmentalism of the poor campaigns have been shaped and led by women. From 1985 Medha Patkar attempted to prevent the building of the Sardar Sarovar hydro-electric dam on the Narmada River in India. Her tactics included protests and hunger strikes to draw attention to the plight of displaced villagers. The protests managed to delay the building and caused the Indian government to reject World Bank funding, although the project has now reached a state of partial completion. Patkar spurred a movement which continues to protest to protect villagers from environmental degradation. While these actions often drew little Western media attention, they show that the concern for natural environments was a truly global phenomenon. Many environmentalism of the poor campaigns are about alleviating the excesses of capitalism. This focus suggests that corporations often have little concern for externalities like entrenched poverty or the environment, while governments often act liberally in terms of regulation of industry.

The 1980s saw the formation of environmental political parties in many nations which brought green issues closer to the mainstream, although they often remained minor. Often called the 'Greens', these parties initially emerged in Germany, Great Britain, France and Belgium. They united a broad range of groups including animal rights campaigners, anti-pollution groups and anti-nuclear campaigners under a single banner. In Germany a particularly strong Green Party emerged from 1979, gaining representation in the Bundestag in 1983. The 1970s had seen an upswing in activist groups at the local and national level with protests against runways, refinery expansions in the

---

[91] Keck and Sikkink, *Activists Beyond Borders*, 140.

Rhineland and a longstanding campaign against nuclear power such as in Wyhl, where winegrowers and environmentalists campaigned through the mid-1970s against the building of a new nuclear power plant. From the 1980s, as Frank Uekötter argues, the green movement in Germany grew in strength and Green politicians were able to convince policy makers to take environmental action.[92]

Environmentalism became increasingly professionalised through the 1990s and 2000s with the UN Earth Summits held in Rio de Janeiro in 1992 and 2012. Many of the global NGOS opened offices in Brazil from the 1990s. Brazil has drawn the focus of environmentalists the world over because of its huge area of rainforest, which acts as a carbon sink and has been seen as a vital part of the Earth's environment. But often parliamentary Green movements lacked widespread popularity. In Germany the Green Party lost all their seats in December 1990, failing to reach the 5 per cent threshold for representation at the national level, although they did share power in several states. Following the end of European communist regimes from 1989 transnational co-operation between activists increased. At the Rio Earth Summit in 1992 governments proclaimed their intentions to take decisive action on climate change, deforestation and biodiversity. However, often the delivery on these promises was lacking. Some nations saw backtracking on green promises, with German media labelling green campaigners 'do-gooders' and seeing green issues generally as a barrier to economic growth in the face of globalisation.[93] By the end of that decade, however, attitudes began to change and in 1998 the Green Party became the minor party in a coalition with Gerhard Schroeder's Socialists. While the coalition was tenuous and problematic, the Greens were able to introduce a tax on energy to subsidise jobs and the transition towards renewable energy, as well as limitations on nuclear reactors. While these advances were modest, it showed that environmental campaigns could begin to achieve political success. During this time environmental activists became more interconnected than ever before and lobbied governments and general populations on a national and international scale about the need to act faster to defend the environment.

The twenty-first century saw the emergence of new Green parties across a number of African nations with Kenya's Mazingira Green Party the most prominent. In the West the Greens' electoral success continued with the British Green Party attaining parliamentary representation from 2010. Green parties were able to poll relatively high numbers, sometimes double percentage points, often helped by socialist ideas. International co-operation to tackle climate change continued, with extensive lobbying by scientists, activists and opinion polling convincing an increasing number of politicians around the world that something needed to be done. The Paris Agreement drafted in

---

[92] Frank Uekötter, *The Greenest Nation? A New History of German Environmentalism* (MIT Press, 2014), 21.

[93] Uekötter, *The Greenest Nation?*, 142.

2015 after the UN Climate Change Conference was the most substantial charter to date, aiming to limit the increase in global temperature to an average of 1.5° centigrade and lowering carbon emissions.

The 2010s perhaps showed the limitations of activism from climate campaigners. When Donald Trump was elected to the White House in 2016, he quickly set about tearing up climate treaties, declaring that the USA was going to withdraw from the Paris Accords. Naomi Klein suggests that Trump is one of a group of wealthy people who essentially believe that climate change is happening, but that they simply do not care. Their wealth will enable them to shield themselves from the adverse effects by buying the services of 'luxury disaster response' businesses such as the Seasteading Institute which has utopian aims to create floating communities for the wealthy that are independent of government regulation. For Klein the denial of climate change is a form of cognitive dissonance; the deniers run counter to scientific evidence and all logical conclusions. But their desire to protect their wealth, and the economic neo-liberalism which enabled their profits, requires lax regulation, low taxes and market primacy.[94]

Wherever people have campaigned for the environment, business and others have fought back against the measures. Focussed on short-term profitability, they have sought to deny the impact of industry on the environment. Others have aimed to 'greenwash' their reputation by claiming that they are supporting environmental measures; these include the German carmaker Volkswagen which in 2015 fraudulently lowered its emission values to make out that its cars were more environmentally friendly than they actually were. Campaigns have also been launched to prevent the building of clean technologies like wind power on the grounds that they are a 'blot' on the landscape. The objectives of societies like the USA and Western Europe, whose industrial infrastructure has largely been outsourced because of globalisation, allows governments to discuss reducing carbon production. While Western governments can talk about achieving 'carbon neutrality', they are effectively lying to themselves and their citizens because globalisation of supply chains means that their carbon deficit is merely displaced elsewhere—in nations that are essentially being asked to clear up the biproducts of the consumption of the more developed nations.

Environmental politics were not defeated by President Trump. When he made his anti-environmentalist announcements the rest of the world pressed on with their commitment. Campaigners were also reinvigorated to lobby their government and to attempt to get the USA to re-commit to the agreements. Several state governments in the USA made a collective commitment to the Paris Accords. Ultimately the election of the less extreme Joe Biden in 2020 led to the United States re-engaging with the international community. Part of this new policy meant joining the Paris Agreement once more. Attempts to limit the increase in global temperatures through political agreement, however,

---

[94] Klein, *No is not Enough* (London: Haymarket Books, 2017), 77–82, 164–6.

have rarely led to concerted action, with international legislation often being watered down by nations who have particular interests in the petro-chemical industry, as happened in the 2023 COP conference held in Dubai. It was revealed that the conference hosts intended to use the conference to discuss fossil fuel deals with other nations, and the agreement did not include the phasing out of fossil fuels.

Activism on climate has spread through nations as the scientific and naturalist ideas have spread around the world, hastened by the growth of mass media from the later twentieth century. While action has become internationalised, with global organisations campaigning and co-ordinating action, there has always been a large degree of localised action. These local groups have often networked with similar organisations in other countries, showing that the environmental movement has developed the sense of an international imagined community with a shared concern for the planet as well as the people within it.

Globalising Activism

The post-war era saw political activism go global. Aided by international news technology, travel, translation and later by the democratisation of the means of communication, ideas have become one of the main entities that travel across borders. As the world began to seem smaller many global citizens, often motivated by the horrors of World War Two, developed a keen sense of international solidarity, and sought to build a global civil society either to pressure individual governments or to force global action. Many of these campaigns continued in the twenty-first century. Activists, however, realised that these issues cannot be tackled on their own. A new form of activism, intersectionality, built on ideas from the 1980s. This concept had its roots in the realisation that marginalisation of sections of society such as gender, race, class, ability and sexual orientation were all part of the same division. Intersectionality has now expanded to include alliances with environmental and economic activists who seek to change the systems that can make the world a fairer place for all. Klein argued strongly for organisations to follow this path in her 2017 book *No is Not Enough*. Inspired by Crenshaw's concept of intersectionality, she hopes that a worldwide organisation can form that seeks to benefit all of these groups, and that governments and parties will adopt parts of a common manifesto in order to benefit all interests. The single-issue transnational networks that characterised the latter twentieth century had by the second decade of the twenty-first given way to more coalition-based groups who agreed on certain common goals.

The ability to build a global civil society has a faced number of barriers. Political divisions like the Cold War often prevented activists from meeting and talking freely. But even when free discussion was enabled activists may have thought the others inhabited different worlds, not just a different part of the same one. The differences in mentalities, most commonly seen between activists from the Western developed world and the global majority South, have been perhaps the greatest barrier to organisations planning and acting together. The process of learning about each other has enabled people from different cultures to overcome divisions and to work together to achieve their mutually supportive but sometimes diverging aims.

> **Discussion Questions**
>
> What caused activist groups to become global?
> What are the kinds of tensions that emerge in global activist groups and how do organisations overcome them?
> What is intersectionality and why has it become important?
> How effective are transnational groups at achieving their aims?
> How do governments, corporations and international institutions respond to publicly led transnational activism?

CHAPTER 5

Encounters at the International Expositions

Governments have long sought to promote their national way of life. One way of doing this has been through installations, exhibitions and museums. The most high-profile of these is the International Exhibition or World's Fair, where nations display items of culture and goods they want to trade. These exhibitions allow governments to reinforce ideas about national identity and to promote their values. Assigned national days punctuate the 'expo' calendar but exhibitors also display national symbols such as flags, folk products and food and drink. The exhibitions promote mobilities through tourism, or more frequently, as a form of 'virtual mobility' where domestic visitors experience a representation of other national cultures through these displays. Visitors encounter the culture of many different nations and continents within hours. In the second part of the twentieth century these exhibitions became known as Expos and many of them became sites of the Cold War. Post-war Expos, however, also allowed developing nations to promote their nationhood internationally. The Expos became a site where people could encounter different cultures; the fairs allowed nations to showcase their identity, sometimes becoming a point of 'convergence'.[1] The fairs allowed hybrids to develop as new cultures were forged from learning about other nations. However, at other times some nations' displays were imperialist, while former colonised nations hoped to assert their post-colonial national identity. In this way they had potential to simultaneously become sites of convergence and of divergence as differing ideologies completed for predominance.

---

[1] Katherine Smits & Alix Jansen, 'Staging the Nation at Expos and World's Fairs', *National Identities*, 14.2 (2012), 173–188.

The International Expositions have their root in the imperial cultures of the nineteenth century. There were several attempts to hold international exhibitions before Britain hosted its Great Exhibition in 1851, which is commonly regarded as the original World's Fair. The event was intended to display the products of the world, with other industrial nations, such as the USA, participating. The fair also featured stands representing Britain's colonial subjects, albeit these representations were created by the British exhibitors. The philosopher Karl Marx felt that the Great Exhibition was symbolic of the growth of the industrial class, with the bourgeoisie deemed to have 'erected in the modern its Pantheon, where, with self-satisfied pride, it exhibits the gods which it has made for itself'.[2] This form of what he later termed 'commodity fetishism' was clearly visible in the nineteenth century as consumerism grew. Marx also recognised that the display represented the predominance of a bourgeoise class that was set to become global, writing 'This exhibition is a striking proof of the concentrated power with which modern large-scale industry is everywhere demolishing national barriers and increasingly blurring local peculiarities of production, society and national character among all peoples.'[3] A consumer identity had emerged and the fairs catered to this idea with the ideologies of liberalism, trade and patriotism on display. Although the exhibitions appealed beyond the middle class, their primary aim in the mid-nineteenth century was to show off the products of the industrial revolutions and to encourage others to modernise along similar lines to the European nations.[4] The fairs were an example of public culture which promoted the nation and its technological advancement not only to foreigners but also as a tool to educate populations about their own cultures and promote patriotism at a time when nation states were becoming the predominant form of government.[5] The Great Exhibition was an outcome of European nationalism and displays of imperial status, particularly from the British;[6] but it was also symbolic of the world becoming globalised.

The early fairs promoted ideas which have remained central to the project of globalisation into the late twentieth and early twenty-first century. The

---

[2] Karl Marx and Friedrich Engels, 'Review: May–October 1850', *Neue Rheinische Zeitung Revue*, at https://www.marxists.org/archive/marx/works/1850/11/01.htm Accessed 9 July 2020.

[3] Karl Marx and Friedrich Engels, 'Review: May–October 1850', *Neue Rheinische Zeitung Revue*, at https://www.marxists.org/archive/marx/works/1850/11/01.htm Accessed 9 July 2020.

[4] Jeffrey A. Auerbach, *The Great Exhibition of 1851: A Nation on Display* (London: Yale University Press, 1999), 4.

[5] Robert Kargon, Karen Fiss, Morris Low & Arthur Molella, *World's Fair on the Eve of War: Science, Technology & Modernity, 1937–1942* (Pittsburgh, PA: University of Pittsburgh Press, 2015), 4.

[6] Jeffrey A. Auerbach, 'Introduction', in Jeffrey A. Auerbach and Peter H. Hoffenberg (eds), *Britain, the Empire and the World at the Great Exhibition of 1851* (London: Ashgate, 2008).

Expos have sought to promote internationalism, with the sharing of ideas about how a society can be organised, and display of technology and goods. The ideologies of capitalist trade were displayed, with competition between nations being encouraged and numerous prizes awarded for pavilion architecture and outstanding exhibitions. But from the 1880s and the European scramble for Africa many of the Expos, especially those held in Europe, celebrated the cultural encounter formed by colonialism, depicting their actions as a 'civilising mission' that justified their exploitation of people and resources.

In the nineteenth century Paris became a regular host for the fairs and represented some of the romance associated with the expositions hosting the events in 1855, 1867, 1878 and 1889. The Eiffel Tower was built as a viewing platform for the 1889 fair; a number of monarchical countries including Britain refused to participate because it commemorated the overthrow of the French monarchy in 1789. Their last World's Fair of the nineteenth century was in 1900. France's position as an imperial world power helped it to maintain the world's interest in displaying at these events. Belgium was also keen to prove its imperial position. King Leopold II (1835–1909) encouraged a number of Expos including the World's Fairs in Brussels in 1897, which housed a large colonial exhibit displaying items including a Maxim gun (an early machine gun) which had aided the conquest of much of Africa. The Belgians also exhibited subjects from the Congo, whose display prompted much interest from the public and press who discussed their uncivilised status and felt they were encountering an exotic subject.[7] Belgium's next fair in Liège in 1905 celebrated the nation's independence but also 40 years of Leopold's rule. The World's Fair returned to Brussels in 1910, with the last Expo before World War One held in the Belgian city of Ghent in 1913. Its theme of 'Peace, Industry and Arts' echoed some of the earlier themes, but it seemed to mark the growing international turbulence. In the twentieth century the fairs became an opportunity to exhibit national cultures and historical narratives, replacing the nineteenth-century display of 'colonial' work, which often meant displaying colonial plunder (something which several countries still do in their national museums). By using their exhibitions as a form of cultural diplomacy, certain nations presented their world visions, often in competition with rival nations for influence, and attempted to convince the rest of the world about the superiority of their ideas.

During the twentieth century the Expos became more officially organised. An international organisation, *Bureau International des Expositions* (BIE) was founded in 1931 with a view to formalising the allocation process and ensuring that hosts of the World's Fairs were able to deliver on their promises. This organisation pronounces which fairs officially count as 'International Exhibitions' and which are classed as specialised exhibitions. In the twenty-first century the fairs have become an expensive undertaking and most nations that

---

[7] Adam Hochschild, *King Leopold's Ghost: A Story of Greed, Terror and Heroism in Colonial Africa* (London: Macmillan, 1999), 175–177.

take part build their own pavilion. The award-winning British pavilion at the Milan Expo in 2015 resembled a beehive and its design demonstrates how these events have become showcases for the aesthetics of architecture. The reward for the investment in expensive pavilions is cultural diplomacy and the opportunity to impress people of other nations. The fairs remain an exercise in soft power but this has at times moved beyond the idea of 'nation', with regions and identities sometimes becoming paramount.

The interwar years saw a stuttering start to the resumption of International Expositions amid a period of economic recovery and rebuilding of states. When they did restart in 1929 the site of Barcelona underwent a renovation of its city space and welcomed other, mainly European, nations. Opening in the year of the Wall Street Crash, however, was not the most fortuitous timing and a downbeat economic outlook hung over the event. From 1933 to 1934 Chicago celebrated the 'Century of Progress'. This theme marked a tendency that became more common after World War Two by celebrating new technologies and science.

The Expositions soon became influenced by global politics. At the Paris World's Fair of 1937, against the backdrop of the Eiffel Tower, the showpiece building from the 1889 World's Fair, two totalitarian nations stood in hostile opposition. The monumental pavilion of Stalin's USSR, crowned by a statue of a factory worker and collective farmer, faced Nazi Germany's building, topped by an imperial eagle and swastika. Both encompassed their nations' visions of modernity but embedded them within classical architecture, with the Soviets encasing their structure in marble as a response to the German use of Bavarian granite. Inside, the Nazis displayed their industrial accomplishments including a Mercedes Benz branded with a swastika and oil paintings of German factories. Alongside these modern icons was the use of stone and classical chandeliers, which Danilo Udovički-Selb sees as a contradiction between conservatism and modernity, with the regime rooting its ideology in the myth of a resurgent past Germanic era. The Soviet pavilion was based on its image of a utopian future, but its use of neoclassicism reflected the increasing conservatism of the regime under Stalin and the claims of Bolshevism to be rooted in Greek democracy and the French Enlightenment.[8] Its style was also influenced by American modernity with the Soviet architect Boris Iofan visiting New York to examine their skyscraper construction techniques.[9] The Soviets' exhibition included a Ford limousine, which was rebranded as GAZ on licence. Soviet modernism was reliant on international ideas and products to advance.[10] This use of mass-produced technology was part of a future modernism that the

---

[8] Danilo Udovički-Selb, 'Facing Hitler's Pavilion: The Uses of Modernity in the Soviet Pavilion at the 1937 Paris International Exhibition', *Journal of Contemporary History*, 47.1 (2012), 13–47, 28.

[9] Deyan Sudjic, *Stalin's Architect: Power and Survival in Moscow* (London: Thames & Hudson, 2022), 197–202.

[10] Susan Buck-Morss, *Dreamworld and Catastrophe: The Passing of Mass Utopia in East and West* (London: MIT Press, 2002), 164–168.

Soviets hoped to deliver. Each utopia set out to show why its version of modernity was superior and would win the world struggle.

The ideological conflict continued between these totalitarian nations and extended to the democracies. Spain had had been plunged into civil war as fascist forces led by General Franco sought to overthrow the democratically elected socialist government. German and Italian forces had supported Franco and on 26 April 1937 conducted a major air raid against civilians in the Basque town of Guernica. The destruction at Guernica was reimagined by the artist Pablo Picasso who had been approached to produce an artwork for the Spanish Republic's pavilion. The result was his masterpiece *Guernica*, finished two months later and displayed in Paris for the world to see. The Spanish Republican government maintained its presence at the Paris World's Fair and its use of art made a powerful ideological statement. This act of cultural diplomacy helped to raise awareness about the destruction their nation was suffering and to enhance their legitimacy in the wake of invasion. In doing so they highlighted the divergence between the democracies and the dictatorships, setting the scene for the next five decades.

World War Two and the Early Post-war Period

Six months into the next World's Fair, held in New York in 1939, the European powers became embroiled in World War Two. No more fairs were held for the duration of the conflict. Afterwards, with a world undergoing reconstruction and uncertainty over economic recoveries, there was little appetite for a large-scale World's Fair. Instead the BIE organised several specialised Expos and a World Expo in Port-au-Prince, Haiti in 1949, which was relatively small with twenty exhibiting nations and around 70,000 attendees. Britain held its own Festival of Britain in 1951. At a time of austerity and recovery the event aimed to help kickstart the nation's economy. This exhibition was a celebration of Britishness at a time of rebuilding following a destructive war. A nearly bankrupt country undertook the display of the goods that would become available in the coming years. Critics often paired the official slogan 'Britain can make it' with 'but Britain can't have it' to highlight the lack of availability of goods as rationing continued. The festival drew crowds from around the nation and spurred the imagination of what Britain could achieve. It promised an age of affluence in the UK, and symbolised the British government's belief in the 'New Jerusalem' of opportunity for all, supported by the welfare state. This less internationalised event, however, was more inward looking than many of the later global showcases or even earlier events like the Great Exhibition of a century earlier. It seemed the nations of the world lacked the confidence to produce such showcase exhibitions.

It was only when the Expos returned to Europe with the Brussels Exposition in 1958 and its theme of 'a new humanism' that the world began to show its confidence in re-engagement and re-build connections. The theme of humanism allowed a new kind of encounter in the age of decolonisation with some newly independent nations able to present their self-defined image to the world. In a special edition, the *UNESCO Courier* stated:

> The face of the World is changing literally before our very eyes. Its most visible elements, once considered as traditional are disintegrating. Others are striving to establish themselves. People which for centuries have slumbered, are now awakening. The demand for social progress now universally echoed has aroused a desire for independence which has sometimes assumed the form of virulent nationalism.[11]

The exhibition was positioned as symbolic of a world in flux and one where the yoke of imperialism, which was celebrated in the early exhibitions, was now being cast off. The world of 1958 appeared to be embracing the modernity of the age and hoped to challenge traditional social structures. The article continued,

> But if demographic expansion and that of the needs which it carries with it may be considered as the most determining forces of the political and social changes which we are now witnessing, they still only bring about these changes through the equally irresistible growth of human genius, expressed through inventions and discoveries in sciences and technical skills.

The *Courier* presented the Expo as an encounter at which new nations could participate on equal terms. Colonial domination by Europeans was receding; developing nations were spurred on by their newly gained independence. But above all else the UN, who had their own pavilion at the exhibition, sought to celebrate human ingenuity and the development of new technologies. The new international organisation hoped to use its participation to promote ideas of peace, progress and humanism.

Ideological differences took centre stage. The historian György Péteri depicts the Brussels fair as one of Cold War convergence where 'different cultures (and different cultural- and social-political projects) meet one another and where *rivalry, confrontation and contestation* take place'.[12] The shadow of nuclear weaponry hung over the world. The fair's centrepiece, however, was the Atomium, a building of metallic spheres connected by tubular walkways. It was a model of an atom magnified many millions of times and was designed by the Belgian hosts to showcase the peaceful uses of nuclear technology. At the same time the older ideas of Europe were still part of the world's engagement with Belgium. The opening event was noted by the USA's *Life* magazine for its Royal ball hosted by King Baudouin, the first such event since 1936.

---

[11] Maurice Lambilliotte, 'Humanism for a Modern World', *Unesco Courier*, July 1957, 13.

[12] György Péteri, 'Sites of Convergence: The USSR and Communist Eastern Europe at International Fairs Abroad and at Home', *Journal of Contemporary History*, 47.1 (2012), 8.

The images of European royalty in the crystal chandelier ballroom formed a contrast to the modernity of the Atomium. The magazine depicted a raucous atmosphere where, 'guests were seen to climb on tables. Later the press around buffet tables laden with caviar and champagne became so ardent that the food was spilled and jewels were ripped from gowns and uniforms.'[13] The new humanism was presented as struggling to emerge alongside older traditions (Fig. 5.1).

The Brussels Expo saw the communist nations in a state of change. Under the leadership of Nikita Khrushchev, the USSR hoped to move away from belligerency between East and West and turn the fair itself into part of the moralistic context of the Cold War. The Cold War was now characterised by a policy of peaceful coexistence, which effectively meant competition between two systems of production. This rivalry meant that the Brussels Expo was depicted as a proxy for the Cold War. The French pictorial magazine *Paris Match* emphasised the opposition between the USSR and the Vatican pavilion by juxtaposing images of the two and situating the conflict as between two opposing belief systems rather than as a geopolitical conflict between the

Fig. 5.1 The Atomium, Brussels

[13] *Life*, 12 May 1958, 5.

Soviets and USA.[14] Where they did compare the Soviets and USA they saw the USSR pavilion as a 'reel of propaganda', but the USA's as one with an 'atmosphere of relaxation: pools, drug-stores, ice cream sellers against a backdrop of jazz music'.[15] While this message ignored America's propaganda in attempting to show an idealised way of life, the French magazine portrayed the USA as trying to demonstrate its culture to the rest of the world in what Susan Reid sees as a more subtle way of disarming European criticisms of 'vulgar consumerism'.[16] *Life* magazine contrasted what it saw as the 'graceful pleasure dome housing a very soft sell indeed', from the USA's exhibition with the USSR's described as 'Hard Hard Sell'.[17] It had previously commented that 'the U.S. and the Russians in giant pavilions would each try to show fair visitors that its way of life was superior'.[18] *Life* presented all forms of engagement between the superpowers as part of the Cold War, seeing confrontation at every turn. The Cold War was hard to avoid when the two superpowers' pavilions had been placed in close proximity. As one of the earliest cultural encounters between the two and when both were attempting to build their soft power it is little surprise that commentators found it difficult to move away from the simmering conflict.

The organisers hoped to avoid an ideological confrontation and believed that by placing the American and Soviet pavilions opposite each other they would be able to create a space for the rhetoric of peace in the plaza dividing the two. Each side used its pavilion to demonstrate why its ideas were superior: the 'new deal' market economy of the USA against the state capitalism of the USSR. The Soviets saw the event as two world systems in competition and ensured that they received equal display space.[19] In 1957 the Soviet Union had launched the first satellite into outer space, shocking many people in the West and causing many to declare that the Soviets had won the space race. The USA's press and political class felt the moment was humiliating, believing that they needed to catch up. The Soviet pavilion capitalised on this supposed lead and showcased its technology with agricultural machinery, aircraft and television on display, but the centrepiece of their exhibition was a display of models of its various space craft and a replica Sputnik was the star of the show. The Soviets also used the exhibition to showcase the living conditions of the

---

[14] See 'Face à l'U.R.R.S., la prière de Pie XII', *Paris Match*, Numéro Spécial, Mai-Octobre 1958, 36–48.

[15] 'Chez les Américains mot d'ordre: relaxe', *Paris Match*, Numéro Spécial, Mai-Octobre 1958, 49.

[16] Susan E. Reid, 'Cold War Cultural Transactions: Designing the USSR for the West at Brussels Expo '58', *Design and Culture*, 9.2 (2017), 130.

[17] *Life*, 12 May 1958, 56.

[18] *Life*, 31 March 1958, 23.

[19] Lewis Siegelbaum, 'Sputnik Goes to Brussels: The Exhibition of a Soviet Technological Wonder', *Journal of Contemporary History*, 47.1 (2012), 120–136.

Soviet Union and their (often as yet undelivered) improvements in consumption and leisure, giving a nod to the exhibitions of the consumerist nations like the United States, but also their system of social provisions.[20] The display of a model home was a technique which the Soviets learned from American touring exhibits, but which they did not use at Brussels. The pavilion itself marked a break with the past. Whereas Stalin had opted for monumental architecture in the neo-classical style, this pavilion was more utilitarian, reminiscent of the modernism that the USSR hoped to present. Its glass front represented openness with smaller archways near the entrance that appeared less imperialistic than Stalin-era architecture.

The USA also opted for a glass-fronted pavilion with a circular roofless design that indicated a sense of openness. However, scholars have also suggested that, because the USA assumed the leading role in the world economy during the post-war era and became an empire, this design also represented a sense of the neo-classical, and its pavilion has drawn comparisons to the Colosseum in Rome.[21] Displays of consumer goods and daily fashion shows aimed to showcase an idealised version of everyday American life, focussing on family and domesticity. Meanwhile 'high' culture in the form of abstract Impressionist art and jazz were intended to demonstrate to Europeans that America offered more than consumerism. For Sarah Nilsen the USA pavilion was notable for its use of film to 'project' an impression of American identity, which she sees as an extension of Eisenhower's psychological warfare programme designed to win support for its ideology in Europe and the developing world.[22] Film acted as one of the USA's main forms of cultural diplomacy throughout the post-war period and the success of Hollywood in overseas markets was seen as part of creating a positive encounter between international audiences and the American way of life. Films screened at the exhibitions included Walt Disney's *USA in Circarama*, which showcased America's landscape and cityscapes using the latest cinematic technology to create a 360-degree immersive experience inside a circular cinema. The enlistment of America's top entertainer helped this film to become the sensation of Brussels.[23] The projection was reused in exhibitions across America and beyond, including the American National Exhibition in Moscow in 1959. Some of the displays, however, were not appreciated and survey data found that the fashions and abstract art were the least popular elements. This distaste accounted for American surveys that suggested that despite

---

[20] Reid, 'Brussels Expo '58', 123–145.

[21] Cathleen M. Giustino, 'Industrial Design and the Czechoslovak Pavilion at Expo'58: Artistic Autonomy, Party Control and Cold War Common Ground', *Journal of Contemporary History*, 47.1 (2012), 185–212, 186.

[22] Sarah Nilsen, *Projecting America, 1958: Film and Cultural Diplomacy at the Brussels World's Fair* (Jefferson, NC: McFarland & Co: 2011). 20.

[23] Nilsen, *Projecting America*, 5, 22.

some condescending reviews of the Soviet pavilion by Western journalists, it appeared to be more popular with the visiting audience.[24]

America's display aimed to sell its ideology of 'people's capitalism'. Part of the battle of ideology was directed at the African and Asian nations, with both sides using cultural diplomacy and hoping to draw these often newly independent nations into the American or Soviet sphere of influence. However, the USA's Achilles heel was its terrible record on race relations and the fact that its Southern states remained segregated, with black people legally defined as second-class citizens. In 1957 black students who had enrolled at the previously all-white Little Rock Central High School were prevented from attending by the National Guard at the behest of state authorities. The outrage prompted President Eisenhower to federalise the guard and use them to escort the students to school. The global media coverage of this ongoing civil rights crisis turned America's racial divide into an international talking point. The American State Department recognised that this issue aided those who portrayed America as a negative force in the world and they hoped to change minds at Brussels.[25] An exhibit called *Unfinished Business* did not try to hide this aspect of its culture but sought to address the issue head on. The display was designed to show the 'progress' of black Americans over the past 50 years and to suggest that the gradual de-segregation was indicative of American ideals at work. However, the display was controversial and Southern American senators objected to its content, particularly a large photograph which showed white and black children holding hands while playing ring-a-roses as a 'hope for the future'.[26] Another area that focussed on the Little Rock incident was also problematic and soon after opening, the display was closed for seventeen days, when it was completely changed to refocus on issues of public health. The failure to address this issue showed the limits of openness and was not in line with the theme of humanism. The display, however, was not the only aspect of the exhibition that sought to show more harmonious race relations; Jazz music was used as the performing section, including a high proportion of performances by African Americans. Jazz was seen by most Europeans as an African-American artform but also had the benefit of showing American freedom through a style of music that was suppressed in the Eastern Bloc.[27] The USA's divisions were laid bare, causing an encounter between different American communities and the values that organisers and politicians held; Americans were forced to confront their segregationist policies. In this instance they did so by presenting a more sanitised national image to the world.

Péteri sees Brussels 1958 as a Cold War site of convergence. He writes,

[24] Cited Reid, 'Brussels Expo '58', 133.

[25] Michael L. Krenn, '"Unfinished Business": Segregation and U.S. Diplomacy at the 1958 World's Fair', *Diplomatic History*, 20.4 (1996), 591–2.

[26] Krenn, '"Unfinished Business"', 602.

[27] Nilsen, *Projecting America*, 134.

We are now able to show that international fairs were indeed major sites of interaction between different nations and systemic camps. They were 'sites of convergence' in the admittedly (and deliberately) ambiguous sense that they promoted the mutual assimilation of norms, values and standards, at the same time as they prompted with renewed force the efforts among elites of state socialism to articulate and assert the distinct and independent nature of socialist modernity.[28]

For Péteri these World Fairs were not so much solely about the battle of ideas; instead they saw nations from each sphere learning from each other. He suggests that the communist leaders hoped that their technicians would see what they needed to do to catch up, as well as gaining from technical transfer. He sees the Brussels Expo as creating a sense of hybridity between the blocs, with the Eastern Bloc showing itself as being not so isolationist after all. Péteri emphasises the role of aesthetics. These mattered as much as the message that each nation portrayed and how these were assimilated by the other side was part of the contest. We should keep in mind David-Fox's description of the Iron Curtain as a semipermeable membrane: during the fairs the curtain was at its most permeable, and ideas and goods crossed it.[29] Multidirectional conversations took place and influenced designers with stylistic borrowings and hybrids emerging.

At Brussels'58 'convergence' between the blocs could be seen in other ways. Cathleen Guistano sees such an encounter between Czechoslovakian politicians and its artists. While artistic expression had been supressed in order to produce items of 'Socialist Realism', artists and designers were more freely able to express themselves during the exhibition as a means of negotiating national identity.[30] In order to create a worthwhile display they were able to build a space of free expression. For Guistano overt propaganda was avoided by many of the artists, allowing Czechoslovak national culture to come to the fore and making the exhibition and its multimedia shows very popular with visitors. The pavilion designed by Franišek Cubr, Josef Hrubý and Zdeněk Pokorný was in a modernist style of architecture, seemingly free from the ideology of the Stalin era. A pamphlet produced for the Czechoslovakian National Days on 23 and 24 July demonstrates these ideas.[31] The main articles concern Czechoslovakian culture and celebrate performances by the National Opera and the Czechoslovakian Philharmonic Orchestra, marionette displays

---

[28] Péteri, 'Sites of Convergence, 3–12.

[29] Michael David-Fox, 'The Iron Curtain as Semipermeable Membrane: Origins and Demise of the Stalinist Superiority Complex', in *Cold War Crossings: International Travel and Exchange across the Soviet Bloc, 1940s-1960s*, edited by Patryk Babiracki & Kenyon Zimmer (College Station, TX: Texas A & M University Press, 2014), 14–39.

[30] Giustino, 'Czechoslovak Pavilion', 185–212.

[31] Bodhan Posvic (ed.)., *La Tchécoslovaquie a Bruxelles 58: Les Journées Nationales Tchécoslovaques à l'Expo 23–24 Juillet 1958*.

and Lúčnica, the Slovak National Folklore Ballet. The pamphlet also downplays some of the tenets of communism with an article on the restoration of the churches after World War Two. Other articles follow the themes of the display, discussing Czechoslovakian glass, fashion and the production of Skoda cars. State socialism, however, occasionally occupies a key position, with one article highlighting scientific and technological co-operation with the Soviet Union, although this was towards the back.[32] Little wonder that the Czechoslovakian pavilion won the *Grand Prix* for Best National Pavilion.

Perhaps the most evident way that the Czechoslovakian government turned the Brussels World's Fair into an encounter for its country was by learning from the other exhibits. Groups of designers, loyal to the Communist Party,[33] were sent to Brussels to examine the goods on display in other countries' pavilions, both East and West, as well as in Brussels stores such as *Au Bon Marché*.[34] The result was the emergence of the 'Brussels Style', which became a Czechoslovakian form in architecture, design and arts. This trend, which was similar to the Western 'mid-century' style, was borrowed from their experiences in Belgium, and became popular in Czechoslovakian design as the country sought to increase the availability of consumer goods. After 1959, when the party reaffirmed their commitment to socialist realism, the 'Brussels Style' was still tolerated, allowing a hybrid culture to develop.

The Brussels World's Fair, however, was not just a Cold War exhibition: it allowed nations from the developing world such as Thailand and Brazil to showcase their modernisation and their traditional cultures. Decolonisation of European empires was a key feature of the time and newly independent nations such as Tunisia, Morocco and Jordan were able to demonstrate their independent national culture on the world stage. For the first time they could showcase themselves as equal world partners and many former colonised nations asserted their identity. The focus of previous scholarship on the Cold War aspect has meant that these pavilions and their meanings have been underexplored.

Not all of the displays of the developing world were stories of independence. The Belgian displays of their colonies ensured that these subjects did not represent themselves and were often shrouded in Orientalism. The 'Congorama' and the display of Ruanda-Urundi continued the tradition of European colonial displays. Belgian colonisation of the Congo had been brutal, with King Leopold II responsible for the deaths of between eight and ten million people as he sought to run the colony's rubber plantations at a profit, with the violence peaking between 1890 and 1910.[35] Throughout the

---

[32] 'Plus Jamais Le Fascisme', *La Tchécoslovaquie a Bruxelles 58: Les Journées Nationales Tchécoslovaques à l'Expo 23–24 Juilet 1958,* 54–5.

[33] Kimberly Elman Zarecor & Vladimir Kulić, 'Socialism on Display: The Czechoslovak and Yugoslav Pavilions at the 1958 Brussels World Fair', in Laura Hollengreen et al. *Meet Me at The Fair: A World's Fair Reader,* (Pittsburgh: Carnegie Mellon Press, 2014), 228–9.

[34] Giustino, 'Czechoslovak Pavilion', 209–212.

[35] Hochschild, *King Leopold's Ghost.*

years of colonisation, but especially in the late nineteenth century, Europeans had displayed colonial subjects in 'human zoos' at exhibitions like the World's Fairs under the guise of anthropology. Here the focus was on the display of bodies rather than culture.[36] By the mid-twentieth century most of these displays had ended, especially as decolonisation accelerated. However, a form of the 'human zoo' was repeated in the Congo Exhibition. Matthew Stanard shows how the Congolese subjects were kept separated from Europeans and recounts one uncomfortable moment when a visitor threw a chocolate bar to a Congolese child, only for the child to throw it back.[37] The display was a work of colonial propaganda that presented the Congolese as inferior and attempted to justify a sense of mission that contained more than a hint of nineteenth-century 'civilising' ideology. The inability of the Congolese to represent themselves was an exercise in the creation and re-affirmation of knowledge about them and removed their agency. However, by the mid-twentieth century such displays were seen as dehumanising and while some areas of the Belgian press lauded the display, others criticised the practice. The Congolese actors felt that they were treated unfairly and left after three months because of the way that the visiting public had responded to them. The exhibition became an encounter between colonial cultures and a newly emerging independent national culture with the Congolese seeking their right to represent themselves.

The Brussels fair signalled that global trade was resurgent, but it also showed humankind that the post-war world was going to be one of rapid technological advancement. It captured the imagination of what the human race could achieve at a time when memory of destruction remained paramount for many in Europe. In the twenty-first century it has become romanticised in popular literature: Jonathan Coe's *Expo 58* satirises national identities that remained static in the face of internationalism and modernity, while a graphic novel, *Sourire 58* by Patrick Weber and Baudouin Deville, published in the twenty-first century, adds an element of espionage in the style typical of Belgian *bande dessinée*.[38] The 1950s were an age where mass travel was in its infancy and television, while spreading in America and Europe, had still not made images of other nations part of an everyday experience. The World's Fairs evoked romance and seemed to have recaptured their heyday.

Cold War exhibitions also became more direct encounters between the two sides. In an interview with the TV channel CBS on 2 June 1957, Nikita Khrushchev asked Americans to 'do away with your iron curtain' and

---

[36] Walter Putnam., '"Please Don't Feed the Natives": Human Zoos, Colonial Desire, and Bodies on Display', in Jeff Persels (ed.), *The Environment in Francophone Literature and Film* (Amsterdam: Rodopi, 2012), 55–68.

[37] Matthew Stanard, '"Bilan du monde pour un monde plus déshumanisé": The Brussels World's Fair and Belgian Perceptions of the Congo', *European History Quarterly*, 35.2 (2005), 267–298.

[38] Jonathan Coe, *Expo 58* (London: Penguin, 2014); Patrick Weber & Baudouin Deville, *Sourire 58* (Brabant: Editions Anspach, 2018).

submitted a proposal for exchange of technical, industrial, scientific and artistic products which appeared to open the door to warmer relations, as part of his 'peaceful coexistence'. The Soviets made agreements with various Western nations to host reciprocal national fairs. First, they hosted their own World Festival of Youth and Students in Moscow in 1957. This communist-led event provided 30,000 young people from around the world with heavily subsidised visits to the Soviet capital. Walter Hixson argues that this exposed the Soviet public to Western fashions, music and ideas at a scale not experienced before. Eventually the Soviets organised reciprocal national exhibitions with a number of nations including the USA, France and the UK. When the USA opened its national exhibition in Moscow in 1959 it carried forward many of the ideas that it had learned at Brussels. One of these was the training of 75 guides, including four African Americans, with particular coaching in how to deal with questions from Soviet visitors about racial inequality in the USA. But again, displays which showed integration between black and white ethnicities had to be closed due to protests from American segregationists.[39] At Moscow's Sokolniki Park the Americans displayed their consumerist nation by rehousing Disney's Circarama display and distributing free Pepsi Cola to visiting Soviets (with very few asking if they had Coca-Cola instead). In a televised debate between Vice President Richard Nixon and a jocular Nikita Khrushchev, the Soviet leader stated that the Americans were ahead in consumer production but that soon the Soviets would catch, pass and wave at the Americans as the international working class usurped the bourgeois business-owning class. This exhibition has been variously seen by scholars as a moment when the liberal-democratic worldview greatly influenced the Soviet population,[40] or something about which visitors were more sceptical, responding with politeness to the Americans.[41] But it became another Cold War site of convergence where nations, and in particular the technicians of the USSR, could learn what the other side was doing and seek to develop and catch the West.

The Soviets' return display in Washington met with a mixed response from the American press. While it was possible to laud the Soviets' scientific achievements, if only to continue the trend to emphasise America's supposed complacency in this area, the accompanying cultural exhibits, particularly the Soviets' fashion displays, drew cynicism from the American press.[42] When the

[39] Walter Hixson, *Parting the Curtain: Propaganda, Culture and the Cold War* (New York: St Martins Griffin, 1998), Epub 182, 190, 202–4.

[40] Hixson, *Curtain*; Robert Haddow, *Pavilions of Plenty: Exhibiting American Culture Abroad in the 1950s* (Washington, DC: Smithsonian, 1997).

[41] Susan E. Reid., 'Who Will Best Whom?: Soviet Popular Reception of the American National Exhibition in Moscow, 1959', *Kritika: Explorations in Russian and Eurasian History*, 9.4 (2008), 855–904.

[42] Frederick Charles Barghoorn., *The Soviet Cultural Offensive: The Role Of Cultural Diplomacy in Soviet Foreign Policy* (Princeton, NJ: Princeton University Press, 1960), 92; Djurdja Bartlett, *Fashioneast: The Spectre That Haunted Socialism* (London: MIT Press, 2010), 138–9.

Soviets exhibited a similar display in London in 1961, however, they were able to capitalise on their next space endeavour and had Yuri Gagarin, the first man to orbit the Earth, visit their display. This led to a near frenzy as people attempted to glimpse the cosmonaut. While space captured the British imagination, the exhibition's consumer goods fell flat, with neither fashions nor furniture meeting the stylistic expectations of the 1960s. Over time the Soviets' displays remained rooted in the success of Sputnik and Gagarin but also in displaying their idealised way of life, something which Verity Clarkson has labelled the display of a 'dreamworld' rather than the reality.[43]

INTERNATIONAL EXPOSITIONS IN THE 1960S AND 1970S

The next International Exposition in Seattle in 1962 expanded on the themes of modern technology that Brussels had reified. The Seattle fair, however, was less international in scope and presented an image of the world shaped primarily for Americans. The overarching theme of 'Century 21' and its attention to science and space travel seemed designed to fit with the Cold War, with the USA firmly catching the USSR's supposed lead in space technology. The fair took this theme further and aimed to present a blueprint for the next century. The focus on science reduced the appeal of the fair, with humankind and culture less prominent. Besides the USA, only the Republic of China (ROC), Britain and Sweden built their own free-standing pavilions; the others took space within pre-built exhibition halls. The Walt Disney company's participation was visible with their design for the site making it a smooth-running fair.[44] The designers worked to redevelop Seattle city centre, especially the central business district, with a monorail and the new Seattle Centre with its futuristic 'Space Needle' revolving restaurant as the landmark exhibition centre. With convention halls, amusements and green spaces added to the city, Seattle's people were set to benefit from the Expo.

What was missing from the Seattle fair was the participation of the Soviet Union, People's Republic of China (PRC), Vietnam and North Korea. The Cold War was in one of its hottest phases with the recent Berlin Crisis and escalation of the USA's invasion of Vietnam. The American organisers ensured that their propaganda messages would be amplified. Legislation that permitted the public funding of the fair forbade the participation of the communist governments of the Pacific Rim, including Vietnam, PRC and North Korea, while the USSR and Eastern European communist states declined to host

---

[43] Verity Clarkson, '"Sputniks and Sideboards": Exhibiting the Soviet 'Way of Life' in Cold War Britain 1961–1979', in A. Cross (ed.), *A People Passing Rude: British Responses to Russian Culture* (Cambridge: Cambridge University Press, 2012), 285–300.

[44] Stacy Warren, 'To Work and Play and Live in the Year 2000: Creating the Future at the 1962 Seattle World's Fair', in Laura Hollengreen et al., *Meet Me at The Fair: A World's Fair Reader* (Pittsburgh: Carnegie Mellon Press, 2014), 473–484, 474.

exhibits.[45] The ROC (Taiwan) was represented by a pavilion earning ample mention in the official guidebook, largely because USA recognised this as the State of China instead of the communist-led PRC that controlled the mainland. The exclusion of PRC helped to spread the USA's political worldview. The guidebook talked of the 'free Chinese' and the 'culture of the island republic' showing how the Cold War shaped participation at the American Expo.[46] Their display of traditional handicrafts and furniture contrasted with the nearby British demonstration of its engineering and scientific advances.[47] Unlike the 1958 fair, which organisers hoped would create an open encounter between East and West that might build open dialogue and peace, the door was firmly closed to anything outside of the liberal Western system. Among the pavilions, aiming to raise its international presence, was one from the Western sector of Berlin, the Cold War hotspot with its newly erected Berlin Wall. When the guidebook proclaimed that the fair was 'conceived as a festival of the West' their intended meaning was America's West, recalling the 1909 Alaska-Yukon-Pacific Exhibition, but they certainly presented the world as limited to those nations that fitted into the USA's vision of the Cold War West.[48]

The United States Science Pavilion allowed the USA to show off its advances in science, including space exploration, while the inconvenience of the USSR launching the first satellite and man into space could be ignored. The USA displayed its dreams of the future, science could solve everything and outer space was the hope of the twenty-first century. At the end of the official programme the authors declared 'Now that you've seen…the charm….the beauty… the richness of our way of life and the power of our growing empire…why don't you come back and share them with us!'[49] Such a brazen embrace of the intentions of the USA in the 1960s might have worried foreign visitors but would have delighted the mainly American viewers of the fair. Other American exhibits included displays by international corporations such as Ford, General Electric, IBM, Pan American and General Motors, with the latter displaying their 'space-age' Firebird III. The Seattle fair was designed to signal the USA's advances in science but also the globalising intentions of its corporate leaders.

Where the fair departed from the focus on science, visitors could engage with high art or seek more risqué forms of entertainment. The World of

[45] Centre for the Study of the Northwest, 'Lesson Twenty-five: The Impact of the Cold War on Washington, The 1962 Seattle World's Fair', https://www.washington.edu/uwired/outreach/cspn/Website/Classroom%20Materials/Pacific%20Northwest%20History/Lessons/Lesson%2025/25.html, Accessed 1 Feb 2023.

[46] Washington State Department of Commerce & Economic Development, *Seattle World's Fair: Official Souvenir Program*, 1962, 36.

[47] Warren, '1962 Seattle World's Fair', 478.

[48] Washington State Department of Commerce & Economic Development, *Seattle World's Fair: Official Souvenir Program*, 1962.

[49] Washington State Department of Commerce & Economic Development, *Seattle World's Fair: Official Souvenir Program*, 1962, 98.

Art section displayed fine arts focussing on paintings and sculpture. Five galleries displayed Art since 1950 (American and international galleries), ancient Eastern art, Northwest Indian art and American Masterpieces. This section was a sedate departure from the relentlessness of the scientific advances. The nearby World of Entertainment featured circus acts, opera, ballet and even water-skiing demonstrations. The relief from science could be extended by heading to the Gayway. This area featured amusement arcades, fairground rides and Gracie Hansen's 'Showstreet' as well as the incongruously placed Japanese and Spanish exhibitions. Showstreet was dedicated to 'adult entertainment' and some of its shows included nudity. The area proved controversial and several exhibits were temporarily closed by Seattle's city officials for violating standards of decency.[50] Showstreet, however, proved popular, with more daily visitors heading there than to the science zone.

In 1964 New York held an unofficial World's Fair that was not sanctioned by the BIE, who stipulated that a country could not hold more than one fair in ten years and that they must not charge rent to the exhibiting nations. The fair took place over two six-monthly sessions in 1964 and 1965. The Walt Disney company's influence was ever present, and the exhibits and rides they designed turned the fair into a showcase of the 'American dream'.[51] Corporate involvement was huge with America's top companies such as General Electric, IBM, Kodak and Coca-Cola hosting their own pavilions in order to market their goods. The 1964 World's Fair was a more commercial display aimed towards Americans, with European nations not showing up because of its unofficial status, and the fair eventually ran at a loss.

When the World's Fair reached Montreal in Canada in 1967 the sixties were swinging and the perception that the age of affluence would keep delivering ever more consumer goods to the world's population (especially in the West) was widespread. With 67 countries exhibiting, the fair was the biggest to date and over 50 million people eventually visited. Staged to coincide with the 100th anniversary of Canada's confederation, the fair celebrated 'Man and his World'. It was immensely popular and drew over 50 million visitors. A series of 28 weekly lectures sponsored by Noranda Mines aimed to 'metamorphose some of the native copper and gold from the Canadian shield into jewels for the mind'. Speakers came from around the world, supporting the sense of the Expo as a truly international event. The lectures were published in a book with a peace symbol on its cover. The opening chapter by the former UN Secretary General Paul-Henri Spaak, titled 'How to make peace in the World', helped to reiterate the intentions of the organisers that this encounter could help promote understanding and reconciliation.[52] The *UNESCO Courier*

---

[50] Warren, '1962 Seattle World's Fair', 480.

[51] Lawrence Samuel., *The End of the Innocence: The 1964–1965 New York World's Fair* (New York: Syracuse University Press, 2010).

[52] Paul-Henri Spaak et al., *Man and His World: Noranda Lectures 1967* (University of Toronto Press, 1968).

described the Expo as engaging with humankind's 'struggle—and coming to terms – with his environment: learning to survive in frozen lands, combatting disease and hunger, coping with the problems of life in a modern city and now facing the results of a world population explosion'.[53] Having given this positive slant to scientific and economic progress, the periodical raised emerging environmental concerns, warning that 'only now is he learning to conserve natural and mineral wealth; to replant forests and preserve wildlife; to reclaim the arid lands; to clean the air; to share food and knowledge'. Here the promise of a technological fix to the world's environmental issues seemed at hand. Human ingenuity could conquer all: the fair's site was built on two artificial islands constructed for the Expo. Humankind's encounter with nature was framed as progress.

Perhaps one aspect of Expo'67 that has endured to the present is an apparent divergence from homogenised national identities. In particular Canadians were presented with an encounter between communities. Their national identity was challenged as the displays by Indigenous nations caused many to question the treatment of native Canadians and their place in the nation. At previous World's Fairs Native Americans 'performed' Indianness often in line with the expectations of white Canadians and Americans. Yet, as Rutherdale and Miller argue, at Expo 67 the representation of First Nations changed to reflect a more questioning approach towards colonialism.[54] They suggest that representation and prominence became an issue for indigeonus Canadians, with some decisions about what to include taken out of the hands of native councils, who were attempting to present a critical narrative about the arrival of Europeans in Canada, and the placement of the 'Indians of Canada' pavilion as the least prominent of the Canadian displays. Quebec's pavilion emphasised the federated nature of Canadian identity. The fair led Canadians to consider the hybrid nature of their culture. Furthermore, the uncomfortable presentation of the policies of control of First Nation Canadians led many Canadians into an encounter with part of their own nationhood.

The Expo continued to foster the creation of hybrid cultures, with the opposing superpowers displaying their latest designs and innovations. While not as prominent as at Brussels, the Cold War rivalry still featured. Overall the Soviet Union 's pavilion was the most popular, drawing over 13 million visitors whose curiosity was piqued by the chance to view the alternative communist way of life.[55] The Soviets continued to display their space technology, especially replicas of rockets. *Paris Match* featured smiling models in modern Russian fashions complete with heels, headscarves and shopping

[53] 'Expo 67: The World in a Thousand Acres', *Unesco Courier*, April 1967, 11.

[54] Myra Rutherdale and Jim Miller, '"It's Our Country": First Nations' Participation in the Indian Pavilion at Expo 67', *Journal of the Canadian Historical Association/Revue de la Societé Historique du Canada*, 17.2 (2006).

[55] Voices of East Anglia, 'The Most successful World Fair – Expo '67', November 2011, http://www.voicesofeastanglia.com/2011/11/the-most-successful-world-fair-expo-67.html, accessed 27 May 2023.

baskets, with some gazing in wonderment at the latest Soviet spacecraft. The consumer age was spreading. Across the river stood what was perhaps the most eye-catching pavilion at Montreal: the USA's geodesic dome designed by Buckminster Fuller. Inside, the USA displayed their space technology, aiming to show that they had surpassed the USSR and the astronaut Thomas Stafford gave live talks. Other parts of the American pavilion focussed on film, with *Paris Match* declaring that 'Here the cinema is king', and giant portraits of Marilyn Monroe adorned the display.[56] Along with the customary display of film, the dome contained mechanical rides adding a new level of interaction for visitors. The architectural historian Jonathan Massey sees the design as aiming to enable a 'deliberative forum' that could deliver a more equitable distribution of global resources as a response to the communist threat to the American system. Others took this criticism of the American system further and the pavilion became the site of protests against the continued war in Vietnam. The American presence and news of the death of American soldiers and Vietnamese allowed the protest movement in the USA to grow. On the opening day of 28 April, a group of Americans held a sit-in protest under a portrait of President Lyndon Johnson. Their T-shirts bore slogans such as 'Peace in Vietnam', and one burned a draft card. The pavilion's organisers responded by offering them drinks and chairs, unlike other American fairgoers who confronted the group. The protesters raised awareness of the physical encounter taking place in Asia that the American pavilion had omitted.[57] The domestic political currents spilled over to impact the American projection of nationhood abroad.

The Expo was also an encounter of the Anglophone and Francophone worlds that encapsulated the hybrid nature of Canadian identity that was influenced by both of those European nations. France's bowl-shaped pavilion told the story of the nation's culture and arts. *Paris Match* boasted of their display containing 'Ten centuries of French art, from the modern age to avant-garde'.[58] The pavilions also housed a restaurant with a menu of the best of French food, which drew on dishes from some of the most famous restaurants of Paris and encapsulated the designer's image of French identity.[59] This identity was also projected through France's association with fashion, with numerous shows by designers including Paco Rabanne, whose unconventional designs were seen as futuristic and projected French identity onto the spirit of the 1960s. The British pavilion was situated opposite and featured a huge

---

[56] *Paris Match*, 20 Mai 1967.

[57] Jonathan Massey, 'Buckminster Fuller's cybernetic pastoral: the United States Pavilion at Expo 67', *The Journal of Architecture*, 21.5(2016), 796, 812.

[58] *Paris Match*, 20 Mai 1967, 76.

[59] Rhona Richman Kenneally, '"The greatest Dining extravaganza in Canada's history": Food, Nationalism and Authenticity at Expo 67', in *Expo 67: Not Just a Souvenir*, edited by Rhona Kenneally and Johanne Sloane (Toronto: University of Toronto Press, 2010), 29.

tower filled with a jet engine from a Concorde airliner showing Anglo-French co-operation and in keeping with the general focus on science and technology. The British also displayed modern art including Mario Armengol's *Family of Man,* which were six-metre-tall sculptures of stick-like men. With a cinema showing 21 films, a pub, theatre and ballet, this display aimed to make the most of Britain's changing identity but remained rooted in its traditions and older position as a world leader. Britain's display aimed to cement its place at the centre of the *Zeitgeist:* Beatlemania was capitalised upon and women in miniskirts were photographed next to a Mini Cooper car, and the fashions of Carnaby Steet were displayed. The 1960s were gratuitously flaunted. As Britain sought to project its leadership of the Commonwealth in one of its former colonies, it was important for Britain to have a statement pavilion that represented the era.[60] France and Britain aimed to show off their postcolonial cultural heritage and ostentatiously projected their vision of the 1960s onto the modern consumerist world.

The less internationally powerful nations made strong statements, with notable displays from Czechoslovakia and Cuba, the latter's pavilion formed from stacked rectangles and semi-circles rising over a tributary of the river. It depicted its revolution with an element of excitement as opposed to the staid image of the Soviet Union. These nations were proponents of different forms of socialism and showed that the USSR was not the only nation that offered an alternative to capitalist economic systems. The Czechoslovakian Communist Party was easing its control and intellectuals were beginning to challenge the system as part of a liberalising movement that in 1968 became known as the Prague Spring. The Czechoslovakian display retold the nation's history but paid notable attention to the display of folk arts, calligraphy and handicrafts, celebrating its Moravian and Bohemian past. As befitted a communist nation, much was made of the revolutions of 1848, the rise of the industrial proletariat and the anti-fascism of the Czechoslovakians during World War Two. The communist era was tied to modernity, progress and industrial production but the images of folkand modern arts, as opposed to socialist realism, prevailed throughout the display.[61] With cinema, puppetry and the return of the magic lantern, the exhibition built on earlier successes and enhanced Czechoslovakia's independent appearance.

Other nations used the fair to show their continuing pathway to development. South Korean architect Swoo-Geun Kim blended traditional Korean influences with modern ones in a wooden pavilion and accompanying pagoda.[62] With 4000 years of Korean culture on display including ancient

---

[60] Elizabeth Darling, '"Britain Today" at Expo 67', in *Expo 67: Not Just a Souvenir,* edited by Rhona Kenneally and Johanne Sloane (Toronto: University of Toronto Press, 2010), 54.

[61] Oldřich Beneš (ed.), *Czechoslovakia: Ancient and Modern: A Conception* (Orbis: Prague, 1967).

[62] Myengsoo Seo, 'Architecture as Medium: The Korean Pavilion at the Montreal Expo '67', *Journal of Asian Architecture and Building Engineering,* (2017), 271–278.

relics, masks and fabrics alongside modern art, the nation hoped to exorcise the memory of the war-torn 1950s with which many Westerners predominantly associated them. The encounter with Western influences allowed them to display a hybrid identity that blended aspects of Western business culture with their own traditions to display their own form of modernity. Venezuela and Jamaica hosted pavilions, and a large showing by thirteen African nations signified something of a decentring of the world away from the superpowers. On 10 August the fair celebrated Rwanda's national day, with its president Grégoire Kayibanda attending. Their participation, along with the Democratic Republic of Congo, marked a distinct change in the nine years since Brussels, when the Belgians had determined how the people of these African nations would be represented: now these Africans chose the terms of the encounter and crafted their own narrative.

The Expo also celebrated something that chimed with the increasingly globalised age: youth. Canada hosted the pavilion of youth which celebrated one billion young people worldwide and their ability to travel and meet each other. Photographs showed young people sporting new universal icons, like the 'Ban the Bomb' symbol, suggesting that ideas including peace and anti-nuclear sentiment were now transcending nationhood.[63] The pavilion hosted daily sporting activities and a Folk and Jazz Festival, with acts including exponents of counter-culture and psychedelia; The Grateful Dead and Jefferson Airplane, who performed live, linked the fair with the idea of a transnational movement of youth, which was growing during the 1960s. The Boy Scouts hosted an exhibition, with troops attending from around Canada. The Scouts, however, focussed on a more traditional version of youth, with the focus solely on boys being 'physically strong, mentally awake, morally awake'.[64] While Expo 1967 celebrated the coming of age of the post-war generation and the teenager, there were limits to the embrace of the 'youth revolution'.

1970 saw the first major Asian World's Fair, hosted in Osaka. Japan's economy had expanded and it had the world's third-highest gross domestic product, becoming one of the beneficiaries of the Age of Globalism. A previous fair had been awarded to Tokyo in 1940, but World War Two and Japan's invasion of China led to its cancellation with the nation becoming an international pariah. The location of this fair allowed the world to continue its encounter with South-East Asia and followed the success of the Olympics in Tokyo in 1964, which we visit in the next chapter. This encounter, however, was not entirely positive, with the American war in Vietnam continuing and entering its most destructive phase. However, for the Japanese the main aim was the assertion of a new form of national identity in which the relationship

---

[63] Au Pavilion de la Jeunesse. 1968. VM94-EX137-0833. Archives de la Ville de Montréal. http://archivesdemontreal.com/2017/08/04/expo-67-au-jour-le-jour-aout/, Accessed 30 May 2023.

[64] 'Tomorrow's Men in the Making', *Scouting's Expo'67*, (St Louis, MO: Hendle Press, 1967).

between state and population was shown to be mutually beneficial rather than coercive. Japanese culture was celebrated throughout. The centrepiece of the pavilions was Japan's Tower of the Sun, a building adorned with several faces of the sun with different expressions. It simultaneously celebrated mankind's progress, but also commemorated the tragedies of history. Japan's pavilion celebrated nature, traditional culture and modern life but like many exhibits of the era had a heavy focus on science, technology and the exhibition's theme of progress. Numerous Japanese multinationals built free-standing pavilions to stake their claim to the global marketplace; these included Mitsubishi, Fujipan, Hitachi and Sanyo, with the latter displaying amachine for washing humans,[65] a labour-saving hygiene device that summed up some of the dreams of the future that were shown throughout the fair. The exhibition was primarily aimed at the Japanese, with around 50 per cent of their population visiting.[66] A hybrid culture combining Japanese work ethos with globalised capitalism was displayed to visitors. However, a strong theme of regional pride and attempts to appear better than Tokyo's recent Olympiad also shone through. The high-tech economy and advanced society were inexorably tied to Japan's new national identity.

In this period the world was beginning to decentre and new hybrids were on display. The Australian pavilion broke from the traditional focus on its national identity and incorporated elements of Japanese culture such as the lotus shape built into the roof. The result was a culturally sensitive pavilion that helped to show that Australia's international engagement was shifting away from the Western nations to rising Asian nations such as Japan, who were already their largest trading partner.[67] The fair also allowed the Japanese viewing public to engage with a form of hybridity created by its diasporic community in Hawaii. A special exhibition from the US state paid particular attention to the Japanese population. Using hostesses of Japanese descent, the Pacific state aimed to draw on this hybridity to build tourism and business investment from its regional neighbours.[68] The Osaka Expo's theme of progress and harmony expanded on the ideas of growth, invention and

---

[65] Nobumichi Ariga, 'Presenting the Past, Present, and Future of Technological Innovation', in *Behind the Exhibit: Displaying Science and Technology at World's Fairs and Museums in the Twentieth Century*, edited by Elena Canadelli, Marco Beretta and Laura Ronzon (Washington, DC: Smithsonian Institution Scholarly Press, 2019), 223.

[66] Sandra Wilson, 'Exhibiting a new Japan: the Tokyo Olympics of 1964 and Expo 70 in Osaka', *Historical Research*, 85.227 (2012), 159–178.

[67] Carolyn Barnes and Simon Jackson., 'Creature of Circumstance: Australia's Pavilion at Expo'70 and Changing International Relations', *Proceedings of the XXIV Conference of the Society of Architectural Historians Australia and New Zealand*, (2007), 5.

[68] Sanae Nakatani, 'Staging Democracy and Multiculturalism: The 1970 Osaka Exposition and the Hawai'i Pavilion', *Asian Diasporic Visual Cultures and the Americas*, 1.3 (2015), 40–62.

globalisation as beneficial for humankind, but its intentions to create interconnections, especially through trade and promotion of cultures, remained key to many presentations.

Western nations still displayed their cultures in Osaka. The American pavilion was less conspicuous than at previous Expos, taking the form of an ellipse that blended into the landscape. With cars on display as well as an exhibition of photography by the USA's most famous documentary photographers, including Diane Arbus, Ansel Adams and Garry Winogrand, the Americans presented their growing artistic heritage. The images were displayed in lightbox form, emphasising the modernity of this medium. Other more traditional artforms on display included painting and displays of cars and more irreverent inventions such as a gyrocopter. The obligatory display of space capsules took up the largest space in the US exhibition. They could now celebrate America landing men on the moon following the USSR previously boasting of launching the first satellite and man into space. For the first time an exhibition included a display of samples of moon rock, doubling down on America's lead in the space race. But the USA also made much of 'folk art' and displayed masks, weaving, pottery and totem poles from native Americans, who were described in the guide as Indians and Eskimos. The USA's exhibition was accompanied by a guide in which President Richard Nixon described Japan as 'a friend and neighbour'.[69] While the Americans hoped to build up a positive image of their nation, they also wanted to forge links with the Japanese and the display was less imperialistic than others such as at Seattle.

The USSR, by contrast, built the tallest pavilion with a sloping roof that culminated in a 102-metre tower topped by a red star. The shape was supposed to evoke an unfurled banner. It included its customary display of busts of Lenin and space technology. But instead of the regular displays of machine tools and agriculture the Soviets' display had a different focus. As their English language magazine *Soviet Life* explained, the attention instead was on 'the social evolution, the ethical and cultural growth of Soviet man'.[70] One of its exhibits focussed on Siberia, stretching into Asia. It juxtaposed the natural beauty of the area with the exploitation of resources including iron and oil, and situated the region as an area of great technical production with models of new power and hydroelectric stations that the Soviets had built. The conquest of nature was celebrated, as was the building of new towns like the university enclave of Akademgorodok. Images showed Indigenous Siberians becoming Soviet citizens, with a photograph of fur-clad women next to a child in a school: the caption read 'Today the grandchildren of reindeer breeders and hunters go to school and crowd university lecture halls'.[71] This version of progress and Soviet modernity, alongside a narrative of a communist civilising

[69] Richard Nixon, quoted *United States Pavilion Japan World Exposition Osaka 1970*, Souvenir Guide.

[70] 'Soviet Pavilion at Expo 70', *Soviet Life*, March 1970, 52.

[71] *Soviet Siberia*, (Moscow: Progress Publishers Moscow, 1970).

mission, aimed to build connections with Asian nations by emphasising the Soviets' links to continental identity.

The Osaka fair was the last World Exposition for 22 years, with the BIE preferring to grant Specialised Expos status during this period. But in an age of television, multimedia and mass tourism, the opportunities to promote new products had multiplied so that waiting for the next fair was hardly practicable. Globalisation had made the fair less romantic. The location of this fair, however, showed that the world was modernising and that globalisation was producing new economically powerful nations that by the twenty-first century would challenge American, let alone European predominance.

International Expositions in the Post-Cold War World

The next official Expo in 1992 returned to Europe with Seville as the host. While the fair was part of the commemoration of Columbus's journey to the Americas it was the first of the post-Cold War era and marked the rise of a neo-liberal political order in the USA and much of Europe. Reunified Germany displayed columns of the now dismantled Berlin Wall, the Cold War was seemingly confined to history. Spain had transitioned from dictatorship to democracy since the Osaka World Fair and its economy was expanding. It had recently joined the European Economic Community and the Expo cemented Spain's place as a leading democratic nation. With its theme of 'the age of discoveries', the Spanish organisers looked back to Columbus's voyage. The fair, therefore, had a transatlantic outlook that celebrated a shared Hispanic heritage, but also appeared to commemorate European empires in an era of post-colonialism. For Guilia Quaggio, Spain was able to define a modern progressive Western democratic identity against the former imperial and nationalist-authoritarian incarnation of Spanishness. At a time when smaller nationalisms such as Basque, Catalan and Galician were newly empowered because of the ending of the dictatorship, the annunciation of a broader Spanish identity was intended to show modern post-Francoist Spain to foreign and Spanish visitors. Quaggio sees the representation of Columbus's voyage at the Expo as the start of an encounter between two different worlds, rather than of conquest and Spanish glory. This was an Expo for the post-colonial era and Spain's relationship with the Southern American nations was reimagined as a democratic mutually supporting partnership.[72] The imperial encounters of the last 500 years had been replaced by a new global relationship. However, several

---

[72] Guilia Quaggio, 'A Transatlantic Iberian Peninsula: Exhibiting the nation through the commemoration of renaissance voyages of exploration in Spain (1992) and Portugal (1998)', *Journal of Iberian and Latin American Studies*, 26.3 (2020), 317–340, 329.

'third-world' nations raised concerns about the pro-Western-dominated narrative presented at the fair, and some indigenous American groups protested at the repackaging of their customs as a 'circus spectacle'.[73]

The fair can be seen as representing the era of neo-liberal globalisation. For the anthropologist Richard Maddox, this extended to the values on display as Spain was being fully reintegrated into the liberal political economic system. He argues that the Expo represented the hegemony of 'cosmopolitan liberalism' with a suggestion of a new world order that would fit this ideology.[74] His term refers to the 'rapid transformations of the global political and economic order', especially following the collapse of communism. In practice this amounted to the domination of ideas of 'ethical humanism of individual rights and freedoms' and the significance of 'pluralism and cultural diversity'. Maddox argues that these universal values were primarily about taming the world, celebrating cultural diversity while eliminating the differences that lead to conflict and prevented the expansion of trade. His research examines how these Expos acted to expand global trade and the capitalist economic system: his example of folk art and masks from Papua New Guinea that may be bought by an American suggests that display items acted to extend the 'cash nexus' to people previously outside its scope.[75] Within this interpretation, however, is the role of the state. Individual nations, he suggests, lost some of their power to transnational organisations and corporations but also to smaller-scale identities such as nationalism including the Catalan and Basque nations in Spain. But for Maddox this challenge to large-scale nationhood necessitated the expansion of the repressive state apparatus, such as police and military, as they mediated the new differences, and contradicts the neo-liberal belief that conflict will be eliminated in the course of delivering new individual freedoms. For Maddox, when these values were brought to the southern Spanish city by global elites and local bureaucrats, they came into conflict with more localised populist values that rejected this globalised vision, and felt that the local identity was threatened.

Among the 112 countries who displayed in Seville some of the South American nations were seeking to remake their national image at the Expo. However, colonialist attitudes sometimes came to the fore. Chile, which was transitioning from the neo-liberal dictatorship of Augusto Pinochet, with a less direct move to democracy than had happened in Spain, chose to build a separate pavilion away from the purpose-built Americas building. Their commissioner declared this was to avoid being associated with black and

---

[73] Anthony Gristwood, 'Commemorating Empire in Twentieth Century Seville', in *Imperial Cities: Landscape, Display and Identity*, edited by Felix Driver and David Gilbert (Manchester: Manchester University Press, 1999), 169.

[74] Richard Maddox, *The Best of All Possible Islands: Seville's Universal Exposition, the New Spain, and the New Europe* (Albany, NY: Suny Press, 2004), 31.

[75] Maddox, *Seville*, 32.

Indigenous peoples inside the plaza.[76] Chile displayed a 100-ton ice sculpture carved from its Antarctic territory. In the searing heat of Seville the ice raised the need to protect the Earth's natural resources. Many Chileans interpretated the ice otherwise: One of the curators, Guillermo Tejeda, felt it was a comment on past colonialism and that the ice was 'the only booty Europeans didn't carry out of America, because they couldn't'.[77] The Chileans displayed their technology, including the ability to cool the ice, alongside traditional national products inside a pavilion made of pine to represent their nation's natural resources.

In the post-Cold War era the US pavilion was beset by budget constraints and lacked novelty. High-profile appearances such as Whitney Houston's were cancelled and replaced by a TV link-up to Arnold Schwarzenegger. The Spanish press ridiculed the US show, including their display of the US Bill of Rights, which portrayed American democracy as an inspiration to the rest of the world. The USA's self-depiction fared badly, drawing comparisons to the arrogance of imperial Rome. Little wonder that Canada and Puerto Rico were among the nations of the Americas whose exhibits were lauded while the USA's was roundly denigrated by reviewers. Instead, fairgoers engaged with some of the national symbols on display. The days of honour of each nation, region or company allowed the affirmation of what Maddox terms the 'structures of common difference' at the various ceremonies. The similarity of these events meant that nationhood was proclaimed but also the connections to the world; nations proclaimed their identity in relation to the other participants.[78] The Spanish press lauded supposedly exotic displays including the Mexican 'Voladores de Papantla', an acrobatic dance consisting of men dressed in bird feathers slowly descending from a rotating pole.[79] This and similar national rituals allowed visitors to have encounters with the chosen versions of different cultures. But in many ways these encounters represented the presentation of a type of tradition that is deemed to be authentic and presented in terms of the national vision of culture packaged in a similar way to the tourist encounters discussed in Chapter 3. At Seville and other International Expositions, the exhibitor's gaze often replaced that of the tourist.

The mega-event coincided with that year's Olympics in Barcelona (discussed in the next chapter) and both saw cities transformed as economic development became a key aim of these events, with new transport infrastructure facilitating visitor mobility. The Expo was costly for Seville and its

---

[76] Penelope Harvey, 'Nations on Display: Technology and Culture in Expo '92', in *The Politics of Display: Museums, Science, Culture*, edited by Sharon Macdonald, (London: Taylor and Francis, 1998), 125.

[77] Cited in Erika Korowin, '" Iceberg! Right Ahead!": (Re)discovering Chile at the 1992 Universal Exposition in Seville', Spain', *Studies in Latin American Popular Culture*, 28 (2010), 49.

[78] Maddox, *Seville*, 189–190, 161.

[79] Maddox, *Seville*, 138.

main aim was to generate a legacy of tourism and business. The 41 million visitors were mainly from Spain, but around one-third were foreign, showing that the World's Fair still aroused great interest. The Spanish social-democratic government of Felipe González used the opportunity to tie the new Spanish nationhood to its party's leadership. The Expo was seen to be a socialist act, with the party working to transform Spain following its general election victory in 1982 and steering the nation into the EEC. Spanish history was sanitised at the display and empire and discovery were repositioned as technological innovation while conquest was replaced with the promotion of harmony among peoples.[80] The Spanish pavilion aimed to reshape historical narratives to focus on the legitimisation of the Spanish state and avoid dwelling on its history of conquest, and the persecution of Jews in the fifteenth century. Maddox sees the event as one where families sought to cram in as much as they could during their visit and viewed the other visitors as antagonists, rather than being open to encountering different cultures.[81] Many felt that their encounter with the unfamiliar was limited. While the Seville Expo embedded a sense of Spanish nationhood and hoped to present it to the rest of the world, its impact on audiences was more limited.

In the twenty-first century the World's Fairs have had something of a resurgence due to their mega-event status and potential for cultural diplomacy. The first International Exposition of the twenty-first century took place in Hanover in 2000. While some of its themes of man, technology and nature were familiar, it marked a change in the ideology of the World's Fair to a new set of principles and reflected on the contemporary social and environmental problems that humanity was facing. The focus became about the global community working together, rather than competition to create ever more products.[82] It managed to attract a record 184 countries to house displays, either building their own pavilion or in one of the exhibition halls. Overall, however, it drew fewer numbers than some of the previous Expos and the average spend per visit was down, generating a DM 2.4 billion loss. Part of the reason for its lack of attractiveness, according to John and Margaret Gold, was the loss of wonderment at new technologies, with environmentalism providing a downbeat message with which the global public are less willing to engage.[83] The next fair at Aichi, Japan in 2005 had the theme Nature's Wisdom. This theme fit the twenty-first century change from assuming all progress was good; sustainability was at the forefront of its conception. With pavilions built out of

---

[80] Anthony Gristwood, 'Commemorating empire in twentieth century Seville', in *Imperial Cities: Landscape, Display and Identity*), edited by Felix Driver and David Gilbert (Manchester: Manchester University Press, 1999), 155–173.

[81] Maddox, *Seville*, 257–8.

[82] Alfred Heller, *World's Fairs and the End of Progress* (Corte Maderia, CA: World's Fairs Inc, 1999), 207.

[83] John Gold & Margaret Gold, *Cities of Culture: Staging International Festivals and the Urban Agenda, 1851–2000* (Aldershot: Ashgate, 2005), 251–2.

recycled material, the future was imagined differently to the space-age dreams of the 1960s. In part the Expo warned of potential disaster and stressed the need to imagine a new way for humanity to live that did not destroy the planet. Some of the pavilions departed from this message: the American pavilion highlighted the technological fixes that would solve the climate crisis and praised innovation and the conquest of outer space.[84] In the Global House new technologies were at the core of the exhibition, with robots displayed by Toyota in its celebration of economic globalisation.

In 2010 China marked its rise to globalism by hosting its first Expo. Following the Beijing Olympics of 2008 the event brought global attention to this rising power in a similar way to Spain, Japan and Canada with their hosting of these mega-events. Yet, like Beijing, Shanghai was on a previously unrealised scale and designed to project Chinese influence, depicting China as a modern global nation. The city was further modernised and infrastructure such as underground railways extended. Promotional images were projected onto skyscrapers connecting the whole of central Shanghai into the exhibition centre. With a cost of 45 billion dollars and drawing 73 million visitors, Shanghai delivered the largest Expo yet, suggesting that as the world decentred from the West, other regions remained immensely interested in these events.

Shanghai continued some of the traditional organisational aspects of Expos with pavilions divided by continents. Asia was at the centre: this was not just about projecting Chinese soft power but showcasing the continent's rise to prominence. The shift in global power relations meant that Western nations invested heavily in their pavilions in the hope of attracting investment. None more so than Australia. With China as its biggest trading partner by 2010, the Australian state hoped to expand the connections between the two. The pavilion cost over 83 million Australian dollars and the organisers hoped to support the increased building of business ties and mutual investment between the two nations.[85] The Expo also boasted pavillions from multinational corporations such as Coca-Cola and numerous NGOs. Fitting with the Expo's theme of Better City Better Life, numerous cities including Venice, Liverpool and Ningbo exhibited in the Urban Best Practice section. Many of these cities hoped to expand their status as global cities and draw foreign direct investment from Chinese enterprises. In the case of Liverpool, its participation followed its year as European Capital of Culture in 2008 and marked its transformation from post-industrial decline to a globally recognisable city. It leant heavily on the presence of a large Chinese community in the city that dated

---

[84] Fred Nadis, 'Nature at Aichi Wold's Expo 2005', *Technology and Culture*, 48.3 (2007), 575–581.

[85] Hilary Hongjin He, 'I wish I knew: Comprehending China's cultural reform through the Shanghai Expo', in Tim Winter (ed.), *Shanghai Expo: An International Forum on the Future of Cities* (London: Taylor & Francis, 2012), 52–3.

back several centuries. The sense of a Chinse diaspora was promoted to draw investment.

The visitors were almost entirely Chinese and most would never have travelled overseas before. Tim Winter sees their encounter with the pavilions of much of the world as a form of 'virtual tourism' that allowed Chinese people to engage with other cultures without travelling to them.[86] Visitors collected stamps in an Expo passport that gave them the sense that they had visited the world; completed passports became much coveted items in China.[87] With nations and cities presenting what Winter sees as utopian images of the future, including pristine beaches, robotic solutions to water shortages, solar cars and lost civilisations; the Expo fitted the previous 'dreamworld' presentation, whereby visitors are treated to a nation's imagined reality of how it could look. The dream of sustainability has become one of the overriding pre-occupations of the Expos, replacing the mid-twentieth-century celebration of humankind's conquest of nature.

Dubai in the United Arab Emirates hosted the first official Middle Eastern World Expo in 2020. The event offered the kingdom, which had a dubious human rights record, a chance to build its international reputation. With environmentalism at the centre of the International Exposition's twenty-first century project, it may have seemed odd to host the Expo in an oil-producing Emirate that lobbied against plans to reduce fossil fuel usage. In addition to the traditional arts, culture, business, food and the continuation of the smart cities section, the festival centre featured a section on sustainability. This district mainly focussed on, with recreations of the rainforest, waterfalls and the Czechia pavilion, which featured a display on using solar energy to produce water out of the desert air.[88] Part of the sustainability pavilion focussed on encouraging individuals to change their consumption patterns rather than the need for international governmental legislative action. While there were some attempts at promotion of green energy and water preservation, the Expo could have gone further in promoting the need to reduce fossil fuels.

Dubai was not the first exposition in a Middle Eastern country, but was the first officially sanctioned by BIE. Since 1954 Syria had hosted the Damascus International Fair, which aimed to promote an international face of the nation. It also regularly displayed at the Expos, including the first of the post-war era in Port-au-Prince, 1949. While the fair had to break between 2012 to 2017 due to the Syrian civil war, it has remained an ongoing attempt to promote Syrian industry and culture to an international audience. The first fair, known as the Damascus International Exposition, was in part an attempt to associate Syria with the modernity of the post-war era and increase the role of

---

[86] Tim Winter, 'A Forum on the Future of Cities', in Tim Winter (ed.), *Shanghai Expo: An International Forum on the Future of Cities* (London: Taylor & Francis, 2012), 8.

[87] Hongjin He, 'Shanghai Expo', 49.

[88] Expo 2020, Dubai UAE, 'Sustainability District' https://www.expo2020dubai.com/en/understanding-expo/sustainability-district Accessed 30 June 2023.

middle class-based nationhood in the post-colonial nation. With the USSR and USA in competition, both invested heavily in their national pavilions. The USA debuted its Cinerama immersive video display for the first time outside America, before it became the star of so many Expositions during the 1950s and 1960s. Syria's government promoted tourism and eased entry requirements during the fair, resulting in increased numbers of visitors and a subsequent upswing in foreign trade. The government, however, had to control the behaviour of Syrians to create a good impression in the environs of the fair, including the removal of beggars and hawkers from the capital.[89] This mediation of culture, therefore, represented an imagined view of Syria that was designed for the consumption of foreigners. While the Dubai Expo was directed to a twenty-first-century international community, it continued the encounters that Middle Eastern nations had built since the start of the Age of Globalism.

Not all exhibitions hope to facilitate international reconciliation, and some have marked divergence from previous international links. In 2018 British Prime Minister Theresa May announced that in recognition of Britain's withdrawal from the European Union a Festival of Brexit Britain would be held in 2022. This festival was set to celebrate a nation that was withdrawing from a relationship that developed links among states that had once warred over many centuries. In a world that had become multicultural and diverse a homogeneous British culture was to be celebrated. Critics attacked this monolithic British ideal. The cartoonist Martin Rowson drew a vision of how such a festival might look on the South Bank of the Thames, which housed the Festival of Britain in 1951,[90] complete with a 'Bullshit Tower', non-existent hall of global trade, a 'latest Boris bridge' (after the former cabinet minister Boris Johnson who had suggested that bridges might be built from Scotland to Northern Ireland) and a missing pavilion that had 'relocated to Dublin, Frankfurt, Vilnius etc.'. The image took aim at the deglobalising world that Brexit seemed to symbolise, while harking back to the Festival of Britain. The twenty-first-century festival was intended to be more akin to the spectacle nationalism discussed by Mary Kaldor. When it arrived, however, overt references to British culture were removed, often as a demand by artists as part of their participation. The festival was re-packaged as 'Unboxed: Creativity in the UK'. Notwithstanding the pandemic restrictions, its poor engagement rate partly reflected a population that rejected the idea of a singular British culture and a cultural class that wanted little to do with Britain's withdrawal from Europe.

Throughout the Age of Globalism the International Expositions created encounters between East and West; coloniser and colonised; and between

---

[89] Kevin Martin, 'Presenting the "True Face of Syria" to the world: urban disorder and civilisational anxieties at the first Damascus International Exposition', *International Journal of Middle Eastern Studies*, 42 (2010), 391–411.

[90] Martin Rowson, *The European*, 5 Oct 2018.

diverse national cultures. These events were forms of spectacle nationalism that allowed visitors to engage with foreign cultures they might never have otherwise encountered and promoted a sense of global harmony with themes such as progress, humanism and latterly environmentalism uniting the displays. Modern, however, perhaps lack the romance of previous fairs held before mass transport and communications technology made encountering other cultures somewhat easier. Yet mega-events still hold a big attraction for many because of the spectacle they promise, which is perhaps seen more directly in the Olympic Games.

Discussion Questions

What kinds of people gain an encounter with other cultures at International Expositions?

What types of culture are on display, who influences what is displayed and who is it presented for?

What are the lasting legacies of International Expositions?

How far can the displays be said to be authentic representations of national cultures?

What have been the impacts of the globalisation of economics, mobilities and communications on International Expositions?

CHAPTER 6

Olympian Encounters at the Summer Games

International sporting events are forms of 'spectacle nationalism' as well as conduits for globalisation itself. The summer Olympics are the sporting world's greatest encounters between peoples of different nations. The role of global corporations such as Coca-Cola, Nike and numerous media organisations has meant that globalisation expanded alongside the growth in popularity of the Games. Television has turned sports into global events consumed in homes around the world. Other spectators travel to these mega-events, giving them a sense of participation, with festivities, parades and cultural exhibitions as part of the display. For elite athletes the encounter becomes even more intense, and they are removed from their familiar backgrounds and transplanted to another culture. At the opening ceremonies the host nation celebrates its culture, showcasing it to viewing millions internationally. These huge acts of choreography often cost millions of dollars with film directors sometimes recruited to present a positive vision of national cultures. Each participating nation parades in a form of homage behind its own flag. Sport is also one of the key forms of cultural diplomacy which enables nations to build 'soft power'. It is for this reason that massive redevelopment and social cleansing often take place in preparation for the Olympics. The 'best face' of a city is presented to the world, with those aspects or people deemed undesirable hidden or removed.

The Olympics may sometimes be seen as a proxy for war, but this was not the founder's intention. The Games were imagined as increasing understanding between nations and preventing conflict. Pierre de Coubertin, the founder of the modern Olympic movement wrote that,

> Wars break out because nations misunderstand each other. We shall not have peace until the prejudices which now separate the races shall have been outlived.

To attain this end, what better means than to bring the youth of all countries periodically together for amicable trials of muscular strength and agility.[1]

This attempt to build understanding and peace through a common sporting ethos indicates that the Olympics aimed to develop a hybrid culture, taking sports from many different nations and turning them into global entities. De Coubertin's vision was about empowering people with physical exercise, which was part of education. He hoped to create an event in which the youth of the world became conduits for peace.

The early modern Olympics were not the capitalist showpiece of professional athletics that they are today. De Coubertin wanted to celebrate the 'gentlemanly amateur'. He had his doubts about the movement and Goldblatt writes that he was inspired when visiting an 'Olympic' sporting contest in the Shropshire town of Much Wenlock in 1890.[2] Following this competition he arranged the first modern Olympics in 1896, which were held in Athens, the centre of the ancient Games. Professionals were barred; all the cyclists who were due to participate in the Paris-Roubaix race later that year were deemed professional and stopped from competing. Carlo Airoldi, an Italian marathon runner who had undertaken a sponsored run to Athens, was disqualified after being deemed a professional.[3] The gentleman's club that competed at Athens was all male and all white, fitting in with de Coubertin's vision. The next two Olympic Games, Paris (1900) and St. Louis (1904), were part of the World's Fairs held in those cities and lacked the intense coverage of later Games. The Olympics took some time to acquire the mega-event status that they claimed from the late twentieth century.

The make-up of the early twentieth-century Olympic Games would have shocked many modern viewers. With sports including the tug-of-war, they were closer to Scotland's Highland Games than a multinational corporate spectacular. At the 1908 Games in London, which were held concurrently with the Franco-British Exhibition, a USA vs Liverpool Police quarter-final football match caused controversy after the Merseyside team wore their work boots, which it was alleged gave them a better gripping surface. Two other teams—Germany and Greece – withdrew meaning that three teams received a bye to the semi-finals. Amateurism was the order of the day and sports were often not yet codified, with rules being contested.

However, for one country at least the London Games became a metaphor for national prestige. At a time when Germany and the USA were challenging Britain's international pre-eminence (and when jingoism was increasing), many newspapers treated the hosting of the Games in the imperial capital as a

---

[1] Pierre de Coubertin, cited in John J MacAloon, *This Great Symbol: Pierre de Coubertin and the Origins of the Modern Olympic Games* (New York: Routledge, 2008), 302.

[2] David Goldblatt, *The Games: A Global History of the Olympics* (London: Norton, 2017), 34.

[3] David Goldblatt, *The Games*, 48.

chance for Britain to re-assert its international authority, trampling on the ethos of individual endeavour.[4] The internationalism that was embedded in the founding of the movement was already under threat. This nationalist fervour continued during the 1910s, with Sweden enlisting its athletes in the army prior to the 1912 Stockholm Olympiad. They became de-facto professionals, winning 24 golds and the most medals overall. The major nations began to respond with attempts to hire the best coaches, and provide some forms of sponsorship and the best facilities to athletes in order to prove their prowess and masculinity against the other nations.[5] The myth of gentlemanly amateurism was quickly undermined.

Cultural activities were part of the contest until 1948 and prizes were awarded for events including painting, sculpture and literature. Entries were to be based on sports and the contests were an attempt to recreate the ritualistic nature of the Games in Ancient Greece.[6] But these contests showed the heart of the new movement was humanism. With few entries for the Stockholm Olympics in 1912, however, the literature contest was judged by de Coubertin, and he awarded the gold medal to *Ode Au Sport* by Hohrod and Eschbach. It later transpired that Hohrod and Eschbach was a pseudonym for none other than de Coubertin himself. In part this symbolises the 'closed shop' that constituted the early modern Games.[7] Most working-class athletes were unable to take part and women were discouraged from participation.

Women were limited to being spectators in de Coubertin's vision; he felt that their applause for men could be reserved as a prize. The participation of women was only permitted following an IOC vote in 1914 (which de Coubertin opposed). But the decision was hampered by a compromise limiting women's participation. In 1921 women sought to counter this exclusion and formed the International Women's Sports Federation, which held its own world championships to counter the exclusion from the Olympic movement. In order to prevent this 'breakaway' and bring women under control the IOC, now under the presidency of Henri de Baillet-Latour, included women's activities in the main Olympiad. This did not, however, mark a golden age for women's sport. At Amsterdam 1928, having been involved in a lung-busting sprint for the line in the 800-metres final, several women collapsed to the ground as they sought to catch their breath. They were criticised by the press for being unladylike and the furore meant that no women's race over 200 metres featured in the Olympics until 1968. Gender inequality has been a

---

[4] Matthew McIntyre., 'National Status, the 1908 Olympic Games and the English Press', *Media History*, 15.3 (2009), 271–286.

[5] Arnd Kruger, 'The Unfinished Symphony: A History of the Olympic Games from Coubertin to Samaranch', in Jim Riordan and Arnd Kruger (eds), *The International Politics of Sport in the Twentieth Century* (London: Taylor & Francis, 1999), 10–11.

[6] Margaret M. Gold & George Revill, 'The Cultural Olympiads: Reviving the Panegyris', in John R. Gold & Margaret M. Gold, *Olympic Cities: City Agendas, Planning and the World's Games, 1896–2016*, Second Edition (Abingdon: Routledge, 2011), 81.

[7] David Goldblatt, *The Games*, 1–2.

long-held feature of the Olympic Games and the type of encounters available to men and women have differed for much of the period, with women's sports involved in an ongoing struggle to be placed on an equal footing to men's.

During the interwar years the Olympics began to turn into a mass media spectacle. The first live radio broadcasts took place in 1924 at Paris and newsreel cameras filmed many of the events. By 1932, at the Los Angeles Olympics, radio stations were bidding to secure the rights to broadcast live commentary.[8] The creation of a multi-lingual press department meant that the organisers were determined that the world would have a good impression of their Games. The expansion of mass media and broadcasting went hand in hand with the development and later commercialisation of the Games.

The Soviet Union did not take part in the interwar Games. Their aim was for the physicality and ability of this undeveloped nation to catch that of the West and to build a non-bourgeois sporting culture. The Soviets believed that this withdrawal would give a space in which to develop the 'new Soviet man', who would exhibit sporting prowess.[9] During the interwar years a healthy 'Worker Sports' movement also held its own games; these were open to men, women and all social and ethnic groups, and aimed to be a co-operative display that negated the commercialisation of bourgeois sports.[10] The movement originated with Social Democratic parties in Western Europe and focussed on internationalism instead of national competitions. The 1928 Workers Olympics in Moscow became the first Spartakiad, which became a rival Games.

By the time of the Berlin Olympics in 1936, Adolf Hitler had risen to power in Germany and the Games became a propaganda display of spectacle nationalism, the like of which had never been seen. The state funded the Games to a then unprecedented level. A worldwide publicity campaign of posters and pamphlets, reaching as far as Buenos Aires, broadened awareness of the coming spectacle. At the opening ceremony for the first time the torch was lit following a relay of the flame, a ritual that remains central to the 'mysticism' of the Games. The Nazi state heavily controlled coverage, even controlling rights over which photographs could be distributed. The racial ideology of Nazism held that the Aryans were the master race and they intended to prove it on the sporting field. Jesse Owens, the African–American runner, had a final say on that theory as he beat all comers and won four gold medals. Popular mythology contends that Hitler, having invited all medal winners to be congratulated personally, refused to shake his hand. He had, however, stopped greeting the winners before Owens competed. The iconic photograph of the Berlin Games shows Owens on the podium receiving his long jump

---

[8] Arnd Kruger, 'Unfinished Symphony', 11–14.

[9] Susan Grant, *Physical Culture and Sport in Soviet Society: Propaganda, Acculturation and Transformation in the 1920s and 1930s* (Abingdon: Routledge, 2012).

[10] James Riordan, 'The Worker Sports Movement', in Jim Riordan and Arnd Kruger (eds), *The International Politics of Sport in the Twentieth Century* (London: Taylor & Francis, 1999), 105–118.

medal. Owens salutes the American flag while his defeated German rival Lutz Lang holds his arm aloft in the Nazi salute, as do many of the crowd and officials. It looked as though the Olympics had taken an ideological sway with the next contest awarded to the dictatorship of Japan (Tokyo, 1940). The start of World War Two in 1939 overtook this moment of fascist ascendency and the competition was cancelled.

THE AUSTERITY-ERA OLYMPICS

The first post-war Olympiad took place in London in 1948 as the West was still reeling from the physical and economic destruction of World War Two. At a time of rationing, shortages and economic strife, the hosting of such a large-scale event appeared foolhardy to some. But the Labour government hoped to use the Games to generate money from ticket sales and visiting tourists, which would boost Britain's balance of payments. The costs of staging were borne by private companies, not the public. Fifty-nine nations sent athletes. No team was invited from Germany or Japan because of their wartime conduct. German prisoners of war, however, were used as labour to construct the road to the Olympic stadium.[11] The new nations of India and Pakistan competed for the first time since their independence the previous year. Other nations competing for the first time included Burma, Ceylon and Syria plus a number of Central and South American nations. The geographic make-up of participants was diversifying, a trend that would continue through the post-war era as more won their freedom from the European empires. For American athletes the trip allowed them to encounter their fellow countrymen. While travelling in luxury on the *SS America*, US rifleman Arthur Jackson remembered 'I shook hands with my first black American on board ship'. Indeed when photos of black and white athletes mixing on board began to circulate, one newspaper noted that it 'provoked a scandal in the United States',[12] where segregation remained in force.

At these Games the chance to have an encounter was mainly limited to male athletes. There were only 385 women competitors, who were barred from all but nine athletics events. Indeed a new campaign of sex testing had been introduced following the 1946 European Championships, which included inspections of genitalia, making competing for women something of an embarrassing and potentially traumatic encounter.[13] Of the women who were able to compete the Dutchwoman Fanny Blankers-Koen drew headlines by winning gold in the 100-metres final before returning to compete in the hurdles and 200m, winning both. While Blankers-Koen became the exception to the rule of not celebrating women's athleticism, the era remained one of

---

[11] Janie Hampton, *The Austerity Olympics: When the Games Came to London in 1948* (London: Aurum, 2008), 25, 33.
[12] Hampton, *Austerity Olympics*, 48.
[13] Hampton, *Austerity Olympics*, 144.

marginalisation of women in the Western nations and this extended to their continued exclusion and treatment at the Olympics.

Many of the 4000 competitors were placed in rapidly converted housing such as former army bases or schools. Others were found lodgings in the homes of British people. This hosting offered a chance to encounter previously unknown cultures. Jennifer Welson, whose family welcomed three Jamaican athletes, remembered that they 'Introduced a new dish into our home of boiled rice, grated coconut and red beans'. Such encounters offered both host and visitor a previously unseen vision of life beyond their borders. British competitors were introduced to new products like talcum powder, deodorant and aftershave by their American counterparts. The Olympic movement at this time remained heavily focussed on the West with no awareness of the fact that Muslims were fasting during the Games due to Ramadan.[14] Some countries sought familiarity and brought their own chefs and food to guarantee adequate supplies, especially considering the ongoing shortages in Britain. Australians ensured that their athletes received a pint of milk, two eggs and a lamb chop for breakfast, with the Mexican team importing chillies and tripe. Sometimes relations were less than harmonious. James Pilditch, an art student working at the Games, recalls being in an Uxbridge pub where a local picked a fight with some Asian men, because of stories of the Japanese in the war. Unfortunately the men were Korean boxers and wrestlers who did not come off second best in the ensuing fight.[15] Certainly for the predominantly male competitors the Olympics provided an opportunity to mix with people from other cultures, although not always in a peaceful manner. Little accommodation was given to those whose customs differed to those of the West.

Spectators at the opening ceremony and the Games recall an unfamiliarity with anything foreign. One spectator remembered having his first Coca-Cola, a product imported for the Americans.[16] Foreign visitors and their languages proved even more strange with one bar worker reporting the confusion over pronunciation of certain beer brands like Guinness. Even under the auspices of austerity the Games spread the products that would become globalised in the late twentieth century.

When the Soviets joined the IOC in 1951 it was the height of the Cold War. The 1952 Olympic Games in Helsinki heralded the politicisation of the Games according to Cold War rivalries. The geographic location of the neutral Finnish capital meant that it became the target of ideologies from both East and West. Marek Fields has explored how the US State Department saw the arrival of the Soviets as a new front in the Cold War. The American authorities placed new importance on sport and instructed athletes to extend the American message of friendship and goodwill, should they come into contact with Soviet competitors. The CIA were tasked with collecting information

---

[14] Hampton, *Austerity Olympics*, 5.
[15] Hampton, *Austerity Olympics*, 64, 74.
[16] Hampton, *Austerity Olympics*, 81.

on Soviet athletes, including their training regimes and identifying potential defectors.[17] An 'information' office was opened in Helsinki city centre that provided foreign visitors with leaflets and films about life in the USA; the opportunity for national propaganda aimed at potential visitors from the East was not to be missed. With Coca-Cola introduced to the public of Finland for the first time, the American way of life and consumer capitalism was well and truly on show at the Games, with the products of globalisation continuing their conquest.

Certain members of the population, however, had ideas beyond the Cold War. At the opening ceremony Barbara Rotbraut-Pleyer walked onto the field and took the microphone, getting part-way through her speech about peace before police pulled her away.[18] The protest and her desire for the Games to be about reconciliation, not confrontation, suggests that the conflict between governments was not wholly desired by populations. The Helsinki Games didn't quite become the site of internationalism and convergence that had been intended in the spirit of the movement: two Olympic villages were built, one for Western athletes and one for those from the East.[19] The Communist bloc village was a real little Moscow with portraits of Stalin and other Eastern leaders. The Finns arranged meetings between Eastern and Western athletes and the Soviets offered their traditionally opulent feasts of caviar, steak and vodka to foreign guests.[20] With the expansion of radio, film and television coverage, these Games represented the start of a pivot away from being an amateur affair into a more global and commercialised event.

Other nations saw the Helsinki Games as an opportunity to promote themselves on a global scale. The government of the recently created state of Israel believed that sports and diplomacy went together: participation in international sporting institutions would lead to greater international political recognition for their state. Its 25 competitors were Israel's first Olympic participants. The athletes were asked to change foreign names to Hebrew to present an image of cohesive Israeli nationality. They were briefed on their behaviour by their government's Committee for International Sports Relations, who told them to enjoy the local food but adopt a serious persona with the locals who were deemed to 'lack a sense of humour'.[21] The trauma of the recent past remained a heavy burden for this nation of Holocaust survivors. The athletes were instructed to avoid all contact with Germans and to leave the stadium if Germany won a medal and their national anthem was played.

---

[17] Marek Fields, *Defending Democracy in Cold War Finland: British and American Propaganda and Cultural Diplomacy in Finland, 1944–1970* (Leiden: Brill, 2020), 235–6.

[18] Goldblatt, *The Games*, 195–6.

[19] Kruger, 'Unfinished Symphony', 18.

[20] Goldblatt, *The Games*, 216.

[21] Udi Carmi and Orr Levental, 'Ambassadors in Track Suits: The Public Relations Function of Israeli Delegations to the Olympic Games during the State's First Decade', *Sport History Review*, 50, (2019), 17–37, 25.

This was easier said than done, however, and Yehoshua Alouf wrote of three friendly marksmen from the Saar Protectorate (then an individual team) who tried to befriend Israeli team members.[22] For the Israelis Helsinki marked a line which had been crossed: sporting participation was a step to international recognition of their state but in which the recent history meant that there was a wariness of Northern Europeans.

The first Games to be held in the Southern Hemisphere were at Melbourne in 1956. In an era of post-war shortages and spending restraint the public spectacle of later Games was not envisioned. Hotels required modernising for foreign tastes and the city's drinking laws, which prevented the serving of alcohol after six pm, were extended to cater for 'sophisticated' European tastes. The difficulties in travelling to Australia and winter staging meant that participation was lower, with only 3500 athletes. Several countries boycotted the Games because of the geo-political tensions that emerged that year. The Games are remembered as 'the friendly games' despite the decidedly unfriendly atmosphere of some events described below. The tag was a classic piece of national marketing, with Australian friendliness promoted. It was cemented at the closing ceremony, where for the first time, athletes walked unsegregated instead of in national ranks. Friendliness could only stretch so far, however, and the desire of many Australians to exclude their wartime enemies, the Japanese, showed another side to the national character.[23] At these Games and the accompanying cultural festival, Australia presented its image to the world. Criticism, however, has shown that this was an Anglo-centric 'White Australia' on display rather than a multi-ethnic identity including Indigenous Australians.[24]

To create the image of Australian friendliness Melbourne housewives were mobilised as part of 'Operation Hostess'. Homemakers across the city were recruited to host the Olympic guests, with door-to-door recruitment taking place in 1955 as the need to find beds became urgent. Many women enrolled in special Olympic etiquette classes to prepare themselves. These taught housewives the social habits of other nations and trained them in preparing the best of Australian cookery such as grilled lamb chops and billy tea. Inspections of the homes produced a grading system, suggesting that those most in line with the preferred stereotype of Australianness were prioritised. The phenomenon prompted comedian Barry Humphreys to create a new character based on the hostesses: Edna Everage, a satire based on the class and racial snobbery of the imagined middle-class Australian housewife. The preferred form of Australianness – white, European and as aspirational and consumerist as 1950s Melbourne could be – was presented to the visitors. Ultimately the

---

[22] Carmi and Levental, 'Ambassadors'.

[23] Graeme Davison, 'Welcoming the World: The 1956 Olympic Games and Re-presentation of Melbourne', *Australian Historical Studies*, 27: 109, (1997), 64–76, 70, 74.

[24] Gold & Gold, *Olympic Cities*, 49.

endeavour to impress foreign guests was limited: of 8806 provided with these lodgings only 731 fell outside the category of Australians, Americans or New Zealanders.[25] Nevertheless, the showcasing of the Australian family environment provided an opportunity for encounters between the visitors and hosts and to increase understanding about other cultures.

Cold War tensions loomed large at these Games, leading to divergence as international politics took precedence over sport. Despite a change in policy from the Soviet leader Nikita Khrushchev, several global events had inflamed international tensions. On 29 October the British and French joined in the Israeli invasion of Egypt under the auspices of securing the strategically important Suez Canal. This war coincided with the attempted revolution in Hungary, which began on 23 October and was followed by the re-invasion by the Soviet army. These conflicts brought international politics into the sporting arena and led to boycotts with Egypt and Lebanon withdrawing because of the participation of those who invaded the sovereign territory of Egypt. They were joined by Spain, the Netherlands and Switzerland, who protested against the participation of the USSR while they occupied Hungary. The tensions simmered at the Games. The Australian-Hungarian community turned out to support their countryfolk. Many supporters carried the Hungarian flag with the central image of a hammer and sheaf of wheat cut out, as the revolutionaries had in Budapest. On 6 December Hungary played the Soviet Union at water polo. Violence soon erupted in the pool. Both teams aimed punches at opposing players. Hungary won the match 4–0. A dramatic photograph shows the Hungarian Ervin Zádor with blood streaming from his eye. At the poolside the Australian police had to quell the crowd and prevent a riot. The game caught headlines around the world, with newspapers dubbing it the 'blood in the water match'. Hungary went on to win the gold medal. Forty-six members of the Hungarian Olympic team claimed political asylum in Australia, following the example of one of their footballing superstars, Ferenc Puskas, who had defected to fascist Spain earlier in the year. The claims that the Olympics were non-political had proven to be false once more. The Games became divergent: they facilitated clashes of cultures, but also the creation of new migrant communities who used sport to change the cultural encounter of war to new hybrid cultures. The potential of these Games to create a broader encounter was limited to those attending and the athletes, however, because of the television companies' refusal to purchase the screening rights.

THE GAMES CONFRONT THE PAST

The Rome Olympics in 1960 served as the first of the three symbolic rehabilitations of the former Axis powers. Rome used the fascists' EUR model city and Foro Mussolini sports complex, which was renamed the Foro Italico

---

[25] Rachel Buchanan 'The Home Front Hostess, housewife and home in Olympic Melbourne, 1956', *Journal of Australian Studies*, 26.72 (2002), 201–209.

but retained an obelisk bearing the name of the former fascist leader. Little surprise that the 1960 Games have been descried by Goldblatt as an exercise in 'historical amnesia'.[26] Many of the organisers had been active supporters of fascism. With the Games expanding the use of television, they offered the opportunity for Rome and Italy to cast off its fascist taint. The past was conveniently forgotten, with Italy's traditional rural communities being celebrated. But some habits were hard to overcome. The Vatican prevented clergy from attending or watching any women's events and participation from Italian women was woefully low. If these Games were an encounter they remained that of a white, male, amateur and therefore non-working-class group. The post-war Italian state, however, was able to promote its new version of nationhood.

Much of Rome was physically regenerated. Ruined housing, on which shanty towns were built after the war, was pulled down and the squatting population evicted. Modern housing complexes took their place in what became the Olympic village and was later turned into public housing. While the infrastructure of the city was changed, inside the new constructions traditional attitudes prevailed. The Italian and other nations' press sexually objectified the 600 or so women competitors, leading to reports of men attempting to look inside the women's quarters from outside. The result was that the women athletes had to use blackout blinds at all times and live almost in a state of siege to keep them away from male harassment. Other cultural norms sometimes clashed. American competitors complained of the poor quality of the toilet paper that was either waxy or resembled kitchen roll, while a young boxer named Cassius Clay was reported to have mistaken the bidet in his bedroom for a water fountain.[27] But Clay's gregariousness and tendency for self-publicity won him much popularity with other nations' athletes and the world's press. He was able to present the best face of America as he would later do again when, named Muhammed Ali, he was recruited by the US government for a cultural diplomacy campaign. As a black athlete he was able to become the face of modern America, despite the nation struggling to come to terms with its battle for civil rights and desegregation.

With live television screenings in eighteen nations, these Games formed the broadest encounter between audiences and the sports yet. But Cold War tensions loomed large. On the eve of the Games a goodwill message to all athletes from Nikita Khrushchev raised the hopes for a peaceful encounter, even if many dismissed the speech as propaganda.[28] When Soviet athletes visited the American quarters to greet their fellow competitors and share a Coca-Cola, the world's press once again focussed on the warm front of the Cold War. The opening ceremony brought controversy due to the Cold War's

[26] Goldblatt, *The Games*, 244.

[27] David Mariness, *Rome 1960: The Olympics that changed the World* (New York: Simon and Schuster: 2008), 73, 76.

[28] Mariness, *Rome 1960*, 78.

impact on global politics. Under pressure from the USSR and the People's Republic of China (PRC), the IOC declared that Taiwan was no longer able to call itself the Republic of China (ROC). The move led to disagreement between the US government, who recognised the Taiwanese state and not the PRC, and the IOC, with press criticisms of its president Avery Brundage because of the decision. Brundage, the American businessman and elitist who had attacked the government's unwillingness to let General MacArthur use nuclear weapons in Korea, was condemned in America's right-wing media as a communist sympathiser.[29] The IOC declared that Taiwan must march under the banner of Formosa at the opening ceremony, which they duly did, but they also carried a smaller banner saying 'under protest'. Other contentious areas involved the two Germanys. It was decided that a united German team would complete. Instead of the German national anthem, Beethoven's 'Ode to Joy' was played when a gold medal was won. While the German teams presented an image of unity, many divisions remained: when East German Ingrid Kramer won gold in the diving, the communists made much of her being raised in the German Democratic Republic (GDR). For these politically divided nations, the Olympics represented a heightening of tensions.

Developing and newly independent nations were visible on a scale not previously seen: Singapore (as part of Malaysia), Ghana, Tunisia and Morocco were among those competing for the first time. Ethiopian Abebe Bikila ran the marathon barefoot, setting a new world record. His win brought the first gold medal for an athlete from sub-Saharan Africa. The win conveyed a sense of post-colonial fightback from the nation that had emerged from Mussolini's invasion in 1936. These developing nations were able to raise their influence. Many were particularly critical of South African participation. The apartheid regime had raised political tensions. 1960 was the year of the Pass Law protests and the Sharpeville massacre (discussed in Chapter 4) had been reported worldwide in March. On 14 August, the day before the Games began, Brundage and other IOC members heard reports about discrimination in team selection, but they chose to believe the South African account that this was not happening.[30] While the ability of these national teams to influence the IOC was limited, in future Games the issue of participation of apartheid nations would become a contentious issue leading to the withdrawal of some national teams.

In 1964 Japan used the Games as a reconciliatory act to symbolically re-enter the international community.[31] These Olympics were the first to depart from the Eurocentric focus of previous Games and served to kickstart the internationalisation of the events. Japan had rapidly reindustrialised after World War Two and the Games marked its rising economic power. Brundage proclaimed

[29] Mariness, *Rome 1960*, 54–58.

[30] Mariness, *Rome 1960*, 88.

[31] Kay Schiller and Christopher Young, *The 1972 Munich Olympics and the Making of Modern Germany* (Berkeley, CA: University of California Press, 2010), 56.

the nation 'a meeting-point between East and West'.[32] With an opening ceremony that was notable for its absence of traditional dance, arts and theatre, Japan's culture was distinctly downplayed to the mainly Western global audience. However, subtle images of traditional culture such as women dressed as Geishas presenting medals allowed Westerners to maintain their usable image of Asian culture. The opening ceremony featured the release of balloons instead of the traditional 21-gun salute, showing that Japan was now a nation of peace.[33] The Olympic flame was lit by Sakai Yoshinori, chosen because he was born on 6 August 1945, the day that Hiroshima was destroyed by the American nuclear bomb. Sakai was just one of the specially chosen torchbearers during its route around Japan. All were aged between sixteen and twenty: too young to even remember the war, this was the new guilt-free Japanese generation.[34] The symbolic presentation of the new Japanese nation represented the end of war but also hopes that atrocities against humankind would never happen again. Japan's new world image was as a nation of peace powered by roaring economic growth. While the message of peaceful internationalist Japan was projected to the world, Sandra Wilson argues that its biggest impact was on the Japanese audience. Around 70 per cent of Japanese adults watched the opening ceremony and saw the new representation of a national image that had changed from belligerent expansionism to a new benign state.[35] With live satellite television bringing the Games to millions of homes nationally and internationally, these Games marked a change in the audience role: the Olympics now became an encounter between home viewer, spectator and athlete.

Japan's global image was carefully constructed. Tokyo had been thoroughly redeveloped from a post-war sense of making do into a modern cosmopolis. The city was completely modernised: shanty towns that had emerged following widespread destruction during World War Two were bulldozed with new roads, subway lines and a monorail built. Alongside was a new sewage system fit for the world's largest urban area and the start of the high speed 'bullet' train project. Hotels were made appealing to Westerners by copying American standards of comfort in a similar way to that discussed in Chapter 3. But the Japanese also attempted to change the behaviour of its population to accommodate the social attitudes of foreigners: urination in the street was

---

[32] Cited in Sandra Collins., 'The Fragility of Asian National Identity in the Olympic Games', *Owning The Olympics: Narrative of the New China*, edited by Monroe Price and Daniel Dayan (Chicago: University of Michigan Press, 2008), 191.

[33] Olympics, *Tokyo 1964 Olympic Games—Olympic Flame & Opening Ceremony*, Youtube, 3 Oct 2013, https://www.youtube.com/watch?v=JOIYgXzMSC4, Accessed 24 May 2023.

[34] Paul Droubie, 'Phoenix Arisen: Japan as peaceful internationalist at the 1964 Tokyo Summer Olympics', *The International Journal of the History of Sport*, 28.16, (2011), 2309–2322, 2306.

[35] Sandra Wilson, 'Exhibiting a new Japan: The Tokyo Olympics of 1964 and Expo 70 in Osaka', *Historical Research*, 85.227 (2012).

discouraged, beggars and prostitutes were cleared from around the stadium out of the sight of foreign visitors. This wide-scale social control suggests that the tourist gaze was being constructed especially for those visiting, but it also showed that globalising values emerging from the West were seen as modern and could force a change in behaviours. With the Games including judo and volleyball for the first time, some diversification was visible. These sports were popular in Japan and appeared to show the Olympics beginning to diversify away from their Eurocentric hegemony. More importantly judo was shorn of militaristic origins and trappings and was presented as an internationalist Olympic sport.[36]

These Games brought, not for the first time, disabled athletes to the world stage. In so doing the Paralympic Games helped the disabled population of Japan to improve their lives and brought more attention to their conditions. The visibility of disabled people began to change broader attitudes towards them. The Tokyo Paralympic Games had been campaigned for by Hanako Wataanable. She had attended the Stoke Mandeville Games in London in 1948 (a forerunner to what is now the Paralympics). When Japan won its bid she led a campaign for the parallel contest. Japan's participation in these Games vastly increased; they went from zero disabled competitors at Rome to building a new athletes' movement that grew as more Japanese saw the athleticism of the foreign disabled sportspeople. One woman swimmer had to be carried to the pool by her husband. Once her race started the other competitors left her behind. She slowly progressed down the pool. At several points rescue staff began to intervene but her husband gestured for her to be left. After three minutes she completed her 25-metre race.[37] Examples like this led the Japanese government to treat disabled sportspeople as athletes with proper training and equipment provided. They also helped to change the attitudes of Japanese physicians, with more attention paid to recovery. Over time the rest of Japanese society became more accepting of people with disabilities.

With the accompanying arts festival, the theme of modern Japan stood alongside that of traditional culture. Folkloric art works were displayed alongside more modern ones. The photography exhibition was limited to colour images showcasing the advancement of Japanese photographic technology. The building of Japan's empire and World War Two were omitted. The desire to forget the recent past and reinvent the international vision of Japan shaped the decision. When the war was shown images focussed not on Japanese expansionism but on the nuclear bombs that ended the conflict. Some critics

---

[36] Jessamyn Abel, 'Japan's Sporting Diplomacy: The 1964 Tokyo Olympiad', *The International History Review*, 34.2, (2012), 203–220.

[37] Roy Tomizawa, *1964, The Greatest Year in Japanese History: How the Tokyo Olympics Symbolized Japan's Miraculous Rise from the Ashes* (Carson City, NV: Lioncrest, 2019), 94–105.

believed that this recast the Japanese as victims and covered up their culpability during the 1930s and 1940s.[38] The national memory of the Japanese during this time looked to forget the interwar years with the nuclear bombing of Hiroshima and Nagasaki being seen as a focus for remembrance instead.

While nation states have used the Games as a proxy for international relations or to promote their ideology, individuals have sometimes used their ability to grab global headlines. 1968 is remembered as a year of worldwide cultural 'revolution' among students in Western nations including France and Germany as well as some behind the Iron Curtain such as Czechoslovakia. This global revolt inspired Mexican youth to protest against the authoritarianism of the National Revolutionary Party (PRI). Ahead of the opening ceremony young urbanites organised against the party's corruption. A series of strikes and protests that followed the heavy-handed policing of riots meant that the protests grew throughout July and August 1968. President Gustavo Díaz Ordaz was determined to crush the movement and ordered riot police to storm the National Autonomous University of Mexico in September. The protests and fighting that followed led to a 10,000-strong crowd rallying at a housing complex. A major protest then took place on 2 October in the Tlatelolco district. Here police fired into the crowd and killed up to 250 protesters. This mass murder of Mexicans by their government was followed by the imprisonment and torture of protesters, with many being held for the duration of the Games. The Olympic authorities drew a veil of silence over the massacre, ensuring that the Games went ahead. Reports of the violence barely reached the global audience. These Games showed the spread of ideas around the globe but also the ability of governments to repress protests meaning that the sanitised façade that was shown to the world hid a real human cost.

Mexico City's Olympiad had been foreshadowed by attempts to moderate the behaviour of the population and change the world's impression of Mexicans. The Mexican government hoped to throw off the image of it being underdeveloped and present a modern face that engaged with international cosmopolitan attitudes. At the opening ceremony the Olympic flame was lit by twenty-year-old Norma Enriqueta Basilio, the first woman to be given the honour. She represented a different image to the 'short and fat' stereotype that persisted about Mexicans.[39] Mexicans were warned about their behaviour and the national image was redefined for the new generation. The popular comedy character Cantinflas, played by Mario Moreno, fronted a series of TV shorts, which showed him as the policeman Patrolman 777, who rounded up different objectionable figures in each episode including an overcharging

---

[38] Droubie, 'Phoenix Arisen'.

[39] Michael Barke, 'Mexico City 1968', in John Gold and Margaret Gold, *Olympic Cities: City Agendas, Planning and the World's Games, 1896–2012* (Abingdon: Routledge, 2007), 183.

taxi driver, football hooligans and hippies.[40] The messages of compliance were aimed at all Mexicans to adjust their behaviour in preparation for their encounter with foreign visitors. After the initial thrill of winning the Games, many members of the population began to question their cost. Encounters between rich and poor showed that the Olympics could be a curse as well as a blessing. Hawkers were removed from the city streets, a routine which has become familiar for Olympic Games the world over, and laws forbade their operation in tourist-heavy areas. The city was physically changed, including a new motorway between facilities (which were spread out over 30 kilometres), a water and sewage system and a new underground railway (which was completed behind time, only partially opening in 1969).

With many people around the world and at home questioning Mexico's preparedness to host the Games there was a great desire to show otherwise. The Mexican authorities hoped to challenge the image of 'the south' as lazy and disorganised. The cultural festival was unprecedented for an Olympics. The displays of art, film, music and theatre which started ten months before the Games focussed on internationalism, with the participation of 97 countries.[41] By the time of the Games Mexico City was dressed for the occasion with a 'route of friendship' branding the progressive Mexican identity for visitors and foreign journalists. Bright colours depicted Mexico as exotic, but also echoed the Pop Art movement that was at the forefront of global arts. Advertising boards that normally hosted commercial branding now showed images of activity around the Games, family portraits, and messages of peace and friendship. The Mexicans made much use of their peace dove emblem, an abstract design that also resembled a flower and differed from that made by Picasso. It was hoped this image would show Mexicans as peacemakers, especially in the Central and Southern Americas. The Op Art logo of Mexico '68 became ubiquitous and aimed to show Mexico as progressive and cosmopolitan, in contradiction to the state violence at Tlatelolco. Specially trained hostesses were dressed in modish uniforms, including mini-skirts and trouser suits, channelling the nation's hope to show advances for women as part of Mexico's modern image.[42] It was clear that the developing nation intended to show the world that it was every bit equal to those parts labelled 'first world'.

The Olympics struggled with its Eurocentrism and the presence of high-profile racists in the IOC. The first two post-war IOC presidents, Sigfrid Edstrom (1946–1952) and Avery Brundage (1952–1972) were sympathetic to racism. With the Olympic Project for Human Rights and a number of

---

[40] Keith Brewster, 'Teaching Mexicans how to behave: Public education on the eve of the Olympics', *Bulletin of Latin American Research*, 29, (2010), 46–62.

[41] Barke, 'Mexico City', 191.

[42] Eric Zolov, 'Showcasing the "Land of Tomorrow" Mexico and the 1968 Olympics', *The Americas*, 61.2 (2004), 159–188.

African nations threatening to boycott the Mexico Games over the participation of South Africa and Rhodesia, the desire to remain aloof from politics was hard to achieve. When a 1967 fact-finding mission by the IOC found no issues, the racial state's participation in Mexico 1968 was permitted by a committee that had just one black member.[43] Brundage refused to send an invitation, however, not because of South Africa's politics, but because of fear of the disruption that boycotts from other nations would cause. The conflation of international politics and sports marked a change in how many of the subsequent Olympiads were framed. As decolonised nations acquired more influence, they were able to apply pressure on the IOC to enforce a ban on South Africa. South Africa was fully expelled from the IOC in 1970 in a move that had been delayed as far as possible amid rising indignation from governments and internationalised civil society groups.

During the Games the American athletes Tommy Smith and John Carlos, who had finished first and third respectively in the 200-metres final, turned their medal ceremony into a political protest. They stood on the podium wearing the badge of the Olympic Project for Human Rights. They wore black socks and no shoes, to symbolise the poverty in which black people in America had to live. As the American national anthem played, the two held aloft their hands in a clenched-fist Black Power salute. Each wore one black glove. Their statement was of support not just for the civil rights campaigns that were currently being waged in the USA but for a more radical form of black nationalism. Avery Brundage was angry because the pair had breached the Olympic principle that claimed the Games were non-political. The event threatened to spread discord through the American ranks and other athletes were warned not to follow the example of the two sprinters, with the hero of Berlin, Jesse Owens, being used to convince athletes to moderate their behaviour.

Smith and Carlos received an outpouring of support from athletes of developing nations, many seeing them as part of a wider fraternity of black people who had suffered centuries of oppression: the moment highlighted their plight. The Cuban 4 × 400-metres team donated their medals to Stokely Carmichael, the prominent pan-Africanist and civil rights campaigner. Simon Henderson suggests that Smith and Carlos embodied a pan-African ideology, a movement whose origins were inspired by the intellectual W.E.B. Du Bois and connected black Americans to Africans.[44] Smith and Carlos were sent home from the Olympics by the United States Olympic Committee with outrage directed towards them, often under the claim that they had breached the non-political status of the Games. But their stance, which they maintained was in support of all human rights, meant that their message was heard around the world and drew some support, even if many preferred to ignore it. With their

---

[43] Goldblatt, *The Games*, 238.

[44] Simon Henderson, '"Nasty Demonstrations by Negroes": The place of the Smith-Carlos Podium Salute in the Civil Rights Movement', *Bulletin of Latin American Research*, 29.1 (2010), 78–92.

sporting careers cancelled, it was only from the late 1980s that Americans began to heroise these figures, but the damage done to them by the Olympics and national sporting authorities was irreversible. At a time of attempted social revolution, the Games were used by various groups to highlight state oppression. Activists in Mexico were brutally murdered, while those in the USA were able to shine a light on the structural violence that black people suffered because of the nation's legacy of slavery. The international focus on the legalised violence of the racial state in South Africa meant that the Games became the focus for an international coalition for change.

By the 1970s Germany had re-emerged as an economic power in Europe. Politicians in the Federal Republic of Germany (FRG), or West Germany, hoped to use its first Games in 1972 to present the world with a German identity rooted in democracy, friendliness and modernity. The Munich Olympics hosted 7121 athletes from 121 countries and were the biggest to date. Terror, however, stole the headlines amid conflict born out of the divisions in Israel between the Jewish population and the Palestinian organisations (the origins of which are discussed in Chapter 2). A charm offensive by the organisers to the African nations of Ethiopia, Kenya, Somalia, Uganda, Malawi and Egypt included a reception attended by Ethiopian emperor Hailie Selassie. The campaign underlined the German intention of building its reputation overseas, especially with nations that had recently achieved independence. At the same time Germany increased its foreign aid to African and other developing nations to help build its global reputation.[45] Even here there was no guarantee that these nations would participate. The presence of Rhodesia, a newly independent state which had embedded white minority rule within its system, caused the threat of a boycott. Up until the eve of the Games, when Rhodesian athletes had already arrived at the Munich Olympic village, there was no guarantee that African, South American or black US athletes would participate. Eventually on 22 August the IOC voted to exclude Rhodesia, ensuring the participation of the concerned nations.

The Games were designed to be progressive and look to the future.[46] Munich had undergone massive regeneration with a new underground railway built. The arena was developed on a brownfield site near the city centre: the blank slate allowed a modern vision to come to fruition. Architect Gunter Behnisch built an Olympic complex which broke with the monumental style of the Nazi era. The result was an interconnected park with each building sunk into hollows and appearing complementary to the whole campus. Covering the stadium was a Plexiglas roof, which became much celebrated in West Germany. The modern design angered some traditionalists who disapproved of Germany's apparent break with architectural customs. Munich itself catered to tourists offering new forms of 'tat' souvenirs: beer Steins featuring 'Mad'

---

[45] David Clay Large, *Munich 1972: Tragedy, Terror and Triumph at the Olympic Games* (London: Rowman and Littlefield, 2012), 93.

[46] Schiller and Young, *Munich Olympics*, 22.

King Ludwig (Ludwig II, 1845–1866) and the Olympic rings were on sale alongside Ludwig music boxes.[47] At the Games and the cultural exhibition Olympic hostesses wore traditional dirndls. The folkloric image that many visitors gained was certainly out of keeping with the modernism of the new Munich. The accompanying 40-day-long arts programme drew on worldwide art, music and literature, showcasing the best in classical, contemporary and avant-garde sections along with an international folklore festival. The festival angered Brundage, who had requested it be scaled down to a national festival, but the Germans had presented an outward-looking image, which helped to boost their internationalist credentials.[48] The FRG projected an image of a global nation that fitted with the era and their political and economic aims.

With the organisers promoting Munich as 'the friendly Games', there was a distinct lack of security.[49] On 5 September members of Black September, a splinter group from the Palestinian Liberation Organisation (PLO), gained access to the Olympic village and murdered two Israeli athletes, taking nine others hostage to bargain for the release of Palestinian prisoners and members of Germany's terrorist organisation the Red Army Faction. The world's media televised the ensuing siege of the Israeli complex. All of the athletes, and the kidnappers, were later killed in a shootout with police. The Israeli state responded by attacking bases of the PLO and its leadership. The world had tuned into their televisions for the sporting event, but this celebration of sporting prowess had been hijacked by the spectacle of terrorism.

When Chancellor Willy Brandt expressed his distress that Jewish people had once again been murdered on German territory it was clear that the Games had been overshadowed.[50] The Munich Olympics had presented Germany with the opportunity to repair its international reputation following World War Two. Hosting its first Olympiad since 'the Nazi Olympics' gave the FRG the opportunity to remove the Nazi legacy and challenge global opinions of Germans. Many sports fans and members of the IOC looked back on the Berlin Games as a great success, which subsequent Olympics had sought to emulate.[51] However, not all of the legacy of 1936 or the Nazis was removed. Buildings which had served the Nazis such as the Haus der Kunst, which hosted the cultural exhibition, were denazified and reused. This was partly pragmatic, because the building had suffered little wartime damage, but it also helped to rehabilitate German art. The organisers hoped to forget the past and, as the official report stated, to 'demonstrate a new cosmopolitan

---

[47] Clay Large, *Munich 1972*, 128.

[48] Schiller and Young, *Munich*, 94.

[49] Kruger, 'Unfinished Symphony', 20.

[50] Christopher Young, 'Munich 1972: Representing the Nation', in Alan Tomlinson and Christopher Young eds. *National Identity and Global Sports Events: Culture, Politics, and Spectacle in the Olympics and Football World Cup*, (Albany, NY: State University of New York Press, 2006), 118.

[51] Schiller and Young, *Munich Olympics*, 60.

understanding of art'.[52] The site of the former Dachau concentration camp, 35 kilometres away, hosted three memorials during the Games as a means of atonement. The East German government accused the West of allowing fascist sport to dominate, with the continuity of board members and rehabilitation of several former Nazis as organisers, especially when several 1936 medal winners were used as personalities at the launch. The organisers fought back by hiring Jesse Owens to promote the Games. The medal winner helped Germany to exorcise the ghost of the Nazi past.

Owens became controversial among African–American athletes. The 400-metres medallists Vincent Matthews and Wayne Collett refused to face the American flag during their ceremony due to the continued inequality that faced African Americans. Instead they fidgeted and talked between themselves as the anthem played. Owens was once again called in to try to bring the recalcitrant athletes to heel and make them apologise, leading many black athletes to see him as helping to silence them. Matthews and Collett refused and the IOC gave them both lifetime bans. Protests against injustice continued at these Games and were seen as negative by the organisers, who had zero tolerance and maintained their non-political façade, despite the challenges that were frequently levelled.

The overarching memory of the Munich Games is the act of terrorism committed against the Israeli athletes. But this is certainly not the only legacy of the Games. They allowed an encounter between the peoples of divided Germany, although this was not always seen as positive. From Melbourne onwards the German sides had competed as a unified team under the German tricolour with the Olympic rings at its centre, with 'Ode to Joy' replacing the national anthem. But the desire to present the best face of the FRG raised the state's desire to use national symbols. The GDR had been recognised by the IOC in 1968. As part of its attempts at reconciliation the FRG permitted the participation of the GDR as a separate team.[53] Willy Brandt's *Ostpolitik* was bearing fruit in building diplomatic understanding between the two sides, while still claiming that the West represented the whole of Germany. At a time when most communist states were open to rapprochement and cultural exchange with Western nations, the GDR attempted to convince its allies to be wary and limit these contacts to those areas in which the East was clearly ahead. With no desire to promote its Western counterpart, the government of the GDR attempted to persuade its allies to boycott the torch relay, something which was overruled by Moscow.[54] The hopes of a unified Germany seemed to be fading and the Games appeared to represent one of the earliest

---

[52] *Die Spiele: The Official Report*, Cited Schiller and Young, *Munich Olympics*, 84.

[53] Jørn Hansen, '"The Most Beautiful Olympic Games That Were Ever Destroyed" (Munich 1972)', in *Surveilling and Securing the Olympics: From Tokyo 1964 to London 2012 and beyond*, edited by Vida Bajc (London: Palgrave, 2016), 144–161, 148.

[54] Schiller and Young, *Munich Olympics*, 181.

times that the Eastern side could obtain diplomatic recognition, leading to an oppositional encounter between Germans of either side.

It was important for both German states to assert their form of national identity and accompanying stereotypes both internationally and to their own people. The GDR targeted funding to sports in which they thought they had most chance of winning medals: swimming, track-and-field and gymnastics. The funding for team sports or those with less history of success was reduced.[55] Not to be outdone, West Germany increased its funding for elite sports. With the FRG ending the Games fourth in the medal table with 40 overall and GDR third with 66 it was clear that the political division had crossed into the world of sports. The Games became a form of legitimisation and competition for German identity by the two Cold War states.

The Olympics and the Coming of Neo-liberalism

As the spotlight fell on North America in 1976 it was the turn of the Canadian Francophone city of Montreal to the host the Games. Having hosted a successful and popular International Exposition in 1967, surely Montreal would deliver a glorious Olympics. Yet the legacy of 1967 was a costly debt with which the provincial capital was saddled. The Games themselves were similarly beset by costs and construction issues. The city's mayor, Jean Drapeau, was determined to turn Montreal into a global city, using mega-events and building modernist architectural legacies. Along the way he awarded contracts to political and business allies and spent money on follies (including eight million dollars on a fountain near the stadium). With building costs and time over-running, the Games were forced to open in an unfinished stadium. The Olympic Park itself was estimated to cost 150 million dollars but rose to 1.2 billion dollars, with budget-sapping interest payments taking the cost to over two billion dollars.[56] The debts were not paid back by the city until 2006. For all its expense, the result for the host nation was poor; in a Games where the Soviet Union and GDR excelled, Canada won a grand total of eleven medals but zero gold. It was the first host nation to lose by such a margin and at such expense.

The chances of sporting encounters between competitors from different nations were reduced at the Montreal Olympics. As with previous Games of the global era, international politics mediated the encounter between peoples. The division of China remained problematic and the Taiwanese team hoped to enter as the Republic of China (ROC), the name of the nation the IOC officially recognised. In 1970 Canada's Prime Minister, Pierre Trudeau, had offered diplomatic recognition to the PRC. Yet the PRC was not recognised by the IOC and would not compete at Montreal. The threat of a boycott

---

[55] Gerd Horten, *Don't Need No Thought Control: Western Culture in East Germany and the Fall of the Berlin Wall* (Oxford: Berghahn, 2020), 39.

[56] Goldblatt, *The Games*, 300.

from nations including the USA, Australia, UK and FRG emerged if Taiwan was barred. Canada and the IOC offered several compromises, from allowing Taiwan to compete as a neutral team to offering similar options to those of the Rome Olympics with the team marching under the name Taiwan, but with no mention of China. None were acceptable to Taiwan, who withdrew their team from the Games.[57] The other major boycott issue concerned South Africa. By 1976 they were firmly banned from Olympic participation but attention turned to others who maintained sporting contacts with them, despite the UN boycott of the apartheid nations (discussed in Chapter 4). New Zealand's 'All Blacks' Rugby team was touring South Africa, causing much ill feeling. With the Soweto uprising against apartheid rule breaking out in June and the resort to lethal violence against children by authorities, the calls to further isolate South Africa and its supporters grew. The boycott threats began just two days before the opening ceremony, when thirteen African nations wrote to the recently appointed president of the IOC, Lord Killanin, threatening to withdrawunless New Zealand were banned, or the All Blacks returned from South Africa. The IOC refused to back down and New Zealand's Olympic Committee claimed it was powerless to influence the rugby team. With no movement, the African teams withdrew. Opposition to racial politics in Africa once more grabbed headlines and impacted on the sporting encounter.

The Games may have been judged a financial disaster for Montreal but scholars such as Darel Paul suggest the real legacy lies elsewhere. For Paul the Montreal Games, along with its earlier Expo, were part of its building of global city status.[58] He suggests that Montreal cast off the mantle of provincialism and linguistic nationalism, with these mega-events being the first steps in becoming a cosmopolitan global city, as many Olympic cities since the 1960s have sought to do. But at the same time these Games were part of Canada's battle for its national identity. Trudeau was seeking to create a multicultural Canadian identity. The divergence between the Francophone and Anglophone parts of the country, combined with the historic marginalisation of Indigenous peoples, necessitated creating a Canadian identity for the late twentieth century as well as a new global one. All did not necessarily go to plan. The torch relay became a fraught inter-cultural competition. It was dominated by the Canadian English-speaking capital Ottawa and the route took it mainly through Ontario, only entering Francophone Quebec shortly before reaching Montreal. In the battle for domination of Canada by these European-oriented cultures, the voices of the First Nations were drowned out, with Indigenous Canadian dancers choreographed at the opening ceremony by white Canadians.[59] Their direction followed stereotypes created by white

---

[57] Xu Guoqi, *Olympic Dreams: China and Sports, 1895–2008* (London: Harvard University Press, 2008), 164–196.

[58] Darel Paul, 'World Cities as Hegemonic Projects: the politics of global Imagineering in Montreal', *Political Geography*, 23 (2004), 571–596.

[59] Goldblatt, *The Games*, 298.

Canadians, continuing with the escort role created for the closing ceremony where 'North American Indians' would form an arrowhead before gathering together in the shape of the Olympic rings.[60] Of the 450 'Indian hosts' only 200 were Aboriginal peoples, with the remainder being non-Indigenous local dancers who had been given the role and dressed in native American costume. The cultures on display were often stereotypes and non-representative with little consultation with First Nation groups. First Nation, Anglophone and Francophone were all part of the formation of the new Canadian identity that was presented to the world, but which were certainly not harmonised.

During the 1980s the Games became a proxy for Cold War tensions as international politics became paramount. The USSR's first hosting of the Games at Moscow in 1980 is best remembered for the USA-led boycott in which they were joined by 64 nations. The protest, over the Soviet invasion of Afghanistan in 1979, fully subsumed the Olympics. The division was not completely West versus East, however, with Britain among those whose governments did not insist on a full ban. The Americans attempted to spread their boycott: Jimmy Carter enlisted the help of the former world heavyweight boxing champion Muhammad Ali to convince the governments of Tanzania, Kenya, Nigeria, Liberia and Senegal to join in the boycott. Many of these nations were part of the non-aligned bloc of nations which attempted to stay outside the superpower conflict; most had no desire to allow the Cold War to cause them to miss their second consecutive Olympics. The issue of South African apartheid was much more pressing for these nations and most of them, including Tanzania, rejected Ali. Many press outlets in these nations asked why Africans should join with America's boycott when the USA had rejected their 1976 action against New Zealand.[61] Kenya and Liberia, however, announced the day before Ali's arrival that they would join the boycott. The latter was closely allied to the United States and the extension of the boycott to nations such as South Korea, the Philippines, Canada and West Germany showed that international political alliances held much sway over the decision not to participate. Indeed a similar desire to build relations with the USA, as well as worries about the Soviets creating instability in Asia, were behind the decision of the Chinese to join the boycott. With the boycott campaign taking in many of the USA's allies the first opportunity for a communist nation to use the Games to showcase its system was severely limited.

With the Cold War heating up during the early 1980s, the new Soviet leadership decided to boycott the 1984 Los Angeles Games, claiming they were concerned about athlete safety in an anti-communist environment. They were joined by the Eastern Bloc countries and some African nations including

---

[60] Christine O'Bonswain 'Indigenous Peoples and Canadian-Hosted Olympic Games' in *Aboriginal peoples and sport in Canada: historical foundations and contemporary issues* edited by Janice Forsyth and Audrey Giles (Vancouver: UBC Press, 2013), 39.

[61] James Ivey, '"Welcome, Ali, Please Go Home": Muhammad Ali as Diplomat and African Debates on the 1980 Moscow Olympic Boycott', *African Studies Review*, 66.2 (2022), 490–508.

Ethiopia, South Yemen, Libya and Angola who boycotted following the deterioration of their own relationship with the USA. However, the Games saw the participation of 140 nations, making them the biggest ever. Among them was China who returned to the international sporting arena having last competed in 1952. The Soviet boycott of the American Games was more limited, with international politics seemingly preventing the Games from achieving their aim of promoting peace through friendly competition.

These two Olympiads became showpieces for the rival ideologies. Spectacle nationalism was supplemented by ideological displays aimed at showing each side's supremacy. At Moscow's opening ceremony the Soviets used flash cards to have spectators form a huge flag emblazoned with Lenin's image, with dancers on the field choreographed in a human hammer and sickle. The communist nation showed off some of its development with a live broadcast featuring their two cosmonauts in the Salyut 6 space station. Competitors and visitors were entertained by the Bolshoi and Kirov ballet companies as well as being able to visit newly built cinemas and discotheques. With Moscow's redevelopment these Games were about modernising the city, as with many previous hosts. The Games allowed those who attended to mix and see their cultures catered for in Moscow. Lord Killanin recalled going to Catholic Mass in the Olympic village and being joined by Soviet colleagues, despite the state's official atheist status.[62] Regardless of the boycotts, the Soviets pushed ahead with their attempts to showcase their way of life to those nations of the world who were still watching.

In turn the Los Angeles Olympics of 1984 have been dubbed 'the first neoliberal Olympics' by Goldblatt, with ideology as much a feature at these Games as at Moscow's. With a private organising committee led by business instead of the city authorities, profit was the priority. The LA authorities ensured that they were able to get full television rights and sell these to the highest bidders. They used sponsorship deals with global brands like McDonalds to refurbish older buildings like the LA Coliseum, constructed for the 1932 Games. Public investment was minimal with the role of multinational corporate sponsorship expanded to an unprecedented level. The refurbishment of the area around the Olympic Park allowed LA to hide its industrial decline, pollution-ridden air and the crack-cocaine epidemic that had raged for the past decade. Many of the staff at the events worked for free as volunteers, their wages turned into corporate profit.[63] With an eventual profit of around 215 million dollars, the LA Olympics reversed the trend of the last 40 or so years of the Games being a costly show.

A less politicised Olympics was required by the time Seoul was due to host the Games in 1988. Under the authoritarian leader Park Chung Hee (1961–70) South Korea had undertaken a programme of rapid development

[62] Michael Morris, Baron Killanin, *My Olympic Years* (New York: Morrow, 1983), 53.
[63] Jules Boykoff, *Power Games: A Political History of the Olympics* (London: Verso, 2016), 132.

with the leadership determined to catch up with the living standards of the West. Just over a year away from the Games, trade unions, student groups and church groups led a successful revolution against the military junta. Amid in-fighting among the opposition the junta's leader, Roh Tae Woo, was able to win the presidential election and claim a democratic mandate. The Games allowed Korea to present its new image of a wealthy and democratic nation. At the opening ceremony in Seoul the Koreans made a showcase of traditional dance and culture mixed with the contemporary and industrial aspects that were praised in the West. This emphasis on traditional Korea (and not the modern divided nation) aimed to appeal to Western tastes by showing them what they believed about Asia. For Sandra Collins this amounted to a form of 'modern hybridity', meaning that Koreans displayed modern technological advancement alongside ancient cultural traditions based on the 'exotic civilisations of the East'.[64] In doing so Collins contends that Korea showed that modernisation need not necessarily mean Westernisation. Collins holds that by tilting towards the Western conceptions of modernity, this form of 'self-orientalism' allowed Koreans to be successful within power structures that were dominated by Western nations. South Korea made its strongest performance yet and won twelve gold medals, with notable success in judo, table tennis, archery and wrestling; the Euro-American hold on the Games was being challenged. The debut of taekwondo, a Korean martial sport that had been banned by the Japanese in the early twentieth century, marked the globalisation of Korean culture, with its popularity followed by K-pop other among cultural exports in the coming decades.

Many hosts have used the Games to turn themselves into global cities, but few matched the success of Barcelona. Following the model of Los Angeles, the Olympics of 1992 turned the Catalan capital from a run-down deindustrialising city that was beset by the problems of economic globalisation into a tourist trap that would have negative as well as positive impacts for decades to come (Fig. 6.1). As neo-liberalism reached its apex, Barcelona fitted seamlessly into the Age of Globalism. Its bid, sponsored by public–private partnerships, involved the complete transformation of the city. The redevelopment involved changes in use of land with former industrial sites, railways and ports turned into parks, leisure facilities and other amenities. The building of the Olympic village on the waterfront strengthened the city's connections to the sea and regenerated that area. The entire seafront and a further six kilometres of coastline to the north were renewed: having been previously separated from the city by railway lines, they became public spaces for recreation and sports. The redevelopment was augmented by the building of museums and galleries, which

---

[64] Sandra Collins., 'The Fragility of Asian National Identity in the Olympic Games', *Owning The Olympics: Narrative of the New China*, (Chigaco: University of Michigan Press, 2008), 186.

boosted tourism in the city from 4.1 million in 1991 to 6.3 million in 1995.[65] The regeneration was not seen as positive by all, and locals complained of gentrification with living costs rising up to 250 per cent in the six years before the Games, leading to working-class dissatisfaction.[66]

1992 was a year of renewal for Spain. Madrid was European Capital of Culture and Seville hosted its Expo, which was examined in the previous chapter; all were accompanied by massive regeneration. The Spanish government was determined to present a modern, liberalised face to the world. But there were also encounters between nationalities within Spain. Under the Franco regime the Catalan language had been suppressed. Now the opening ceremony was broadcast in Catalan as well as Spanish. King Juan Carlos's opening declaration drew rapturous applause when he began in Catalan and the language continued to be used throughout the Games. During the torch relay through the region the cry of *Independencia* was heard wherever the flame went. When the flame toured Barcelona on its final leg the city's apartments were bedecked with the Catalan flag and sometimes nationalist slogans.[67] The Games allowed the Catalans to express their identity and desire for independence to a Spanish and global audience. The world saw the new Spanish and Catalan identities side by side.

The Barcelona Games marked the coming of the globalised era. The world was increasingly interconnected in terms of mobility, communications and economies. With the breakup of the USSR, the ending of both the Cold War and apartheid, the era of boycotts was over. A record 169 countries sent teams. Multinational companies such as Coca-Cola, Reebok and Visa firmly associated themselves with the Games through sponsorship deals. Their desire for brand promotion meant that the Games had to reach ever-increasing numbers of the world's population in more creative ways. As a school child in Ellesmere Port in Britain, the author collected empty cans of Coca-Cola that had been released to commemorate each Olympiad up to and including Barcelona, only years later realising the marketing ploy. The spread of global media business and increase in television broadcasting time meant that more people could watch more of the events, even if they lived on the other side of the world with time differences. International music stars became involved and Queen's singer Freddie Mercury, was commissioned alongside Montserrat Caballé to write the theme song 'Barcelona'. Mercury's death shortly before the Games added a certain pathos to the song, but it helped to make Barcelona a recognised city of globalised culture. With the commercialisation achieved under the leadership of IOC president Juan Antonio Samaranch, the Games had finally rejected the veneer of amateurism (Fig. 6.1). The fully professionalised Games

---

[65] Francisco-Javier Monclús, 'Barcelona 1992', in John Gold and Margaret Gold, *Olympic Cities: City Agendas, Planning and the World's Games, 1896–2012* (Abingdon: Routledge, 2007), 223–224.

[66] Boykoff, *Power Games*, 139.

[67] Goldblatt, *The Games*, 348.

were elitist and open to sponsorship like never before. Sporting authorities including America's National Basketball Association sent their all-star teams, hoping to spread the global influence of their product. By Barcelona the Olympics had become a truly global mega-event that marked the city's rise as a travel destination and boosted tourism to the area that has increased since.

The 1996 Games in Atlanta continued the commercialisation and privatisation of the Olympics that followed the *Zeitgeist* of the era of neo-liberal globalisation with public funding removed. Whereas the torch relay for Barcelona had taken in all of the continents, Atlanta's was limited to North America. Against a backdrop of continued racial division and widespread poverty in the state of Georgia, the areas that hosted events were spruced up, while other parts were left in decay. The city was decked out in advertising hoardings, often covering entire buildings, as the commercialisation of the Games accelerated. A recent vote to remove the confederate battle flag from the Georgian state flag had been narrowly defeated, meaning this symbol of racial division was highly visible. The official display of African–American art was situated far away from the stadia and the official transport routes avoided the area, meaning visitors were unlikely to reach it, unlike the main arts festival that focussed on world arts.[68] The city centre itself was sanitised for visitors. Homelessness was effectively illegalised through a series of laws banning public urination, camping, begging and even loitering. This legislation was

Fig. 6.1 After the Games: The empty Barcelona Olympic Stadium

[68] Goldblatt, *The Games*, 355.

accompanied by a project giving homeless people one-way bus tickets to other cities where they had relatives. Poorer city centre neighbourhoods near the Olympic venues were cleansed of their population through redevelopment. These population displacements disproportionately affected the 70 per cent black population of the city. At the same time city leaders promoted the image of figures like Martin Luther King Jr to cover up the persisting racial divides. Criticism of these Games has focussed on the invisibility of the city's black majority in order to sanitise it for the Olympic brand and the presentation of Atlanta in the image of a harmonious global city.[69]

Cost-cutting was the order of the day. Unlike many of the previous Games the city of Atlanta did not invest in its public transport. Buses and drivers were instead transferred from the rest of the country. The result was near chaos, with drivers taking wrong turns on their unfamiliar routes and causing delays as officials and journalists, as well as the 1992 Olympic judo champion, David Khakhaleishvili from Georgia (the nation not the state), were unable to get where they needed to be on time. Khakhaleishvili was unable to reach his weigh-in because his bus got lost and he was disqualified. The profit motive that had presided since Los Angeles prevailed at the Atlanta Olympics and did not always result in a smoothly run mega-event. The opportunity for an encounter between divided Americans was lost, with a symbolic image of diversity presented that covered up the structural inequalities.

THE OLYMPICS IN THE TWENTY-FIRST CENTURY

The turn of the century saw Sydney playing host to the Olympics. In contrast to Melbourne in 1956, the Sydney Games departed from the hegemonic narrative of 'white Australia'. The rising historical awareness of injustice committed by the immigrant white population against Australia's Aboriginal groups since the European 'discovery' of the land and their continued mistreatment led to a sense of repentance and reconciliation between these two Australian cultures. The 1990s had seen Australia's past examined with the Bringing Them Home Commission established in 1995 to examine the separation of Aboriginal children from their parents, which was regarded as genocide, and the disproportionate numbers of deaths of Aboriginals in custody.[70] But the issue was far from resolved by 2000 and discontent rumbled, resulting in protest from some Aboriginal groups. The opening ceremony continued the theme of reconciliation with the Aboriginal athlete Cathy Freeman lighting the Olympic cauldron in a mark of symbolism that masked the reality of ongoing discrimination and inequality. In this case the encounter between different groups of a domestic population became more visible than that of global cultures.

---

[69] Seth Gustafson, 'Displacement and the Racial State in Olympic Atlanta 1990–1996', *Southeastern Geographer*, 53, 2 (2013), 198–213.
[70] Goldblatt, *The Games*, 365.

The image of unity presented by the Australian government told only a fraction of the story. Symbols of Aboriginal culture including didgeridoo players and the boomerang were written into Sydney's Olympic bids. Their visibility increased when feedback on previous failed bids suggested that the Aboriginal aspect made an impact with the IOC. Often however these symbols were performed on call to add a sense of inclusion. According to Helen Lenskyj, this amounted to the appropriation of Aboriginal culture through narrow stereotypes to produce a gain for the white population.[71] As the question of protesting at the Olympics against the exclusion of Aboriginal people from society was raised, the communities were accused of being 'un-Australian' and even warned by Samaranch, a former minister in Spain's fascist dictatorship, not to hijack the Games. When the Olympic flame was lit at Mount Olympus in May 2000 a Greek-Australian, Yianna Souleles, had been chosen to run the first leg. However, Greek Olympic Committee members approached an Australian colleague, Kevan Gosper, and asked that his daughter Sophie run the first leg instead because her blonde hair and blue eyes made her more clearly a 'typical Australian' than the brown-haired, brown-eyed Souleles, who was relegated to run a later leg. Gosper happily accepted the offer and boasted of his daughter's achievements, seemingly unaware of the potential impact of the ethnic profiling. He later received much press criticism, prompting him to apologise. Furthermore, inequalities in society meant that Aboriginal Australians' health outcomes and life expectancies lagged way behind that of their white counterparts.[72] In sports, opportunities for progression into funded scholarship programmes were largely denied to Aboriginal youths. Athletes like Freeman, an Aboriginal who was enabled to achieve national and international acclaim, were the exception rather than the rule.

Where these Games did lead to an unquestioned international encounter was in their bringing together of international activists. At a time of the peak of protests against economic globalisation and the practices of organisations involved, there was spillover into the Games with protests for global justice and human rights. The S11 Alliance protests against the World Economic Forum in Melbourne in early September meant that there had been an increased level of organisation by activists in Australia. Another group called Nikewatch organised a tour by a sacked Indonesian union organiser and Jim Keady, an American sports coach who had quit his job in protest at sponsorship by Nike due to their factory conditions. Other groups protested in advance of the 15 September opening against various issues including Indigenous rights, globalisation and environmental issues. Protesters' numbers were certainly far smaller than the numbers of Olympic competitors and spectators, but they showed that the Games were a central point for the coalescence of internationalised civil society and for the voicing of issues caused by economic globalisation

---

[71] Helen Lenskyj, *The Best Olympics Ever?: Social Impacts of Sydney 2000* (Albany: State of New York University Press, 2002), 78–9.

[72] Lenskyj, *Best Olympics*, 10,74.

to the world stage.⁷³ Protest at the Games also came from the Australian band Midnight Oil. Famous for their song 'Beds are Burning', a political song about the treatment of Aboriginal communities. The band appeared at the closing ceremony wearing T-shirts bearing the word 'Sorry'. The presence of this word highlighted the refusal of Australia's Prime Minister, John Howard, to issue a formal apology to Aboriginal communities following the findings of the Bringing Them Home Commission. Midnight Oil brought politics back to the main Olympic stage following several Games which had largely been free from such controversies.

The Athens Olympics of 2004 marked a symbolic return to the home of the Games. Amid a climate of fear of terrorism stemming from the War on Terror and America and its allies' occupation of Iraq, the Games were held under a virtual siege state. The security costs contributed to a massive overspend. When the lateness of building projects was taken into account, the Games did not get off to a good start. Aside from the stadia and Games venues the Greek capital acquired new museums and new pedestrianised spaces as part of the Games, but these offered a limited lasting impact.

When China hosted its first Olympics in 2008 it signalled the nation's ascent to superpower status. The Beijing Games also allowed the Chinese state to redefine modern Chinese identity. The Games were seen as a moment of national history that tied into an underlying theme that the twenty-first century was 'the Chinese Century'.⁷⁴ Like other Asian hosts, China's authorities used their Games to situate their modernised nation at the heart of the world system and showed their accordance with the globalising values of the West. Where China's example differs from previous Asian-hosted Games was that its development was not aided by American military and economic presence, which had enabled Japan and South Korea to modernise their nations in the Western mould. The difference in the Chinese model enabled them to present themselves as a superpower on a par with the USA. The grandiose opening ceremony featured fireworks and light shows to the beat of thousands of drums resounding in absolute unison. Chinese culture was celebrated with a nod to Chinese philosophy and inventions such as paper, gunpowder and typesetting which were represented through dance. As IOC president, Jacques Rogge, declared Beijing to be 'host to the present and the gateway to the future', China's arrival as a global power was cemented.

Beijing underwent a huge programme of development in preparation for this global showcase. The author visited in 2002 and already many of the traditional *Hutong* neighbourhoods were being pulled down to modernise the city: bulldozers and cranes were omnipresent. The city was changed for visiting foreigners with English signage introduced, new hotel developments,

---

⁷³ Lenskyj, *Best Olympics*, 151–182.

⁷⁴ Carolyn Marvin, '"All Under Heaven"—Megaspace in Beijing', in Monroe Price and Daniel Dayan (eds), *Owning The Olympics: Narrative of the New China* (Chigaco: University of Michigan Press, 2008), 232.

building of parks and green spaces, removal of older more polluting cars, the banning of burning coal, and the closure of the giant Shougang steel plant. The city's authorities built new underground lines, road links and an airport terminal as Beijing grasped global city status. Beijing's cultural architecture was also transformed with the building of the jellyfish-shaped National Centre for the Performing Arts. The destruction of *Hutong* neighbourhoods, however, proved controversial as the demolition of these single-story dwellings was accompanied by the relocation of 1.5 million people to high-rise accommodation on the outskirts of the city.[75] For the Chinese government, however, the push for globalism accompanied the rise in Chinese middle-class living standards in recent decades and progress could not be halted.

The Chinese authorities had carefully developed the new generation of athletes to make them able to challenge for medals. They had been building their competitiveness since the 1990s. Now they took on Western nations at sports which the latter had often codified and dominated. It was no small task to break the Western nations' grip on the medals. The Chinese eventually won 48 gold medals and 100 in total. The domination of Western sports has led many to see the Games as an exercise in the hegemony of certain codes of sportsmanship. One of the main complaints directed at the Beijing Games by Chinese citizens was that they were a showcase of 'Occidental sport' and that the new buildings often followed a Western style, sometimes designed by Western rather than Asian architects; many Chinese people bemoaned the sense of dilution of Chinese identity.[76] In this respect some Chinese felt that the globalising effect of the Games resulted in a hegemonic sporting culture being projected around the world. However, it is also possible to see the twenty-first-century Olympics as imbuing a multidirectional internationalism that allows different cultures to converse rather than simply imposing Western culture.[77] This allows nations and regions to achieve power without fully assimilating Western ideologies, in effect creating a hybrid Olympic culture. Recent Olympiads held in China, the winter Olympics in Russia (Sochi, 2014) and Korea (PyeongChang, 2018), allowed these nations to negotiate new norms rather than being seen as a form of 'outreach' from the dominant West. But states are not the only part of the negotiated Olympic identity: multinational corporations and actors from global civil society take part in the discourse as they seek to use the Games to promote their businesses or agenda on a global scale. While many of these organisations may be held up as examples of cultural imperialism, an increasing number of the sponsors come from outside the West, suggesting a global oligarchy is taking shape.

[75] Ian G. Cook, 'Beijing 2008', in John Gold and Margaret Gold, *Olympic Cities: City Agendas, Planning and the World's Games, 1896–2012* (Abingdon: Routledge, 2007), 291, 297.

[76] Marvin, '"All Under Heaven"', 244.

[77] Christopher Finlay, 'Toward the Future: The New Olympic Internationalism', in Monroe Price and Daniel Dayan (eds), *Owning The Olympics: Narrative of the New China* (Chicago: University of Michigan Press, 2008), 376.

Do the Olympics Provide a Global Encounter?

While the Olympics often leave what is depicted as a positive legacy, such as improvements in public transport infrastructure or a city's global public relations, critics point out that the financing often comes from taxation and that many cities delay development until the bid is successful, meaning that existing facilities deteriorate. Furthermore, Olympic development often concentrates funding on one city (often a capital city), depriving other areas of much needed finance. Many host cities promise to alleviate pre-existing housing crises, but rarely deliver, sometimes exacerbating the problem by clearing housing of low-income families in their desire to regenerate.[78] Local, often working-class, populations are displaced to facilitate an encounter between the global consumer classes. The benefits to Athens of the 2004 Olympics have been questioned. The nation was one of the poorer states of the EU. Greek development funds were redirected towards the Games. The diversion of central funding was exacerbated when costs rose vastly after the terror attacks of 2001 meant that increased security was required. The Games failed to stimulate the expected tourism and Greece ran a budget deficit in 2004 of 3.2 per cent, exceeding the EU's permitted limit. This led to accusations that Greece could ill afford the Olympics and that they would bankrupt the country so that rich companies could profit. Moreover, prior to the 1992 Barcelona Olympics various groups protested the concentration of public funds on 'elites' that left housing and recreational facilities in working-class districts neglected. The city council reneged on an earlier promise to offer social housing at the Olympic village following the Games and sold the units to professionals as rents rose.[79] The displacement of communities and channelling of funds into a single showpiece event has questionable benefits for societies.

The reshaping of cities and populations to show a favourable image to Olympic visitors has become a firm part of hosting the Games. When London built its new stadium at Stratford for the 2012 Olympics it similarly led to the displacement of communities. This social cleansing of London has been something that has accompanied the globalisation of the city, with increasing house prices forcing less well-paid people to move and cuts in social housing provision meaning that the face of London has been shaped to suit the gainers from globalisation. London 2012 witnessed protests against the flattening of parts of Stratford. The Clay Lane Housing Co-operative was one of the main examples of destruction of social housing to make way for the Olympics. The estate provided homes for low-income families, open spaces and good public transport links. Relocation plans split up much of the community, with participatory sports space for working-class people lost to build the Olympic village, and similar happened over much of East London. These communities, as in

---

[78] Helen Jefferson Lenskyj, *Olympic Industry Resistance: Challenging Olympic Power and Propaganda* (Albany, NY: State University of New York Press, 2008), 16.

[79] Lenskyj, *Olympic Resistance*, 42–43.

other cases, were disrupted and moved in favour of the expansion of the global city.

London 2012 did, however, see the Paralympics gain an increased level of attention. Since their origins in the Stoke Mandeville Games at London 1948 and the first official Paralympics at Rome 1960, these games had gradually grown in stature alongside campaigns by disability rights groups. From 1960 onwards the Paralympics have been organised in the same year as the summer Games. In 2001 an agreement was made between the IOC and the International Paralympic Committee (IPC) that the staging of the Paralympics is included in the bid for the Olympics. This contract gave the Paralympics the opportunity to become more formalised and grow their reputation. The organisers of the London Games aimed to promote the Paralympics not just with the intention of showcasing Paralympians' abilities, but to change public attitudes towards disability. While the Paralympics had been broadcast live in many countries since Sydney 2000, media corporations had taken an inconsistent approach, with the disabled sport often being regarded as secondary to the Olympics. At London an increased number of hours were aired by the British broadcaster Channel 4 which showed over 150 hours, plus free streamed footage. The media coverage focussed on the strengths and abilities of athletes and is hailed by the IPC as creating 'massive shifts in attitudes and perceptions towards persons with disabilities', mainly of the British population.[80] The growth of audiences, broadcasting and sponsorship for athletes from this point on (although the funding is still way behind) meant that awareness of elite disabled sports and of the position of disabled people in society has begun to change in many parts of the world.

The modern Olympics have retained the internationalist ethos embedded in the first Games. At Rio 2016 a team made up of refugees appeared for the first time. Instead of representing their home nations, they paraded under the Olympic flag. These stateless athletes served as a reminder to the world that war had a human cost. The story of one of these athletes, Yusra Mardini, is immortalised in the 2022 film *The Swimmers*.[81] Mardini and her sister Sarah had escaped the Syrian civil war and had later swum alongside a boat of refugees to lighten it and helped to push it to safety in Greece, before telling how she then worked to qualify for the Rio Olympics. The Refugee Olympic Team marked the ability of the Games to transcend nationhood. Events beyond the main summer Games examined in this chapter also continue to point towards the potential for reconciliation. Prior to the winter Olympics in 2018, held in the South Korean city of PyeongChang, the North Korean leader Kim Jong Un announced several reconciliatory measures to his Southern counterparts. His proposals included forming a unified Korean team. The North Korean soft power effort came following a warming of relations

---

[80] International Paralympic Committee, 'London 2012', https://www.paralympic.org/london-2012, accessed 1 July 2023.

[81] *The Swimmers* dir. Sally El-Hosiani (Netflix, 2022).

between the two states and the Peace Treaty on the Korean Peninsula in 2017. The Games in this instance marked a new diplomatic agreement.

De Coubertin intended that the Olympics would create an encounter in masculinity and sporting prowess. The modern-day Games, however, might be seen to be more about encounters between youth, giving more hope to ideas of peace. From the Berlin Games in 1936 hosts sought to cater for the young audiences who wanted to watch the Games by providing youth camps— a space where they might meet other young people from around the world as well as watching the sports. The Games in Mexico, 1968 and Munich, 1972 were influenced by the sense of youth revolution that seemed to be spreading around the world in the late 1960s (disastrously so in the former case). The age saw the rise of 'new left' ideologies and a relaxation of the staid conformist lifestyle that had characterised the early post-war years. With the Olympics taking place in Mexico City in 1968 against a backdrop of revolutionary feeling, the conflict between the generations boiled over. Rather than suppress these ideas the Munich organisers presented themselves as embracing them. An 'Avenue of Games' aimed to cater to the increased freedom of expression that young people had begun to demand. In these exhibits some interactive performances such as musicians, dancers and circus acts were included, which were believed to better engage youth than the gun salutes and flag parades, which traditionally appeared at opening ceremonies. The aim was to reconnect youth to the original Olympic ideals. When London hosted the Games in 2012 the slogan 'Inspire a Generation' left no question about where the encounter should lie.

Nevertheless, it has been claimed that the impact on youth is not wholly positive. The use of athletes as role models for youngsters has been claimed by Helen Lenskyj to entrench the sexism, racism and other modes of discrimination that are inherent in the Olympics. These athletes themselves may not be useful role models, often having been sheltered by heavy training regimes and separated from their communities; they are perhaps not as equipped to talk to young people about shared experiences. People from lower-income homes may be better trying to emulate their professional neighbours or similar than the lifestyles of those few lucky enough to become wealthy from sport. The use of athletes as role models is seen to promote and acculturate the values of capitalist society, which critics like Lenskyj claim promotes the 'myth of meritocracy, with hard work and commitment touted as the route to success in sport and life'.[82] The Olympics have built connections between youths of different nations but have also been used to promote the capitalist values of globalisation and sell the belief that anybody can 'make it' when few actually do.

Academics too have seen the Olympics as a cover for neo-liberal globalisation. For Lenskyj, phrases like 'the Olympic Movement' merely provide cover and add mysticism to what she sees as an industry dominated by multinational

---

[82] Lenskyj, *Olympic Resistance*, 77, 80–1.

corporations where the profit motive holds sway over the needs and desires of the populations of host cities.[83] For her the focus of the movement on youth is part of a model of manufacturing consent, meaning that events and education programmes are used to acculturate children to think uncritically about the processes of hosting the Games. These programmes have grown since the 1970s with changes to school curricula to educate children. The Olympics industry also operates a large-scale public relations industry which aims to control news about the Games, especially by releasing 'filler' items to the major newspapers to keep the Olympics in the news and to prevent negative stories from creeping forward in the media agenda. Notwithstanding this, the mainstream media are often part of the Olympic bids and seek to profit from their coverage, so it is not in their interest to publish stories about the negative impacts on communities.

The values of the Olympics are entrusted to the IOC as a central authority who guard them almost spiritually. The ensuing 'Olympic Spirit' is dictated by the IOC and is not allowed to be changed without their approval.[84] The structure of the Games must be predicable, according to the IOC's definitions of this media event. Encounters between a national or city population and beyond are, therefore, mediated by the IOC. During the television age the idea of the Olympics as a media event can also be seen as one of a number of national and international festivals and pageants: the Olympics make people break their schedules to watch. Millions of people view the same events with a similar script in their own language throughout the world. These people become part of a worldwide audience that engages with the values of the Olympics and whose time becomes ordered according to Olympic time, often not that of their home nation. Globalised ritualistic watching becomes an outcome of the Games.

The Olympics have been the site for political protest. The protests in Mexico, 1968, were augmented with the creation of an 'anti-Olympic committee 'at Munich as well as by critics of globalisation who associate the Games with the excesses of capitalism and its tendency to ignore the human rights records of many host cities. Mainly these protests were about politics in the host nation or its perceived allies, for instance against the Vietnam War in Munich or as part of new left protests. In the twenty-first century a transnational protest movement emerged against the Olympics and other sporting events like the football World Cup.

Globally there are estimates of around 2 million people displaced for various Olympic Games since the 1980s. This excludes the 1.25 million displaced for

---

[83] Lenskyj., *Olympic Resistance*, 1–2.

[84] Daniel Dayan, 'Beyond Media Events: Disenchantment, Derailment, Disruption', in Monroe Price and Daniel Dayan (eds), *Owning The Olympics: Narrative of the New China* (Chigaco: University of Michigan Press, 2008), 391–2.

the Beijing Olympics.[85] Before they were delayed due to Covid, the 2020 Games in Tokyo saw renewed protests because growing numbers of people believed that the Olympics increase poverty by driving up housing costs, forced removal of low-income residents, separation of communities, and harm the environment. Affordable and social housing are often destroyed to make way for more upmarket accommodation designed to impress visitors. The speed of development often prevents due consideration, especially as Olympic projects need to be completed on time. New housing complexes target affluent customers, cutting out former residents. In this instance communities suffer divergence along class lines. This is particularly the case in places like Beijing and Tokyo where the twenty-first century Olympiads have seen housing demolished.[86] In Beijing dissent was displayed over the construction of a new giant CCTV (the state television channel) transmitting tower with protests centring on a 'nail house' which held out against the development.[87] According to the NOlympic movement, a group which protests against the impact of the Games on communities, some of the residents displaced by the 2020 Games had originally been evicted to make way for the 1964 Games; a double eviction in face of the unstoppable Olympic brand. The anti-Olympic movement and the Tokyo protesters were joined by groups against the Games in Paris 2024 and Los Angeles 2028.[88] The movement sees itself as part of responsible global citizenship. However, Rule 61 of the Olympic Charter requires that countries guarantee that there is no political protest while the Games take place. Often this rule has been used to commit human rights abuses as free speech is curtailed by force, especially in the case of Mexico City in 1968, Beijing in 2008 and Rio de Janeiro in 2016.

Conclusion

While the Olympics were designed to bring upper-class male youths together in friendly competitive encounters, they have developed way beyond this. They have become associated with the values of the era in which they take place, often with dubious governments using them as a form of soft power to improve global impressions of their nation. As values have changed, the upper-class male elite has been joined by male and female competitors from across a range of classes with professionalism opening the field to athletes who have the necessary sponsorship to train full time. The Olympics have, from the late

---

[85] Lenskyj, *Olympic Resistance*,16; Centre for Human Rights and Evictions, Mega-Events, Olympic Games and Housing Rights (Geneva: COHR, 2007), 215–18.

[86] '"NOlympics anywhere"' Unprecedented Transnational Protests in Tokyo', *RioOnWatch*, https://www.rioonwatch.org/?p=54888, Accessed 1 Aug 2019.

[87] Marvin, '"All Under Heaven", 240.

[88] Kwiyeon Ha, 'More than 100 people protest in Tokyo against 2020 Olympics', *Reuters*, 24 July 2019, https://www.reuters.com/article/us-olympics-2020-1ytg-protest-idUSKCN1UJ1OW accessed 9 May 2023.

twentieth century, become associated with globalisation. This professionalisation and commercialisation has led various publics to fight against the attempt of the IOC and other organisers to impose their values. The encounters that take place are often those of a global consumer class who can either afford to travel to the Games or a broader spectrum who watch on television. Often, however, locals have paid a price for these encounters through displacement and marginalisation.

Many members of the population, however, see the Games as more of a spectacle. They are depicted as a special event in one's own nation or the opportunity for athletes with whom one shares a national passport (if little else) to compete 'for the nation'. During the period since the late 1940s changes in broadcasting from radio to newsreel and the onset of the television era changed the Games into a collective global event in which athletes and spectators in the stadium or in their homes were conditioned by the emotions of the spectacle. In the 2020s the Games became a solely media encounter. The delayed Tokyo 2020 Games were held in 2021 under a state of emergency as the Covid-19 pandemic paralysed Japan's society and economy. The Games, it seems, were too important to allow the lack of spectators or the rising death toll to delay them any further. With such a global draw it is little surprise that the Games have become politicised, indeed the very hosting of them by a city which represents a nation is a political act. But others have seen the Games as a reasonable site to raise politics and engage with a global audience, often facing the wrath of organisers and national committees.

Discussion Questions

How far have the Olympics enabled people from different cultures to interact with each other?

Can the Games be said to have followed a similar path to globalisation, with an ideology rooted in Western values underpinning them?

How much have the values of the Olympics been undermined by commercialisation?

Why do some people protest about the Games coming to their city and how valid are their complaints?

What kinds of legacies are left after the Games and do they enable future encounters between peoples and cultures?

CHAPTER 7

Conclusion: An Age of Encounter?

Throughout the Age of Globalism cultural encounters brought peoples into greater contact than ever before. The result has been change, adaptation and learning about the world. The Age of Globalism raised a desire in some people for political integration on a regional or even broader level, but others felt repelled by unfamiliar cultures. The era saw the creation of economic and political institutions that spanned borders and often seemed out of the control of many members of the world's population. There were great developments in technology that, along with political forces, enabled greater mobility and interconnections between people. As the era progressed, more people acquired the wealth and freedom to form their own cultural encounters. These encounters, however, were often mediated by corporations, governments and other local, national and transnational authorities.

Many responses to the increased interactions followed some of those set out by Gerard Delanty, which are mentioned in the Introduction. These categories of hostility, divergence, assimilation, acceptance, diffusion (adaptation) and fusion (hybridity) can be seen to produce new global cultures. Some encounters started with one category but through a process of familiarisation and learning moved into others (or sometimes back). Populations have often seen conflict among themselves, or between the population and political leaders, over the values that the Age of Globalism brought, especially cosmopolitanism. In recent decades anti-globalist movements have formed, firstly against the economic aspect of globalisation, secondly and more electorally successful against the mobility of people and ideas associated with globalisation.

The Age of Globalism has been one of increased migration with the centres of economic power requiring labour to enable growth. Migration has been caused by globalisation with jobs devaluing and economies deskilling as production moves; it has also resulted from the effects of economic globalisation including war, poverty and climate disaster. More economically advanced nations projected a utopian image of their lifestyle through globalised culture, such as films, which promised an idyllic lifestyle, drawing in migrants. Some governments encouraged temporary immigration, but the establishment of diasporic organisations allowed incomers to establish new communities. New bonds were formed over time leading to acceptance, adaptation and fusion. Numerous Western metropolises such as London, Amsterdam and New York built global hybrid cultures that were influenced by the diversity of incomers and often appeared different to their national cultures. Despite the hostility from some people, many cities were able to grow to global status through economies that were often powered by immigrant labour. The expansion of cosmopolis like London and New York into global economic powerhouses driven by liberalisation is well known. But a similar globalisation of cities occurred behind the Iron Curtain. The draw of metropolitan cities like Moscow and Leningrad allowed these places to diversify and to secure the labour needed to power the Soviet economy. It led these cities to change culturally but also enabled the Soviets to plan for large-scale economic projects that were labour hungry.

Many groups of migrants, from German-speaking expellees to Algerians in France, found hostility from parts of the local population. German expellees were one of a number of groups including various Europeans, Jews, Indians and Pakistanis who experienced the loss of home through the wartime and post-World War Two reshaping of borders. Their displacement caused the forging of new nations such as Israel, India and Pakistan, and the rebuilding of old ones like Germany. These groups had to work to build a space in which to exist and to allow their culture to grow. Rejection in their new nation sometimes brought negative aspects such as the revanchism of some German expellees or catastrophic violence in the nations of India. It was only when the rejection turned to assimilation that the antipathy between groups disappeared. Incomers were able to work with more accepting members of societies in which they arrived and built hybrid communities and cultures that incorporated aspects of their former lives with those from the new nations.

Migrations were caused by political turmoil, particularly the Cold War. Some groups were subject to forced migration as a tool of domination. The deportation of Baltic and other peoples in the USSR was designed to weaken nationalism and lessen the guerrilla warfare that existed in some states. The forced relocation split communities, and exiles formed new associations in remote parts of the USSR. These, like many other groups, rarely regarded their migration as permanent. Others, including Hungarian refugees fleeing the Soviet invasion of 1956, escaped the instability of the Cold War. Some attempted to leave because of politics or the resulting economic issues. East Germans moved to West Germany in search of a better standard of living or political freedom, destabilising the East German state, until the closure of the border stemmed the flow. The West frequently provided incentives for people to make the illegal move, and the Federal Republic of Germany, backed by the USA and Britain, offered cash inducements to refugees. The welcome and propaganda helped to make up the minds of many who were considering leaving.

The post-war re-establishment and dissolution of empires caused people to move. Some of these migrated under citizenship agreements, such as Caribbeans who moved to the United Kingdom, or Indonesians and Surinamese to the Netherlands. Migrants formed organisations around certain policies and campaigned in exile for their cause, be it anti-communism, anti-dictatorship or independence from the successor state. Other groups formed political communities based on a diasporic similarity, with pan-Arabism leading many Algerians in France to support the Palestinian cause and pan-Africanism as one of the uniting factors among black migrants and their children. Some of these political affiliations have led to the mixing of communities and the building of hybridity in affiliations across borders.

While the response of certain groups to migration has been rejection, hostility and violence, this has rarely been a majority viewpoint. The impact on those affected, however, is not lessened. Violence and discrimination have prompted responses from migrant communities, leading to organisation at various levels from street culture to education. In Britain migrants from the 1950s responded to their rejection by certain groups by building what became known as the Notting Hill Carnival, which is now celebrated by those in the migrant community, their children and others who share values of inclusion. Caribbean migrants have produced numerous works of culture and created a black British culture that in the twenty-first century has formed a hybrid with the mainstream. In many nations the immigration of former imperial subjects meant that the colonial hierarchies were reimposed by certain groups. This was visible in France when Algerians who had migrated, often to escape war, were soon treated as outsiders by many French, especially former colonial workers who took up positions in the police.

The USA holds a national foundation myth of being built on European immigration, with these people deemed to have helped build the nation and many becoming Americanised. However, until the 1960s acceptance of immigrants was largely based on skin colour and the limitation of non-white immigration was a feature of the early post-war period. The policy particularly discriminated against those of Asian origin. While lobbying and pressure from minority rights groups helped to change the minds of some leaders, it took the adoption of a more open immigration policy by liberally minded politicians like John F. Kennedy to change the nationality-based quota system. More migrants were able to become American citizens from the 1960s. However, the economic success was short-lived and across the Western world the 1970s saw a period of economic uncertainty that allowed anti-immigrant organisations to grow. Governments in Europe often responded by absorbing some of the policies of the more extreme groups.

After the Cold War migration in Europe was heavily centred on the former Eastern Bloc nations. As subjects from former 'enemy' states there was a mixture of rejection and acceptance of these workers. Often the tabloid press generated scares around migration that bred hostility among a small but vocal minority. With the communities far from established, many initially regarded themselves as temporary, but over time some began to build lasting relationships in their new countries, starting families and making their moves permanent. The mobility was enabled by the extension of the European Union. Within the former Eastern Bloc nations the presence of large Russian-speaking minorities led to questions around national identity at a time of refocussing allegiances. This was especially notable in the Baltic states where there was a refocussing on a broader Scandinavian-based character and away from the Russian-dominated Soviet identity.

Immigration built long-term engagement between communities and developed hybrid cultures through encounters that ranged from hostility and divergence to assimilation, adaptation and fusion, and which generally led to more diverse societies. By adapting aspects of their old cultures to appeal in their new homes, migrants were able to achieve great success. Be this the Cuban-inspired pop music of Gloria Estevan, the growth of reggae and the emergence of two-tone music in Britain, or foodstuffs like General Tso's chicken in the USA or chicken tikka masala in the UK, hybrids became commonplace and spoke of a level of acceptance of migrant cultures. The 2000s, however, saw several periods that might be regarded as turning points for attitudes towards immigration in many Western nations. The first was the terror attacks of 11 September 2001. This destruction and the ensuing War on Terror gave those across the West who disliked the presence of Muslims, whether immigrants or not, an excuse to become more vocal or violent. Fear of immigration began to grow as a political opinion after this time. The tabloid press fuelled the hostility. At the same time migration between the European nations and between Western nations was buoyant and the building of cosmopolitan communities and cities continued. For many people the opportunities that the period offered were great and they could freely mix in global cities, adopting non-national identities. However, those who felt left behind as others took advantage of the new opportunities sometimes stored up resentment, which the economic downturn from 2008 exacerbated, becoming the second turning point. Anger at decline in living standards, combined with visible changes in the make-up of populations, fuelled populist movements like Brexit and Trumpism that had anti-migration at their heart. Migration has become one of the key mobilising issues of the 2020s, heavily influencing voting patterns in some nations. Other less permanent forms of mobility can be seen to mirror these encounters on a smaller scale, tourism being the chief among them.

Tourism became the most common way for people to encounter other cultures. After World War Two, the industry was kick-started by the American government, which built on pre-existing habits and infrastructure. The boosting of tourism occurred because of Cold War politics and the desire to reshape Western Europe economically, fuelling it with foreign currency. However, it was also believed that tourism would educate both Europeans and Americans about the positive aspects of each other's culture, forming an informal liberal sphere. In the early post-war years. However, most tourism was domestic and took place mainly by road, boat or train. The role of technology, especially flight, is vital in explaining the emergence of mass foreign tourism. As technology and government legislation enabled cheaper airlines and holiday groups to operate from the 1960s, the foreign holiday became a more regular occurrence.

The boom in tourism, especially in Southern Europe, was capitalised on by several dictatorships including Spain, Greece, Yugoslavia and later in the period Bulgaria. The leaders used inbound tourism to help their economies and build better foreign relations as a form of soft power. But for several of these nations the liberal attitudes and practices of holidaying tourists were considered an affront to traditional attitudes, especially in Franco's Spain with its conservative morals. While some relaxation of norms was allowed for tourists there were clear lines: divisions and laws were designed to prevent locals becoming over-familiar with the ways of tourists. Some popular tourist destinations like Spain repackaged their customs such as bull fighting or traditional dancing for consumption by tourists as a way of exoticising themselves. The government wanted the encounter to remain one of acceptance focussing on co-operation and business with a desire by Spanish conservatives to show their divergence from much of European culture. Questions remain over the impact of tourism on these areas, with scholars divided between those who believe that it acted to normalise the regimes and legitimise their rule, and those who see foreign influences as creating a well of liberal attitudes which would place the encounter more in the diffusion and adaptation type than was desired. It is fair to say that tourism was not the cause of liberalisation in the post-dictatorship era, but familiarity with foreign ideas may have eased transitions to democracy and the absorption of Spain, Greece and Portugal into the European Community at a quickened pace.

Throughout the Cold War each side sought to build influence by extending air routes and supporting the building of national airlines. While the reasons for this from the USA focussed on 'nation building' and aiding business growth, tourist industries often benefitted from these creations. The countries involved, and many who built their flagship airlines without external support, were able to promote their national identity, especially through staff uniforms and inflight food offerings. Often this meant showing the customs and 'personality' of a nation, as Singapore Airlines did with its promotion of an image of good service as an Asian trait. Overall, however, the impact of these changes was often limited: until the 1970s protections for national airlines and minimum airfares prevented much travel for most people.

While tourism is often seen as a Western trend it was also a feature of the Eastern Bloc. Most communist nations provided opportunities for domestic and foreign travel. Travel between Eastern European nations, at times China, and non-European socialist nations aimed to deliver the benefits of socialism to their publics while building a broader sense of solidarity with other communist nations, producing a form of adaptation and fusion. This fraternity, however, was sometimes ill thought through; travelling Soviets sometimes came to realise that they had some of the lowest living standards. At other times tourism professionals let their anti-Soviet views be known. The mixing that took place through tourism in the Eastern Bloc was not always harmonious, and sometimes brought antipathy to the fore, meaning that encounters led to hostility as well as increased understanding.

Tourism provided an opportunity for Western people to travel behind the Iron Curtain and encounter the seemingly secretive Cold War 'other'. Yugoslavia, while not solidly part of the Eastern Bloc, built a tourist industry that capitalised on its popularity before World War Two. From the 1960s Bulgaria built a holiday industry as a sunshine destination. Westerners could even travel to the Soviet Union. As with many tourist experiences, professionals and governments attempted to steer these tourists to the right sites, often through organised tours. Over time other communist nations such as China, Cuba and Vietnam opened to tourism, often with the pursuit of foreign currency as their aim. These nations offered a longer-haul experience to Westerners, with some travelling to enjoy cheaper sunshine holidays and others because the East was an adventure. The Cold War division offered the opportunity for an encounter through tourism that often turned to a level of acceptance and familiarisation, even if with a selective version of that culture.

Tourists often seek the 'real' culture of the country that they are visiting, but this can prove elusive. Scholars have criticised the practice of delivering home comforts abroad so that tourists effectively rarely leave their home nation. Cultures are often pre-packaged and certain 'traditions' that are invented or performed solely for tourists can be all that they encounter, rather than members of the population. With lists of the must-see sights and landmarks, the secular homage of a visit to a place follows pre-ordained paths. Perhaps the chance of an encounter with a real culture is lessened by this filtering of tourism. But it should be equally noted that no nation has a single culture and that national symbols, figureheads and suchlike aim to build a sense of national identity, not homogeneous ideals. Longer-stay travel allows for greater opportunity to mix with people from different cultures, especially where it involves language acquisition. Over time tourism has allowed people to mix and build up ideas of fraternity beyond borders which has been credited with increasing ideas of broader regional and international friendship and the adopting of more cosmopolitan identities.

For those who live in tourist-dense places there are mixed impacts. Workers in the tourist industry in poorer nations have increased their incomes. But others are excluded. In many places such as the Dominican Republic, tourism takes place in purpose-built enclaves that ensure that tourists only spend their money in the resort and are shielded from the life outside. Law enforcement is sometimes used to prevent those on the margins from encountering outsiders or creating a business that benefits from tourism. By building the idea of the wild or violent hinterland, suspicion is bred between tourists and locals, thereby limiting encounters. The hybridity that is seen as one of the benefits of tourism is actively discouraged. Overall the types of encounters that tourism enables may be limited to those of co-operation and acceptance. The prompting of learning about other cultures is important but the nature in which most tourism takes place does not allow for more than a fleeting engagement. By the 2020s tourism was being increasingly questioned because of its impact on the environment and communities. When mass travel became possible again after the 2020–21 pandemic, tourism soared, showing that it was as popular as ever, but in certain places it was met with anti-tourist protests.

For the politically aware the age of globalisation meant that their activism might become directed beyond their own borders and many built international alliances. Ideas such as racial equality, women's rights and protection of the environment crossed borders, often adapting to local conditions, building fusion across nations. Sometimes these international campaigns targeted individual governments. As the world slowly embraced ideas of racial equality in the post-war era, the government of South Africa moved firmly in the opposite direction. Solidarity campaigns were created in Africa and the West that sought to influence the general population and governments' relations with South Africa and to use international organisations to fight apartheid. Groups of activists, intellectuals, musicians and sportspeople led the campaign to prevent international interactions with South Africa through trade and culture and to promote the rights of the majority black population. The campaign was tied to broader fights for racial equality, especially the pan-Africanist movement, civil rights campaigners in the USA and black rights activists in the UK.

International support was important for the outlawed African National Congress (ANC). Following Nelson Mandela's incarceration, his persona was used to build international awareness. The ANC called for international consumer boycotts. Initially these had limited success but raised awareness and were followed by sporting and cultural boycotts of South Africa, turning the encounter into one of rejection of the apartheid nation, while embracing its black population. The formalisation of opposition to apartheid through organisations like the UN, IOC and British Commonwealth increased the pressure on the South African government. By the 1980s organisations began to target investments in the divestment campaign. While ultimately the cause of the end of apartheid was black South Africans effectively making the nation ungovernable, the international pressure added extra impetus. The encounters were built through international activists, especially those that were able to visit South Africa, and through awareness raising, but the impact of this activism was to block encounters by South Africans until apartheid was ended.

Women's activism incorporated many longstanding movements from different national contexts whose aims were diverse. With the globalisation of communication and media, activist groups could build networks around common aims and could discuss and borrow campaigning tactics. Over the post-war period these networks expanded, often using international institutions like the UN to engage with groups beyond the Iron Curtain and the developing nations. Often these groups had differing aims: those in the global majority South incorporated wealth distribution and anti-colonialism into their programmes, in addition to legal rights, because they believed that poverty had to be eliminated for equality to be effective. International women's conferences attempted to incorporate the divergent aims of the movements and to build an international sense of mutual support and solidarity for all women. The encounter of co-operation also led to diffusion through the borrowings of objectives and campaign tactics and produced fusion through the sense of international solidarity between women's groups.

By the 2010s the women's movement gained renewed impetus. The target of this feminism has been the abuses of power by men that led to sexual harassment, but also 'everyday' sexism. The uncovering of the scale of sexual abuse committed by the film director Harvey Weinstein and his subsequent trial, alongside the ascent to power of Donald Trump, whose pejorative comments about women and subsequent conviction for sexual assault suggested sexism was ingrained throughout many Western power structures, have convinced a new generation of activists to pursue change. The international women's movement has found a new resurgence and increased interconnectivity allows these groups to be ever more global in scale. Women's organisations often had differing goals but through meeting they were able to find common ground and build a campaigning global civil society that considered differing cultures and perspectives.

Environmental activism was well established by the post-war era. The Age of Globalism saw the integration of movements that had previously campaigned on single issues, with campaigning becoming international through the fusion of ideas. The 1960s became a pivotal decade in campaigning. While localised disasters caused by industrial pollution had previously raised outrage, campaigners increasingly thought about the planet as an interconnected entity. Some campaigners like Rachel Carson still focussed on single issues, but her attack on the use of pesticides in industrialised agriculture was able to reach a global audience and lead to action on certain chemicals. Environmental awareness spanned the ideological divide of the Cold War era. While those in communist nations often had to campaign in semi-official or state-approved groups, they were able to direct pressure towards those in power. In Eastern Europe the Chernobyl disaster in 1986 and the relaxing of controls on activist groups led to the creation of more unofficial environmental organisations. Others in countries such as China were able to target corporations and local authorities on issues and to prompt action. In nations of the global majority South, much of the activism constituted what has been termed the 'environmentalism of the poor'. Activists often targeted industry and governmental actions such as logging or dam building and were able to build international support by creating networks with foreign groups. Some of these produced international figureheads, for example, Chico Mendes, the Brazilian campaigner whose anti-logging activism made him an international figure until his murder. Over time organisations dedicated to the protection of the environment have become more professionalised and globalised. This process allowed them to expand their reach beyond their initial countercultural status. Non-governmental organisations such as Greenpeace were, by the twenty-first century, able to be heard by transnational organisations and national governments. More organised political parties have emerged from these groups and have gained some representation, including in Germany and Britain. Their growth has shown that green issues can draw popular support. Internationalised environmentalists were able to raise awareness of the environmental impact of industrialisation and consumerism and forced politicians in the twenty-first century to commit to taking action to lessen the effects. A hybrid culture was formed that fused around the desire to protect the environment and saw the borrowing of tactics and titles from other groups, despite the divergence of cultures that sometimes existed between nations.

National governments and transnational organisations sought to build formal encounters through the International Expositions, or World's Fairs. These exhibitions represented governments' desire to bring others into an encounter with their idealised culture and to increase trade. Governments desired an encounter of acceptance, with the potential for adaptation and fusion emerging from the mixing of cultures. Members of the public could encounter several nations in close succession. These events were encounters of modernity involving the promotion of national and internationalist ideologies. While they were initially a feature of capitalist economies, the Cold War turned the Expos into part of the global contest for minds. Members of the public hoped to build an encounter of acceptance with the 'other' side in the Cold War, rather than rejection. Others wanted to witness the exotic and nations they would not otherwise visit. While the early Expos were rooted in colonialist attitudes, the post-war era gradually saw post-colonial cultures promoted as new nations won their freedom from European domination. By 1958 many of these nations hoped to show their arrival to the world and to represent their cultures themselves. When they could not represent themselves, as in the case of Congo, which was still under Belgian rule, the exhibitions and methods often drew criticisms. Ideologies and values were at the centre of the displays; Expos were part of a top-down encounter that hoped to influence decision makers and members of the public in the host and other nations.

During the Cold War many press outlets presented the Expos as hostile encounters between East and West. There were, however, moments of friendliness and the events were designed to create dialogue and acceptance rather than hostility. Both sides projected their utopian visions of their ways of life. Other nations within either camp were able to incorporate aspects of international cultures by showing how hybrid influences were at work. The Czechoslovakians displayed their own style and often moved away from an overt promotion of communism, showing themselves as an independent nation based on the culture of their regions, which adapted the styles they encountered around Europe.

Often the Expos provided an encounter between different aspects of national cultures. For the USA this came in the issue of race relations and its 1998 attempt to show that progress had been made. With criticisms directed from those who were against equality for black people, as well as those who felt the issue was not backed up by action, the display was soon sanitised to skirt the issue. The fairs uncovered the desire of some to break the assimilation of different cultures into national identities and make them more diverse. When the Fair moved to the USA in Seattle 1962 it was an almost entirely Western affair. The exclusion or withdrawal of communist nations due to the hostility between ideologies meant that no encounter would take place across the Iron Curtain. The USA took the opportunity to project its idealised self-image to its own population and foreign visitors.

The most celebrated World's Fair of the 1960s was Montreal in 1967. Coming at a time associated with youth, fun and freedom, this image was projected by many nations. The Age of Affluence had arrived in much of the West, and the Cold War was at a relatively sanguine moment, despite the USA's war in Vietnam. Canada experienced something of an encounter with their own hybrid identity: the Anglophone and Francophone provinces produced their own displays and a pavilion dedicated to First-Nation Canadians attempted to boost the assimilation into the predominant European-Canadian identities. The Canadian authorities hoped to use the hybridity of their identity to project a multi-directional image. With Britain and France hosting pavilions next to each other there was potential for Anglophone and Francophone influences to interact. Each celebrated its own culture in a Canada that was influenced by both.

By the 1970s Asian nations like Japan and South Korea were firmly implanted as economic powerhouses. Japan used the Expo at Osaka 1970 to project its idealised self-image. The focus turned to the Asian continent, and it was an opportunity to promote a view of alternative hegemonies. Non-Asian countries sought to tie their displays to Asian identities. The USA focussed on its hybrid communities, especially in Hawaii, and promoted the idea of American-Japanese friendship. The USSR made the most of their Eurasian hinterland and the Eastern parts of the USSR. The Expos helped to promote a fusion of business culture between Asia, America and Europe.

The post-Cold War era saw the domination of neo-liberal politics during the Seville Fair in 1992. The hostility of the Cold War was gone and many nations chose to display new images of the democratic successor states, with the German display promoting its reunified nation. The Spanish hosts saw the encounter in terms of pan-Atlanticism, seeking to build relations with those with a Hispanic linguistic background in South and Central America.

The problem was how to present Spain's colonial past. With empire reframed as discovery and progress, the new democratic Spain promoted the common ties between these continents and showcased the diffusion and fusion that united themselves, South and Central America. This was a mutually supportive pro-liberal identity that they sought to build, with conquest and domination sanitised.

By the twenty-first century questions about industrial progress were weighed against its impact. The organisers of Expos from Hanover 2000 onwards began to promote the need to help the environment with the celebration of technology. A hybrid global culture had emerged that blended technology and 'progress' with ideas of environmentalism. Often this was seen in the celebration of utopian ideas of technological fixes for environmental issues, alongside the promise of a less labour-intensive future that echoed the narrative throughout the Age of Globalism. Notwithstanding this, the Shanghai Expo in 2010 was used to celebrate the rise of China as a new global power. While the encounter was mainly limited to Chinese visitors plus international tourists, many of these felt that they were encountering the world and duly celebrated their Expo passport, which was stamped on arrival at national pavilions. The fair celebrated the global decentring of economies and power and, like the Osaka Expo before it, celebrated Asian identities that could emerge and create hybrids of their own to challenge Western predominance.

The sporting counterpart of the Expo is the Olympics. Although the Games grabs more attention than the industrial and technical encounter in the twenty-first century, many of the earlier Olympiads were organised to coincide with the International Expositions. The early Olympics limited the encounter to men, with women largely reduced to spectators. There was a similar class division, with professional sportsmen barred, effectively limiting competition to leisured upper-class people. In the post-war period this status changed slowly but women competitors were still discouraged from participation. Eventually, despite the disparities in funding in many sports that remain, the Olympics facilitated encounters between both men and women and people from different classes and ethnicities.

The Games sometimes provided the opportunity for people to learn from other communities. At London 1948 and Melbourne 1956 there was a lack of purpose-built accommodation, meaning that locals hosted guests. This accommodation facilitated mixing between cultures. Some of these encounters, however, were strictly mediated, with the Australians selecting those women as hosts that they felt would best depict a favourable image of Australianness. Other cultures were often less well accommodated. London in 1948 was notable for the inability to cater to foreign food habits, meaning that teams had to bring their own supply. The organisers also failed to account for other customs like the fasting of Muslims, prioritising only Europeanised cultural norms. Cultures outside of the Western one in which the Games were founded were subjected to assimilation, with little account taken of tradition. The Games only moved slowly away from Western domination. The Tokyo

Olympics of 1964 were something of a turning point for the inclusion of judo, the first Olympic sport that was codified outside the main Western nations, marking the start of diffusion and the creation of a more modern Olympic culture. The imbalance has not been fully addressed into the twenty-first century, with Western-originated sports being the main competition and encounters largely taking place on the terms of the Western nations.

The admittance of the Soviets to the Olympic movement in 1951 changed the Games into Cold War events, with hostility between East and West eventually coming to dominate and limit the encounter. The political divide led to some competitors, such as Americans, being instructed on how to behave when in contact with their Soviet counterparts. Both sides saw the opportunity to win influence and have their sportspeople present their best image, with an outward face of acceptance. Over time Cold War politics led to a series of boycotts and prevented the intended peaceful encounters from occurring.

Host nations have especially sought to shape the image that visitors gain, with cities undergoing massive re-development. Populations have also been made ready, often by moving elements deemed unsavoury away from where they might sully the reputation of the nation. Manners have been modified with laws around begging, hawking, prostitution and toilet habits introduced at various Games. Public information campaigns have sought to reinforce this behaviour modification. The Games have caused displacement of many members of host cities' populations, which is often seen by opponents as a form of social cleansing. The Games exist for the world's elite and those who are deemed objectionable are rejected.

Some nations have used their hosting of the Games to project a new national identity to the world. The Games in Rome 1960, Tokyo 1964 and Munich 1972 saw the three former Axis powers return to the forefront of the international sphere. Each, to varying degrees, left the past in the shadows and presented a more peaceful image. The Games were used as a form of spectacle nationalism. In this case it was to present an outward and inward face of an acceptable form of national identity that carefully found a usable past, that could encourage engagement with others around the world.

Protest turned the Games into a global encounter for many activists who were either competitors or those often excluded. While the organisers aimed for the Games to be non-political, sportspeople like John Carlos and Tommie Smith felt that their cause, the subjugation of black people in the USA, was more important than the contest and brought their statement to the watching world. Others used their position in official ceremonies to make their feelings known. The band Midnight Oil and with their 'apology' T-shirts at the Sydney closing ceremony helped to raise awareness of the issues facing Indigenous Australians and the failures of the government to alleviate their treatment. In both cases the actions of people with a large audience helped to build connections to those whose voices may not otherwise be heard and to build discourse around these issues.

Others who felt excluded from the world of the Olympics used the Games to make their statement. The protests that anticipated the Mexico Games in 1968 were violently put down by the government and led to something of a media blackout over the protest. The Palestinian organisation Black September used the Munich Games to kidnap and murder seventeen Israeli athletes. The use of the Games for politicised action did not end in the twentieth century. The Rio de Janeiro Games in 2016 saw anti-poverty campaigners and teachers who had not been paid for months protest at the torch rally and opening ceremony. The excluded and poverty-stricken felt that they were being trampled upon to make way for the lavish Games for the world's elite. These encounters that have been enabled by the Games have been unintended and unwanted consequences of the staging of the mega-events.

Globalism has been challenged over the last decade or so. The political tendency for isolationism, rising conflict and the environmental disasters that regularly occur may bring to an end the current Age of Globalism. As a phenomenon that tends to go in waves, however, before long new forms of interconnectivity and mobility of people, goods and ideas will emerge and likely with renewed vigour. The cultural encounters in this book saw different cultures engaging and building transnational communities. All existed before the Age of Globalism but the ever-increasing interconnectivity from the end of World War Two meant that each expanded its scope, impacted on more people and increased contact between cultures. While the spread of cultures through globalised news media, film, literature and television has been in the background of the story, these media worked to bring these different forms of encounter together. While many have suggested this has amounted to the Americanisation of cultures, the encounters examined here have suggested that there has been a large rejection of any form of dominant culture. Indeed, identities have at times moved away from the nation and formed around diasporic and different forms of community and those based on internationalised classes. Nevertheless, underpinning these interactions has often been national identity or the desire to get national government to act.

Throughout the period from 1945 people had opportunities to encounter other cultures like never before, whether face to face, virtually or on the terms of businesspeople and governments. Sometimes the subsequent encounters started with rejection, while at other times more open and friendly meetings occurred, but with the work of people on both sides learning often took place. In the Age of Globalism hybrid cultures emerged that have been embraced by many; the new and diverse face of nations is here to stay, despite the vocal opposition of many in power.

REFERENCES

ARCHIVES AND DIGITAL ARCHIVES

US State Department
Margaret Thatcher Foundation
Marxists Internet Archive. www.marxists.org
Montreal Archives. https://archivesdemontreal.com/
The National Archive

BOOKS

Addison, Paul, and Harriett Jones, eds. 2005. *A Companion to Contemporary Britain 1939–2000*. London: Wiley.
Aissoui, Rabah. 2009. *Immigration and National Identity: North African Political Movements in Colonial and Postcolonial France*. London: Tauris.
Alden, Edward H. 2008. *The Closing of the American Border: Terrorism, Immigration and Security Since 9/11*. New York: Harper.
Anderson, Benedict. 1983. *Imagined Communities*. London: Verso.
Andrews, Kehinde. 2021. *The New Age of Empire: How Racism and Colonialism Still rule the World*. London: Penguin.
Anon. 1967. *Scouting's Expo '67*. Souvenir Guide. St Louis, MO: Hendle Press.
Anon. 1970. *Soviet Siberia*. Moscow: Progress Publishers.
Anon. 1970. *United States Pavilion Japan World Exposition Osaka 1970*. Souvenir Guide.
Audelbert, Cedric, and Mohamed Kamel Dorai, eds. 2010. *Migration in a Globalised World: New Research Issues and Prospects*. Amsterdam: Amsterdam University Press.
Auerbach, Jeffrey A., and Peter Hoffenberg, eds. 2008. *Britain, the Empire and the World at the Great Exhibition of 1851*. London: Ashgate.
Babiraki, Patrick, and Kenyon Zimmer, eds. 2014. *Cold War Crossings: International Travel and Exchange across the Soviet Bloc 1940s–1960s*. College Station, TX: A & M University Press.
Bajc, Vida. 2016. *Surveilling and Securing the Olympics: From Tokyo 1964 to London 2012 and beyond*. London: Palgrave.

© The Editor(s) (if applicable) and The Author(s), under exclusive license to Springer Nature Switzerland AG 2024
N. J. Barnett, *Cultural Encounters in the Age of Globalism*,
https://doi.org/10.1007/978-3-031-68797-6

Barghoorn, Frederick Charles. 1960. *The Soviet Cultural Offensive: The Role Of Cultural Diplomacy in Soviet Foreign Policy*. Princeton, NJ: Princeton University Press.
Baron, Nick, ed. 2017. *Displaced Children in Russia and Eastern Europe, 1915–53: Ideologies, Identities, Experiences*. London: Brill.
Bartlett, Djurdja. 2010. *Fashioneast: The Spectre That Haunted Socialism*. London: MIT Press.
Bauerkamper, Arad, and Grzegorz Rossolinski-Liebe, eds. 2017. *Fascism without Borders: Transnational Connections between Movements and Regimes in Europe, 1918–1945*. Oxford: Berghahn.
de Beauvoir, Simone. 1949. *Le Deuxième Sexe: Les Faits et les Mythes*. Paris: Gallimard.
Beneš, Oldřich, ed. 1967. *Czechoslovakia: Ancient and Modern: A Conception*. Orbis: Prague.
Benton, Gregor, and Edmund Gomez. 2008. *The Chinese in Britain, 1800-Present: Economy, Transnationalism, Identity*. Basingstoke: Palgrave.
Berridge, Virginia, and Kelly Laughlin, eds. 2005. *Medicine, the Market and the Mass Media*. London: Routledge.
Blanton, Michael. 1959. *White and Coloured: The Behaviour of British People towards Coloured Migrants*. New Jersey: Rutgers University Press.
Boehmer, Elleke. 2008. *Nelson Mandela: A Very Short Introduction*. Oxford: Oxford University Press.
Boorstin, Daniel J. 1961. *The Image: A Guide to Pseudo Events in America*. New York: Harper.
Borsay, Peter, and John K. Walton, eds. 2011. *Resorts and Ports: European Seaside Towns Since 1700*. Bristol: Channel View.
Borsay, Peter, and Ruth Elizabeth Mohman, eds. 2000. *New Directions in Urban History: Aspects of European Art, Tourism and Leisure Since the Enlightenment*. New York: Waxmann.
Boykoff, Jules. 2016. *Power Games: A Political History of the Olympics*. London: Verso.
Breyfogle, Nicholas, Abby Schrader, and Willard Sunderland, eds. 2007. *Peopling the Russian Periphery: Borderland Colonization in Eurasian History*. Abingdon: Routledge.
Buck-Morss, Susan. 2002. *Dreamworld and Catastrophe: The Passing of Mass Utopia in East and West*. London: MIT Press.
Bunce, Robin, and Paul Field. 2014. *Darcus Howe: A Political Biography*. London: Bloomsbury.
Burke, Patrick. 2009. *Cultural Hybridity*. Cambridge: Polity.
Buruma, Ian. 2013. *Year Zero: A History of 1945*. London: Atlantic Books.
Butler, Richard, and Roslyn Russell, eds. 2010. *Giants of Tourism*. Wallingford: CABI.
Calvetta, Kitty. 2005. *Immigrants at the Margins: Law, Race, and Exclusion in Southern Europe*. Cambridge: Cambridge University Press.
Canadelli, Elena, et al. (eds.). 2019. *Behind the Exhibit: Displaying Science and Technology at World's Fairs and Museums in the Twentieth Century*. Washington, DC: Smithsonian Institution Scholarly Press.
Caraffa, Constanza, and Tiziana Serena, eds. 2015. *Photo Archives and the Idea of the Nation*. Berlin: de Gruyter.
Carson, Rachael. 1962. *Silent Spring*. Boston, MA: Houghton Mifflin.
Çaykent, Özlem., and Luca Zavagno. 2014. *Islands of the East Mediterranean: A History of Cross-Cultural Encounters*. London: I. B. Tauris.

Chatterjee, Joya. 2007. *The Spoils of Partition: Bengal and India 1947–1967* Cambridge: Cambridge University Press.
Clark, Nancy, and William Worger. 2016. *South Africa: The Rise and Fall of Apartheid*. London: Taylor and Francis.
Cochrane, Janet. 2007. *Asian Tourism: Growth and Change*. London: Routledge.
Coe, Jonathan. 2018. *Expo '58*. London: Penguin.
Cohen, Gerard Daniel. 2001. *In War's Wake: Europe's Displaced Persons in the Postwar Order*. Oxford: Oxford University Press.
Connor, Ian. 2014. *Refugees and Expellees in Postwar Germany*. Manchester: Manchester University Press.
Corbin, Alain. 1994. *The Lure of the Sea: The Discovery of the Seaside in the Western World, 1750–1840*. Berkeley, CA: University of California Press.
Cross, Anthony, ed. 2012. *A People Passing Rude: British Responses to Russian Culture*. Cambridge: Cambridge University Press.
Crumbaugh, Justin. 2009. *Destination Dictatorship: The Spectacle of Spain's Tourism Boom and the Reinvention of Difference*. New York: SUNY Press.
Czigany, Magda. 2009. *"Just Like Other Students": Reception of the 1956 Hungarian Refugee Students in Britain*. Newcastle: Cambridge Scholars Publishing.
Daly, Mary. 1978. *Gyn/Ecology: The Meta Ethics of Radical Feminism*. Boston, MA: Beacon Press.
Davidann, John Thares, and Marc Jason Gilbert. 2013. *Cross-Cultural Encounters in Modern World History*. Abingdon: Routledge.
Davies, Thomas. 2014. *NGOs: A New History of Transnational Civil Society*. Oxford: Oxford University Press.
Davoliūtė, Violeta, and Tomas Bakelis, eds. 2018. *Narratives of Exile and Identity: Soviet Deportation Memoirs from the Baltic States*. Budapest: Central European Press.
Delanty, Gerard, Ruth Wodak, and Paul Jones, eds. 2008. *Migration, Discrimination and Belonging in Europe*. Liverpool: Liverpool University Press.
Douglas, ed. 2020. *Himalaya: A Human History*. London: Vintage.
Douglas, Raymond. 2012. *Orderly and Humane: The Expulsion of the Germans after the Second World War* New Haven: Yale University Press.
Douglass, Carrie B. 1997. *Bulls, Bullfighting, and Spanish Identity*. Tucson: University of Arizona Press.
Driver, Felix, and David Gilbert, eds. 1999. *Imperial Cities: Landscape, Display and Identity*. Manchester: Manchester University Press.
Eichengreen, Barry. 1995. *Europe's Postwar Recovery*. Cambridge: Cambridge University Press.
Endy, Christopher. 2004. *Cold War Holidays: American Tourism in France*. London: University of North Carolina Press.
Engberson, Godfried, et al. 2010. *A Continent Moving West? EU Enlargement and Migration from Central and Eastern Europe*. Amsterdam: Amsterdam University Press.
Favell, Adrian. 2008. *Eurostars and Eurocities: Free Movement and Mobility in an Integrating Europe*. London: Blackwell.
Feifer, Maxine. 1985. *Going Places: The Ways of the Tourist from Imperial Rome to the Present Days*. London: Macmillan.
Feldman, David. 2018. *Boycotts Past and Present: From the American Revolution to the Campaign to Boycott Israel*. London: Palgrave Macmillan.

Fields, Marek. 2019. *Defending Democracy in Cold War Finland: British and American Propaganda and Cultural Diplomacy in Finland, 1944–1970*. Leiden: Brill.
Firmat, Gustavo Pérez. 2012. *Life on the Hyphen: The Cuban-American Way*. Austin, TX: University of Texas Press.
Forsyth, Janice, and Audrey Giles, eds. 2013. *Aboriginal Peoples and Sport in Canada: Historical Foundations and Contemporary Issues*. Vancouver: UBC Press.
Friedan, Betty. 1963. *The Feminine Mystique*. New York: Norton.
Fukuyama, Francis. 2002. *The End of History and the Last Man*. New York: Free Press.
Gartner, Lloyd. 2001. *History of the Jews in Modern Times*. Oxford: Oxford University Press.
Gatrell, Peter. 2019. *The Unsettling of Europe: How Migration Reshaped a Continent*. London: Basic Books.
Gay, Ruth. 2002. *Safe Among the Germans: Liberated Jews after World War II*. New Haven: Yale University Press.
Gemie, Sharif. 2010. *French Muslims: New Voices in Contemporary France*. Cardiff: University of Wales Press.
Gentleman, Amelia. 2019. *The Windrush Betrayal: Exposing the Hostile Environment*. London: Guardian Faber.
Gerber, David. 2011. *American Immigration: A Very Short Introduction*. Oxford: Oxford University Press.
Gerstle, Gary. 2022. *The Rise and Fall of the Neoliberal Order*. Oxford: Oxford University Press.
Ghodsee, Kristen. 2019. *Second World Second Sex: Socialist Women's Activism and Global Solidarity during the Cold War*. London: Duke University Press.
Giddens, Anthony. 1994. *The Consequences of Modernity*. Cambridge: Polity.
Gildea, Robert. 2019. *Empires of the Mind: The Colonial Past and the Politics of the Present*. Cambridge: Cambridge University Press.
Gilroy, Paul, ed. 2000. *Without Guarantees. In Honour of Stuart Hall*. London: Verso.
Gold, John, and Margaret Gold. 2005. *Cities of Culture: Staging International Festivals and the Urban Agenda, 1851–2000*. Aldershot: Ashgate.
Gold, John, and Margaret Gold, eds. 2011. *Olympic Cities: City Agendas, Planning and the World's Games, 1896–2016*. Abingdon: Routledge.
Goldblatt, David. 2017. *The Games: A Global History of the Olympics*. London: Norton.
Gooch, Graham. 1986. *Out of the Wilderness*. London: Grafton.
Goodwin, Matthew. 2023. *Values, Voices and Virtue: The New British Politics*. London: Penguin.
Grandits, Hanes, and Karin Taylor, eds. 2010. *Yugoslavia's Sunny Side: A History of Tourism in Socialism (1950s to 1980s)*. Budapest: CEU Press.
Grant, Nicholas. 2017. *Winning Our Freedoms Together: African Americans & Apartheid, 1945–1960*. Chapel Hill, NC: University of North Carolina Press.
Grant, Susan. 2012. *Physical Culture and Sport in Soviet Society: Propaganda, Acculturation and Transformation in the 1920s and 1930s*. Abingdon: Routledge.
Gray, Fred. 2006. *Designing the Seaside: Architecture, Society and Nature*. London: Reaktion.
de Grazia, Victoria. 2005. *Irresistible Empire: America's Advance through 20th Century Europe*. Ann Arbor, MI: University of Michigan Press.
Greer, Germaine. 1970. *The Female Eunuch*. London: MacGibbon & Kee.

Gregory, Stephen. 2006. *The Devil Behind the Mirror: Globalization and Politics in the Dominican Republic*. Berkeley, CA: University of California Press.
Guha, Ramachandra. 2000. *Environmentalism: A Global History*. Harlow: Longman.
Guoqi, Xu. 2008. *Olympic Dreams: China and Sports, 1895–2008*. London: Harvard University Press.
Haddow, Robert. 1997. *Pavilions of Plenty: Exhibiting American Culture Abroad in the 1950s*. Washington, DC: Smithsonian.
Hammerton, A. James., and Alistair Thomson. 2005. *Ten Pound Poms: Australia's Invisible Migrants*. Manchester: Manchester University Press.
Hampton, Janie. 2008. *The Austerity Olympics: When the Games Came to London in 1948*. London: Aurum.
Hannam, June. 2011. *Feminism*. London: Taylor and Francis.
Hannerz, Ulf. 1996. *Transnational Connections: Culture, People, Places*. London: Routledge.
Hansen, Randall. 2000. *Citizenship and Immigration in Post-war Britain: The Institutional Origins of a Multicultural Nation*. Oxford: Oxford University Press.
Hardt, Michael, and Antonio Negri. 2001. *Empire*. Cambridge, MA: Harvard University Press.
Hayton, Bill. 2010. *Vietnam: Rising Dragon*. London: Yale University Press.
Heller, Alfred. 1999. *World's Fairs and the End of Progress*. Corte Maderia, CA: World's Fairs Inc.
Hillary, Edmund. 1999. *View from the Summit*. London: BCA.
Hixson, Walter. 1998. *Parting the Curtain: Propaganda, Culture and the Cold War*. New York: St Martins Griffin.
Hochschild, Adam. 1999. *King Leopold's Ghost: A Story of Greed, Terror and Heroism in Colonial Africa*. London: Macmillan.
Hochstetler, Kathryn, and Margaret Keck. 2007. *Greening Brazil: Environmental Activism in State and Society*. Durham, NC: Duke University Press.
Hogan, Michael. 1987. *The Marshall Plan: America, Britain and the Reconstruction of Western Europe, 1947–52*. Cambridge: Cambridge University Press.
Hollengreen, Laura. 2014. *Meet Me at The Fair: A World's Fair Reader*. Pittsburgh: Carnegie Mellon Press.
Horten, Gerd. 2020. *Don't Need No Thought Control: Western Culture in East Germany and the Fall of the Berlin Wall*. Oxford: Berghahn.
Hosking, Richard. 2005. *Authenticity in the Kitchen: Proceedings of the Oxford Symposium on Food and Cookery, 2005*. Totnes: Prospect Books.
Huang, Michelle Ying Ling. 2011. *Beyond Boundaries: East and West Cross-Cultural Encounters*. Newcastle-upon-Tyne: Cambridge Scholars Publishing.
Hudson, Simon, ed. 2002. *Sport and Adventure Tourism*. London: Taylor & Francis.
Hunt, Tristram. 2010. *The Frock-Coated Communist: The Life and Times of the Original Champagne Socialist*. London: Penguin.
Huntington, Samuel, and P. 2004. *Who Are We? The Challenges to America's National Identity*. London: Simon and Schuster.
Issawi, Charles. 1998. *Cross-Cultural Encounters and Conflicts*. Oxford: Oxford University Press.
Jain, Devaki. 2005. *Women, Development and the UN: A Sixty Year Quest for Equality and Justice*. Bloomington, IN: Indiana University Press.
Jobs, Richard Ivan. 2017. *Backpack Ambassadors: How Youth Integrated Europe*. Chicago, IL: University of Chicago Press.

Josephson, Paul, et al. 2013. *An Environmental History of Russia*. Cambridge: Cambridge University Press.
Judt, Tony. 2007. *Postwar: A History of Europe Since 1945*. London: Pimlico.
Jupp, James. 2002. *From White Australia to Woomera: The Story of Australian Immigration*. Cambridge: Cambridge University Press.
Kargon, Robert, et al. 2015. *World's Fair on the Eve of War: Science, Technology & Modernity, 1937–1942*. Pittsburgh: University of Pittsburgh Press.
Kaufman, Eric. 2018. *Whiteshift: Populism, Immigration and the Future of White Majorities*. London: Allen Lane.
Kaushal, Neeraj. 2019. *Blaming Immigrants: Nationalism and the Economies of Global Movement*. New York: Columbia University Press.
Keck, Margaret, and Kathryn Sikkink. 1998. *Activists Beyond Borders: Advocacy Networks in International Politics*. New York: Cornell University Press.
Kenneally, Rhona, and Johanne Sloan, eds. 2010. *Expo 67: Not Just a Souvenir*. Toronto: University of Toronto Press.
Kennedy, John F. 2008, [1958]. *A Nation of Immigrants*. New York: Harper.
Khan, Yasmin. 2017. *The Great Partition: The Making of India and Pakistan*. London: Yale University Press.
Klein, Naomi. 2017. *No is Not Enough*. London: Haymarket Books.
Koenker, Diane. 2013. *Club Red: Vacation Travel and the Soviet Dream*. Ithaca, NY: Cornell University Press.
Koenker, Diane, and Anne Gorusch. 2013. *The Socialist Sixties: Crossing Borders in the Second World*. Bloomington, IN: Indiana University Press.
Koram, Kojo. 2022. *Uncommon Wealth: Britain and the Aftermath of Empire*. London: John Murray.
Kuisel, Richard. 1993. *Seducing the French: The Dilemma of Americanization*. Berkeley, CA: University of California Press.
Kynaston, David. 2009. *Family Britain 1951–57*. London: Bloomsbury.
Large, David Clay. 2012. *Munich 1972: Tragedy, Terror and Triumph at the Olympic Games*. London: Rowman and Littlefield.
Le Pen, Jean-Marie. 1984. *Les Français D'abord*. Neuilly-sur-Seine: Michel Lafon.
Legrain, Phillipe. 2004. *Immigrants: Your Country Needs Them*. London: Abacus.
Lenskyj, Helen. 2002. *The Best Olympics Ever?: Social Impacts of Sydney 2000*. Albany, NY: State of New York University Press.
Lenskyj, Helen. 2008. *Olympic Industry Resistance: Challenging Olympic Power and Propaganda*. Albany, NY: State of New York University Press.
Levandai, Paul. 2018. *Orbán: Hungary's Strongman*. Oxford: Oxford University Press.
Lodge, Tom. 2011. *Sharpeville: An Apartheid Massacre and its Consequences*. Oxford: Oxford University Press.
Lovelock, James. 1979. *Gaia: A New Look at the Earth*. Oxford: Oxford University Press.
Lovelock, James. 2006. *The Revenge of Gaia: Why the Earth Is Fighting Back – and How We Can Still Save Humanity*. London: Allen Lane.
MacAloon, John J. 2008. *This Great Symbol: Pierre de Coubertin and the Origins of the Modern Olympic Games*. New York: Routledge.
MacCannell, Dean. 1989 [1976]. *The Tourist: A New Theory of the Leisure Class*. New York: Schoen.
MacKay, Finn. 2015. *Radical Feminism: Feminist Activism in Movement*. Basingstoke: Macmillan.

MacDonald, Sharon. 1998. *The Politics of Display: Museums, Science, Culture*. London: Taylor and Francis.
Maddox, Richard. 2004. *The Best of All Possible Islands: Seville's Universal Exposition, the New Spain, and the New Europe*. Albany, NY: Suny Press.
Mair, George. 1960. *Destination Moscow*. London: Herbert Jenkins.
Maloney, Barbara, and Jennifer Nelson, eds. 2017. *Women's Activism and "Second Wave" Feminism: Transnational Histories*. London: Bloomsbury.
Mandela, Nelson. 1994. *Long Walk to Freedom: Autobiography of Nelson Mandela*. London: Little Brown.
Mann, Michael. 2013. *The Sources of Social Power: Volume 4, Globalizations, 1945–2011*. Cambridge: Cambridge University Press.
Mariness, David. 2008. *Rome 1960: The Olympics that Changed the World*. New York: Simon and Schuster.
Marks, Robert B. 2017. *China: An Environmental History*. London: Rowman & Littlefield.
Marsili, Lorenzo, and Niccolo Milanese. 2018. *Citizens of Nowhere: How Europe Can be Saved from Itself*. London: Zed.
Matthews, Gordon. 2000. *Global Culture/Individual Identity: Searching for Home in the Cultural Supermarket*. London: Routledge.
May, Peter. 2009. *The Rebel Tours: Cricket's Crisis of Consciousness*. Cheltenham: Sportsbooks.
McNeil, J.R., and Erin Maudlin. 2012. *A Companion to Global Environmental History*. London: Routledge.
Milward, Alan. 1984. *The Reconstruction of Western Europe 1945–51*. London: Routledge.
Mirowski, Phillip. 2014. *Never Let a Good Crisis Go To Waste*. London: Verso.
Morgan, Robin. 2016 [1984]. *Sisterhood is Global: The International Women's Movement Anthology*. Open Road Media.
Morris, Michael, and Baron Killanin. 1983. *My Olympic Years*. New York: Morrow.
Nesbitt, Francis Njubi. 2004. *Race for Sanctions: African Americans Against Apartheid, 1946–1994*. Bloomington, IN: Indiana University Press.
Ngai, Mai. 2004. *Impossible Subjects: Illegal Aliens and the Making of Modern American*. Princeton, NJ: Princeton University Press.
Nilsen, Sarah. 2011. *Projecting America, 1958: Film and Cultural Diplomacy at the Brussels World's Fair*. Jefferson, NC: McFarland & Co.
Nyaunpane, Gyan, and Timothy Dallen, eds. *Tourism and Development in the Himalaya: Social, Environmental and Economic Forces*. London: Taylor & Francis.
Olcott, Jocelyn. *International Women's Year: The Greatest Consciousness Raising Event in History*. Oxford: Oxford University Press.
Olusoga, David. 2016. *Black and British: A Forgotten History*. London: Pan Macmillan.
O'Neil, Maggie. 2010. *Asylum, Migration and Community*. London: Polity.
Orchowski, Margaret Sands. 2015. *The Law that Changed the Face of America: The Immigration and Nationality Act of 1965*. Rowman and Littlefield.
Oudenampsen, Merjin. 2020. London. *The Rise of the New Dutch Right: An Intellectual History of the Rightward Shift in Dutch Politics*. Taylor and Francis.
Pack, Sasha D. 2006. *Tourism and Dictatorship: Europe's Peaceful Invasion of Franco's Spain*. New York: Springer.

Patu, and Antje Schrupp. 2017. *A Brief History of Feminism*, Trans. Sophie Lewis. Cambridge, MA: MIT Press.
Paul, Kathleen. 1997. *Whitewashing Britain: Race and Citizenship in the Postwar Era*. New York: Cornell University Press.
Perry, Elizabeth, ed. 2000. *Chinese Society: Change, Conflict and Resistance*. Abingdon: Routledge.
Persels, Jeff, ed. 2012. *The Environment in Francophone Literature and Film*. Amsterdam: Rodopi.
Peterson del Mar, David. 2006. *Environmentalism*. Harlow: Longman.
Phillips, Timothy. 2022. *The Curtain and the Wall: A Modern Journey Along Europe's Cold War Border*. London: Granta.
Pieterse, Jan Nederveen. 2009. *Globalization and Culture: Global Mélange*, 2nd ed. Plymouth: Rowman & Littlefield.
Pilkington, Hilary. 1997. *Migration, Displacement and Identity in Post-Soviet Russia*. Abingdon: Routledge.
Polian, Pavel. 2004. *Against their Will: The History and Geography of Forced Migrations in the USSR*. Budapest: CEU Press.
Posvic, Bodhan, ed. 1958. *La Tchécoslovaquie a Bruxelles 58: Les Journées Nationales Tchécoslovaques à l'Expo 23–24 Juilet 1958*. Amsterdam: Hieremann.
Price, Harry. 1955. *The Marshall Plan and its Meaning*. Ithaca, NY: Cornell University Press.
Price, Monroe, and Daniel Dayan, eds. 2008. *Owning The Olympics: Narrative of the New China*. Chicago, IL: University of Michigan Press.
Rachel, Daniel. 2016. *Walls Come Tumbling Down: The Music and Politics of Rock against Racism, 2 Tone and Red Wedge*. London: Picador.
Richards, Trevor. 1999. *Dancing on Our Bones: New Zealand, South Africa, Rugby and Racism*. Wellington: Bridget Williams Books.
Richardson, Dave. 2016. *Let's Go: A History of Package Holidays and Escorted Tours*. Stroud: Amberley.
Riordan, Jim, and Arnd Kruger, eds. 1999. *The International Politics of Sport in the Twentieth Century*. London: Taylor and Francis.
Roces, Mina, and Louise Edwards, eds. 2010. *Women's Movements in Asia: Feminism and Transnational Activism*. London: Taylor and Francis.
Rosenburg, Jerry, M. 2012. *The Concise Encyclopaedia of the Great Recession 2007–2012*. Plymouth: Scarecrow Press.
Rushdie, Salman. 1988. *The Satanic Verses*. London: Penguin.
Sahadeo, Jeff. 2019. *Voices from the Edge: Southern Migrants in Leningrad and Moscow*. Ithaca, NY: Cornell University Press.
Said, Edward W. 1978. *Orientalism*. New York: Pantheon Books.
Samuel, Lawrence. 2010. *The End of the Innocence: The 1964–1965 New York World's Fair*. New York: Syracuse University Press.
Sandbrook, Dominic. 2005. *Having it So Good: A History of Britain from the Suez to the Beatles*. London: Abacus.
Sassen, Saskia. 1993. *Guests and Aliens*. New York: Norton.
Saunier, Pierre-Yves. 2013. *Transnational History*. London: Bloomsbury.
Scarman, Lord. 1982. *The Scarman Report: The Brixton Disorders, 10–12 April 1981*. London: Pelican.
Schiller, Kay, and Christopher Young. 2010. *The 1972 Munich Olympics and the Making of Modern Germany*. Berkeley, CA: University of California Press.

Schofield, Camilla. 2013. *Enoch Powell and the Making of Postcolonial Britain.* Cambridge: Cambridge University Press.
Selvon, Samuel. 1956. *The Lonely Londoners.* London: Longmans.
Sewell, Tony, et al. 2021. *Commission on Race and Ethnic Disparities: The Report* London: HM Stationery Office.
Shindler, Colin. 2020. *Barbed Wire and Cucumber Sandwiches: The Controversial South African Tour of 1970.* London: Pitch Publishing.
Siegelbaum, Lewis, and Leslie Page Moch. 2014. *Broad is My Native Land: Repertoires and Regimes of Migration in Russia's Twentieth Century.* New York: Cornell University Press.
Skinner, Rob. 2010. *The Foundations of Anti-Apartheid: Liberal Humanitarians and Transnational Activists in Britain and the United States, c.1919–64.* Basingstoke: Palgrave.
Slobodian, Quinn. 2018. *Globalists: The End of Empire and the Birth of Neoliberalism.* Cambridge, MA: Harvard University Press.
Smith, Anthony. 2007. *National and Nationalism in a Global Era.* Cambridge: Polity.
Smith, Terry. 2020. *Whitelash: Unmasking White Grievance at the Ballot Box.* Cambridge: Cambridge University Press.
Sobczak, Michael. 2010. *American Attitudes Toward Immigrants and Immigration Policy.* El Paso, TX: LFB Scholarly Publishing.
Spaak, Paul-Henri., et al. 1968. *Man and His World: Noranda Lectures 1967.* Toronto: University of Toronto Press.
Stradling, David and Richard Stradling. 2015. *Where the River Burned: Carl Stokes and the Struggle to Save Cleveland.* Cornell University Press.
Sudjic, Deyan. 2022. *Stalin's Architect: Power and Survival in Moscow.* London: Thames and Hudson.
Talbot, Ian, and Gurharpal Singh. 2009. *The Partition of India.* Cambridge: Cambridge University Press.
Thompson, Leonard. 2001. *The History of South Africa.* New Haven, NY: Yale University Press.
Thorn, Hakan. 2006. *Anti-Apartheid and the Emergence of a Global Civil Society.* Basingstoke: Palgrave Macmillan.
Tirman, John. 2004. *The Maze of Fear: Security and Migration after 9/11.* New York: New Press.
Tomizawa, Roy. 2019. *1964, The Greatest Year in Japanese History: How the Tokyo Olympics Symbolized Japan's Miraculous Rise from the Ashes.* Carson City, NV: Lioncrest.
Tomlinson, Alan, and Christopher Young, eds. 2006. *National Identity and Global Sports Events: Culture, Politics, and Spectacle in the Olympics and Football World Cup.* Albany, NY: State University of New York Press.
Tooze, Adam. 2019. *Crashed: How a Decade of Financial Crises Changed the World.* London: Penguin.
Turner, Tom. 2015. *David Brower: The Making of the Environmental Movement.* Berkeley, CA: University of California Press.
Uekotter, Frank. 2014. *The Greenest Nation?: A New History of German Environmentalism.* Cambridge, MA: MIT Press.
Urry, John. 1990. *The Tourist Gaze.* London: Sage.
Vleck, Van. 2013. *Empire of the Air: Aviation and the American Ascendency.* Cambridge, MA: Harvard University Press.

Washington State Department of Commerce & Economic Development. 1962. *Seattle World's Fair: Official Souvenir Program*.
Weber, Patrick, and Baudouin Deville. *Sourire '58*. Brabant: Editions Anspach.
Weight, Richard. 2002. *Patriots: National Identity in Britain 1940–2000*. London: Macmillan.
Weiner, Douglas R. 1999. *A Little Corner of Freedom: Russian Nature Protection from Stalin to Gorbachev*. Berkeley, CA: University of California Press.
West, Darrell. 2010. *Brain Gain: Rethinking U. S. Immigration Policy*. Washington, DC: Brookings Institution Press.
White, Anne. 2010. *Polish Families and Migration Since EU Accession*. London: Policy.
Wilke, Manfred. 2014. *The Path to the Berlin Wall: Critical Stages in the History of Divided Germany*. Berlin: Berghahn.
Williams, Elizabeth M. 2017. *The Politics of Race in Britain and South Africa: Black British Solidarity and the Anti-Apartheid Struggle*. London: Tauris.
Wills, Clair. 2017. *Lovers and Strangers: An Immigrant History of Post-War Britain*. London: Penguin.
Winter, Tim, ed. 2012. *Shanghai Expo: An International Forum on the Future of Cities*. London: Taylor and Francis.
Zahra, Tara. 2016. *The Great Departure: Mass Migration from Eastern Europe and the Making of the Modern World*. London: Norton.
Zelko, Frank. 2013. *Make it a Green Peace: The Rise of a Countercultural Environmentalism*. Oxford: Oxford University Press.
Zuelow, Eric. 2016. *A History of Modern Tourism*. London: Palgrave.

Journal Articles

Abel, Jessamyn. 2012. Japan's Sporting Diplomacy: The 1964 Tokyo Olympiad. *The International History Review*. 34 (2): 203–220.
Armstrong, Elisabeth. 2016. 'Before Bandung: The Anti-Imperialist Movement in Asia and the Women's International Democratic Federation.' *Signs: Journal of Women and Culture in Society*. 41.2: 305–331.
Barnes, Carolyn and Simon Jackson. 'Creature of Circumstance: Australia's Pavilion at Expo '70 and Changing International Relations.' *Proceedings of the XXIV Conference of the Society of Architectural Historians Australia and New Zealand*. (2007).
Battilani, Patrizia, and Francesca Fauri. 2009. The Rise of a Service-based Economy and its Transformation: Seaside Tourism and the Case of Rimini. *Journal of Tourism History*. 1 (1): 27–48.
Bingham, Adrian. 2013. "The Monster"?: The British Press and Nuclear Culture, 1945-early 1960s. *British Society for the History of Science*. 45 (4): 609–624.
Bodlos, Anita, and Carolina Plescia. 2018. The 2017 Austrian Snap Election: A Shift Rightward. *West European Politics*. 41 (6): 1354–1363.
Bonfiglioli, Chaira. 2016. 'The First UN World Conference on Women (1975) as a Cold War Encounter: Recovering Anti-Imperialist Non-Aligned and Socialist Genealogies.' *Filozofija Drustovo*, 27.3: 521–541.
Bourne, Jenny. 2013. '"May we bring harmony"? Thatcher's legacy on "race"'. *Race and Class*. 55 (1): 87–91.
Brewster, Keith. 2010. Teaching Mexicans how to behave: Public education on the eve of the Olympics. *Bulletin of Latin American Research*. 29: 46–62.

Breyfogle, Nicholas. 2015. At the Watershed: 1958 and the beginnings of Lake Baikal Environmentalism. *The Slavonic and East European Review.* 93 (1): 147–180.

Broinowski, Alison. 1995. 'Culture and Tourism.' *Media International Australia.* 22–26.

Buchanan, Rachel. 2002. The Home Front Hostess, housewife and home in Olympic Melbourne, 1956. *Journal of Australian Studies.* 26 (72): 201–209.

Buckley, Peter, J. and Stephen F. Witt. 1987. 'The International Tourism Market in Eastern Europe.' *The Services Industries Journal.* 7.1.

Bui, Huong T, et al. 2013. 'The "Imagined West" of young independent travellers from Asia.' *Annals of Leisure Research.* 16.2: 130–148.

Burkett, Jodie. 2012. The Campaign for Nuclear Disarmament and Changing Attitudes Towards the Earth in the Nuclear Age. *British Journal for the History of Science.* 45 (4): 625–639.

Cabezas, Amelia. 2008. 'Tropical Blues: Tourism and Social Exclusion in the Dominican Republic.' *Latin American Perspectives.* 35.3.

Carmi, Udi, and Orr Levental. 2019. Ambassadors in Track Suits: The Public Relations Function of Israeli Delegations to the Olympic Games during the State's First Decade. *Sport History Review.* 50: 17–37.

Conterio, Johanna. 2018 '"Our Black Sea Coast": The Sovietisation of the Black Sea Littoral Under Khrushchev and the Problem of Overdevelopment.' *Kritika: Explorations n Russian and Eurasian History.* 19.2: 327–61.

Correa-Martinez, Carlos et al. 2020. 'A Pandemic in Times of Global Tourism: Superspreading and Exportation of Covid-19 cases from a Ski Area in Austria.' *Journal of Clinical Microbiology.* 58.6.

Crenshaw, Kimberlé. 'Demarginalizing the Intersection of Race and Sex: A Black Feminist Critique of Antidiscrimination Doctrine, Feminist Theory and Antiracist Politics.' *University of Chicago Legal Forum.* 1.8 (1989).

Davison, Graeme. 1997. Welcoming the World: The 1956 Olympic Games and Representation of Melbourne. *Australian Historical Studies.* 27 (109): 64–76.

Delanty, Gerard. 2011. Cultural diversity, democracy and the prospects of cosmopolitanism: A theory of cultural encounters. *The British Journal of Sociology.* 62 (4): 633–656.

Droubie, Paul. 2011. Phoenix Arisen: Japan as peaceful internationalist at the 1964 Tokyo Summer Olympics. *The International Journal of the History of Sport.* 28 (16): 2309–2322.

Freitag, Tilman. 1994. Enclave Tourism Development: For Whom the Benefits Roll? *Annals of Tourism Research.* 21 (3): 538–554.

Funk, Nanette. 2014. A Very Tangled Knot: Official state socialist women's organisations, women's agency and feminism in Eastern European state socialism. *European Journal of Women's Studies.* 21 (4): 344–360.

Guistino, Cathleen. 2012. Industrial Design and the Czechoslovak Pavilion at Expo '58: Artistic Autonomy, Party Control and Cold War Common Ground. *Journal of Contemporary History.* 47 (1): 185–212.

Gustafson, Seth. 2013. Displacement and the Racial State in Olympic Atlanta 1990–1996. *Southeastern Geographer.* 53 (2): 198–213.

de Haan, Francisca. 2010. 'Continuing Cold War Paradigms in Western Historiography of Transnational organisations: The case of the Women's International Democratic Federation.' *Women's History Review.* 19.4: 547:573.

Hansen, Peter. 1995. Albert Smith, the Alpine Club and the invention of mountaineering in Mid-Victorian Britain. *Journal of British Studies.* 34 (3): 300–324.
Harrison, David. 2016. Looking East but Learning from the West: Mass Tourism and Emerging Nations. *Asian Journal of Tourism Research.* 1 (2): 1–36.
Harrison, Mark. 2011. 'The Soviet Union after 1945: Economic Recovery and Political Repression.' *Past and Present.* Sup 6: 103–120.
Henderson, Simon. 2010. "Nasty Demonstrations by Negroes": The place of the Smith-Carlos Podium Salute in the Civil Rights Movement. *Bulletin of Latin American Research.* 29 (1): 78–92.
Ivey, James. 2022. "Welcome, Ali, Please Go Home": Muhammad Ali as Diplomat and African Debates on the 1980 Moscow Olympic Boycott. *African Studies Review.* 66 (2): 490–508.
Kaldor, Mary. 2004. Nationalism and Globalisation. *Nations and Nationalism.* 10: 161–177.
Korowin, Erika. 2010. '"Iceberg! Right Ahead!": (Re)discovering Chile at the 1992 Universal Exposition in Seville, Spain.' *Studies in Latin American Popular Culture.* 28: 48–63.
Krenn, Michael L. 1996. "Unfinished Business": Segregation and U.S. Diplomacy at the 1958 World's Fair. *Diplomatic History.* 20 (4): 591–612.
Kreydatus, Beth. 2008. Confronting the "Bra-Burners": Teaching Radical Feminism With a Case Study. *The History Teacher* 41 (4): 489–504.
Leon, Yolanda. 2007. The Impact of Tourism on Rural Livelihoods in the Dominican Republic's Coastal Areas. *Journal of Development Studies.* 43 (2): 340–359.
Lohmann, Guilherne et al. 2009. 'From Hub to Tourist Destination – An Explorative study of Singapore and Dubai's aviation-based transformation.' *Journal of Air Transport Management.* 15: 205–211.
Martin, Kevin. 2010. Presenting the "True Face of Syria" to the world: Urban disorder and civilisational anxieties at the first Damascus International Exposition. *International Journal of Middle Eastern Studies.* 42: 391–411.
McCarthy, Helen. 2015. The Diplomatic History of Global Women's Rights: The British Foreign Office and International Women's Year, 1975. *Journal of Contemporary History.* 50 (4): 833–853.
Massey, Jonathan. 2016. Buckminster Fuller's cybernetic pastoral: The United States Pavilion at Expo 67. *The Journal of Architecture.* 21 (5): 795–815.
McIntyre, Matthew. 2009. 'National Status, the 1908 Olympic Games and the English Press.' *Media History.* 15.3.
McKenzie, Brian. 2003. Creating a Tourist's Paradise: The Marshall Plan and France, 1948 to 1952. *French Politics. Culture & Society.* 21 (1): 35–54.
Nadis, Fred. 2007. Nature at Aichi World's Expo 2005. *Technology and Culture.* 48 (3): 575–581.
Nakatani, Sanae. 2015. Staging Democracy and Multiculturalism: The 1970 Osaka Exposition and the Hawai'i Pavilion. *Asian Diasporic Visual Cultures and the Americas.* 1 (3): 40–62.
Nehring, Holger. 2002. Westernization: A New Paradigm for Interpreting West European History in a Cold War Crisis. *Cold War History.* 4 (2): 175–191.
Notten, Geranda, and Keetie Roelen. 2012. A New Tool for Monitoring (Child) Poverty: Measures of Cumulative Deprivation. *Child Indicators Research.* 5 (2): 335–355.

Paul, Darel. 2004. World Cities as Hegemonic Projects: The politics of global Imagineering in Montreal. *Political Geography.* 23: 571–596.

Pederson, Sune Bechmann. 2018. Eastbound Tourism in the Cold War: The History of the Swedish Communist Travel Agency Folkturist. *Journal of Tourism History.* 10 (2): 130–145.

Péteri, György. 2012. Sites of Convergence: The USSR and Communist Eastern Europe at International Fairs Abroad and at Home. *Journal of Contemporary History.* 47 (1): 3–12.

Quaggio, Guilla. 2020. A Transatlantic Iberian Peninsula: Exhibiting the nation through the commemoration of Renaissance voyages of exploration in Spain (1992) and Portugal (1998). *Journal of Iberian and Latin American Studies.* 26 (3): 317–340.

Reid, Susan E. 2008. 'Who Will Best Whom?: Soviet Popular Reception of the American National Exhibition in Moscow, 1959.' *Kritika: Explorations in Russian and Eurasian History.* 9.4: 855–904.

Reid, Susan E. 2017. 'Cold War Cultural Transactions: Designing the USSR for the West at Brussels Expo '58.' *Design and Culture.* 9.2.

Roberts, Mike, and Ryan Moore. 2009. Peace Punks and Punks Against Racism: Resource Mobilisation and Frame Construction in the Punk Movement. *Music and Arts in Action.* 2 (1): 21–36.

Rosendorf, Neil Moses. 2006. Be El Caudillo's Guest: The Franco Regime's Quest for Rehabilitation and Dollars After World War II via the Promotion of US Tourism to Spain. *Diplomatic History.* 30 (3): 367–407.

Rutherdale, Myra, and Jim Miller. 2006. "It's Our Country": First Nations' Participation in the Indian Pavilion at Expo 67. *Journal of the Canadian Historical Association/Revue de la Societé Historique du Canada.* 17 (2): 148–173.

Şen, Faruk. 2003. The Historical Situation of Turkish Migrants in Germany. *Immigrants & Minorities.* 22 (2–3): 208–227.

Seo, Myengsoo. 2017. Architecture as Medium: The Korean Pavilion at the Montreal Expo '67. *Journal of Asian Architecture and Building Engineering.* 16 (2): 271–278.

Siegelbaum, Lewis. 2012. Sputnik Goes to Brussels: The Exhibition of a Soviet Technological Wonder. *Journal of Contemporary History.* 47 (1): 123–145.

Simpson, Tim. 2012. 'Tourist Utopias: Las Vegas, Dubai Macau.' *Asia Research Institute Working Paper.* 177.

Smits, Katherine, and Alix Jansen. 2012. Staging the Nation at Expos and World's Fairs. *National Identities.* 14 (2): 173–188.

Stanard, Matthew. 2005. Bilan du monde pour un monde plus déshumanisé: The Brussels World's Fair and Belgian Perceptions of the Congo. *European History Quarterly.* 35 (2): 367–298.

Steiner, Christian. 2010. From Heritage to Hyper-reality? Tourism destination development in the Middle East Between Petra and the Palm. *Journal of Tourism and Cultural Change.* 8 (4): 240–253.

Udovički-Selb, Danilo. 2012. Facing Hitler's Pavilion: The Uses of Modernity in the Soviet Pavilion at the 1937 Paris International Exhibition. *Journal of Contemporary History.* 47 (1): 13–47.

Weiqiang, Lin. 2015. '"Cabin Pressure": Designing Affective Atmosphere in Airline Travel.' *Transactions: Institute of British Geographers.* 40.2: 287–299.

Wilson, Sandra. 2012. Exhibiting a new Japan: The Tokyo Olympics of 1964 and Expo 70 in Osaka. *Historical Research.* 85 (227): 159–178.
Yi, Jacqueline, et al. 2022. 'Ignoring Race and Denying Racism.' *Journal of Counselling Psychology.* 70.3: 258–275.
Zhen, Wang and Ying Zheng. 2010. 'Global Concepts, Local Practices: Chinese Feminism Since the Fourth UN Conference on Women.' *Feminist Studies.* 36.1: 40–70.
Zisner, J. 2002. From Mexico to Copenhagen to Nairobi: The United Nations Decade for Women, 1975–1985. *Journal of World History.* 13 (1): 139–168.
Zovlov, Eric. 2004. Showcasing the "Land of Tomorrow" Mexico and the 1968 Olympics. *The Americas.* 61 (2): 159–188.

Newspapers, Periodicals and Broadcasts

Daily Mail
The European.
The Independent
Guardian.
Life.
New York magazine
Paris Match
Partition Voices, Ep.1 'Division', Broadcast 6 Aug 2017, BBC Radio 4
Partition Voices, Ep.2 'Aftermath', Broadcast 7 Aug 2017, BBC Radio 4
Pathe News, Archive.
SkyNews.com
Time.
UNESCO Courier.

Motion Pictures

Boden, Anna. *Mrs America.* Shiny Penney Productions.
Boyle, Danny. *The Beach.* 20th Century Fox.
Cawston, Richard. 1965. *Shellorama.* Shell Film Unit.
Cragie, Gill. 1951. *To Be A Woman.* Outlook Films.
El-Hosiani, Sally. 2022. *The Swimmers* Netflix.
Lowthorpe, Philippa. 2020. *Misbehaviour.* Walt Disney.

Index

A
Afghanistan, 44, 50, 74, 178
African National Congress (ANC), 89, 199
African Union, 11
Aichi, Expo, 2005, 151
Airtours, 74, 82
Air travel, 2, 5, 62, 63, 68, 76
Alexander, Sally, 100
Algerian War of Independence, 33
Ali, Muhammad, 178
All-India Muslim League, 23
All Russian Society for the Protection of Nature (VOOP), 108
Al Qaida, 50
American art, 134
American Express, 67
American National Exhibition, Moscow 1960, 133
Amsterdam Olympics, 1928, 159
Anti-Apartheid movement, 13, 89, 91, 93
Anti-globalisation, 1, 11, 193
Anti-Islamism, 6, 12
Anti-Russian attitudes, 6
Apartheid, 88–95, 97, 98, 167, 177, 178, 199
Apollo Eight, 112
Arab Spring, 54
Ariana Afghan Airlines, 68
Armengol, Mario, 144
Artists Against Apartheid, 97

Artists United Against Apartheid, 96
Athens Olympics, 1896, 158
Athens Olympics, 2004, 185
Atlanta Olympics, 1996, 182
Attenborough, David, 107
Australia, 15, 31, 36, 74, 96, 108, 113, 146, 152, 164, 165, 177, 183, 184
Australia, immigration, 15, 31
Australia, promotion of housewife identity, 164
Australia, treatment of Indigenous Australians, 204
Australia, White Australia Policy, 31, 164, 183
Austria, 15, 36, 53, 56
Austrian People's Party, 56
Ayatollah Khomeini, 44
Azov Battalion, Ukrainian army, 12

B
Backpackers, 77
Bali, bombing 2002, 84
Baltic nations, forced deportations from, 21
Bannon, Steve, 11
Barcelona, 84, 128, 150, 180–182
Barcelona Olympics, 1992, 187
Basque identity, 129, 148, 149
Beach Boys, The, 96
Beatles, The, 77, 80
Behnisch, Gunter, 173

Beijing Olympics, 2008, 152
Belgium, 3, 24, 25, 79, 127, 130, 136
Bengal, 23, 24, 103
Ben-Gurion, David, 20
Berlin Airlift, 1948, 69
Berlin Olympics, 1936, 160
Berlin Wall, 25, 26, 102, 140, 148
Biden, Joe, 122
Bikila, Abebe, 167
Biko, Steve, 97
Black, Cilla, 96
Blackpool, UK, 61, 62
Black Power Movement, 172
Black September, 174, 205
Blankers-Koen, Fanny, 161
Bloom, John, 73
Boeing, 63, 67
Bolsonaro, Jair, 11
Bossi-Fini Law, 2002, 47
Boycott, Geoffrey, 96
Brandt, Willy, 174, 175
Brazil, 11, 80, 118, 120, 121, 136
Brazil, tourism, 80
Breitbart, 11
Bretton Woods conference, 3
Brexit, 15, 57, 154, 196
Brexit, political violence, 15
Bristol Bus Boycott, 31
Britain, 1, 7, 10, 11, 21, 24, 27–32, 36, 42–45, 47, 52, 56, 60, 62, 63, 77, 91, 94–96, 99, 101, 108, 109, 113, 120, 126, 127, 129, 139, 144, 154, 158, 161, 162, 178, 181, 195, 196, 201, 202
British Lions, 95
British Pavilion, Montreal 1967, 143
Brixton, UK, 42
Brower, David, 117
Brundage, Avery, 167, 171, 172, 174
Brussels Expo 1958, 129, 131, 135
Bulgaria, 18, 35, 52, 70, 73, 74, 197, 198
Bund der Heimatvertriebenen und Entrechteten (League of Expellees and Deprived of Rights), 18
Bureau International des Expositions (BIE), 127
Bush, George W., 50, 53

C
Cable, Vince, 9
Cadbury Schweppes, 117
Canada, 31, 36, 141, 142, 145, 150, 176–178, 202
Canada, European identities, 142, 177
Canada, Indigenous identity, 142, 177
Cantinflas, 170
Carlos, John, 172, 204
Carmichael, Stockley, 172
Carson, Rachel, 110, 111, 200
Carter, Jimmy, 178
Carty-Williams, Candice, 30
Catalan nationalism, 149, 181
Catholicism, 44
Central Intelligence Agency, propaganda at the Olympics, 163
Ceuta, Spain, 46, 54
Charlie Hebdo, 51
Chase Manhattan, 93, 94
Chechia Pavilion, Dubai 2020, 153
Chernobyl nuclear disaster, 72
Chicago World's Fair, 1933–34, 128
Chile Pavilion, Seville 1992, 150
China, 28, 39, 74, 75, 77, 105, 115, 116, 145, 152, 176, 177, 185, 186, 198, 200, 203
China, economic growth, 33
China, emigration, 39
China, environmentalism, 107, 116, 203
China, Four Pests Campaign, 115
China, national identity, 185, 186
China, soft power, 76, 152
Chirac, Jacques, 44
Churchill, Winston, 16, 28
Circarama, 133
Civil Aeronautics Administration, 68
Clapton, Eric, 41, 97
Clash, The, 42
Clay, Cassius. *See* Ali, Muhammad
Clinton, Bill, 50
Coal Smoke Abatement Society, 109
Coca-Cola, 138, 141, 152, 157, 162, 163, 166, 181
Cold War, 6, 7, 15, 16, 26, 36, 38, 39, 46, 64, 68, 72, 76, 102, 104, 106, 123, 125, 130–132, 134, 136, 137, 139, 140, 142, 148, 162, 163, 165,

166, 176, 178, 179, 181, 194, 197, 198, 200, 201, 204
Cold War, peaceful co-existence, 7
Collett, Wayne, 175
Commonwealth, British, 27, 32, 199
Communism, collapse, 46, 74, 149
Communist nations, migration, 35, 37
Communist states, 15, 37, 52, 139, 175
Concorde, 143
Coney Island, 61
Congo, 50, 127, 136, 137, 201
Congo Pavilion, Brussels 1958, 137
Conservative Party, UK, 9, 45
Consumerism, 108, 126, 133, 201
Cornershop, 48
Cosmopolitanism, 9–11, 32, 52, 193
Covid-19, 1, 59, 192
Cox, Jo, 57
Craigie, Jill, 100
Crenshaw, Kimberlé, 107, 123
Cricket, 94–96
Croatia, 72, 80
Cuba, 45, 49, 198
Cuba, emigration from, 49
Cuba Pavilion, Montreal 1967, 144
Cultural divergence, 6
Cultural hybridity, 83, 84
Cuyahoga River, 112
Czechia, 153
Czechoslovakia, 17–20, 34, 36, 45, 71
Czechoslovakia, emigration, 34, 36
Czechoslovakia Pavilion, Brussels 1958, 135, 136
Czechoslovakia Pavilion, Montreal 1967, 144
Czechoslovakia, Soviet tourism, 71

D
Daly, Mary, 105, 106
Damascus International Fair, 153
Dammers, Jerry, 97
de Beauvoir, Simone, 99
Decolonisation, 16, 23, 38, 129, 136, 137
de Coubertin, Pierre, 157–159, 189
Democratic Republic of Congo, 145
Deng, Xiaoping, 74, 116
Disabled sports, 188

Disney, Walt, 139, 141
Displaced persons, 16, 19, 20, 27, 38
Diversity, 7, 9, 57, 149, 183, 194
D'Oliveira, Basil, 95
Dominican Republic, 81, 82, 198
Drapeau, Jean, 176
Dubai 2020, Expo, 153
Dubček, Alexander, 71
Du Bois, W.E.B., 90, 172

E
Edstrom, Sigfrid, 171
Egypt, 21, 74, 165, 173
Eiffel Tower, 61, 79, 127, 128
Eisenhower, Dwight, 133, 134
11 September 2001, terrorist attacks, 6, 50, 84, 196
Empire Windrush, 27
Enclave tourism, 82, 83
Engels, Friedrich, 62
Environmental degradation, 110, 111, 119, 120
Environmentalism, 13, 87, 88, 107, 108, 113, 118, 119, 121, 151, 153, 155
Environmentalism of the poor, 119, 120, 201
Environmental Protection Law (Sweden), 113
Equal Pay Act, 1970 (UK), 100
Estevan, Gloria, 49
Ethiopia, 173, 179
European Coal and Steel Community (ECSC), 3, 24
European Economic Community, 25, 45, 148
European empires, 2, 16, 23, 26, 136, 148, 161
European identity, 66, 67
European integration, 24
European Recovery Plan, 3
European Union, 1, 3, 9, 25, 46, 52, 80, 154, 196
European Voluntary Workers Scheme, Britain, 20
Everage, Edna. *See* Humphreys, Barry

F
Far-right politics, 53, 55

Fascism, 166
Fashion, 7, 44, 133, 136, 143
Federal German Republic (FRG), 25, 173
Federal German Republic, Olympics, 173
Festival of Britain, 1951, 129, 154
Feuchtwangen, Germany, 18
Fidesz, 55
Financial Crisis, 2008–2020s, 54
Food, 1, 7, 17, 36, 49, 63, 70, 82, 109, 125, 142, 143, 162, 163, 197, 203
Ford, 100, 140
Fortuyn, Pim, 53
France, 3, 24, 26, 33, 41, 43, 53, 54, 57, 63, 68, 94, 112, 113, 120, 127, 138, 143, 170, 194, 195, 202
France, Algerian immigration, 26, 41
France, Algerian war of independence, 33
France, Muslim population, 43
France Pavilion, Montreal 1967, 202
Franco, Francisco, 64
Fratelli d'Italia, 15
Freedom Party, 15, 56
Freeman, Cathy, 184
FRG, guest worker programmes, 25
Friedan, Betty, 99, 101, 105
Friedman, Milton, 5
Friends of Nature (China), 116, 117
Friends of the Earth, 117, 118
Front National, 41, 43, 44, 57

Germany, 3, 16, 17, 20, 21, 24–26, 36, 41, 43, 46, 47, 53, 55, 67, 113, 115, 120, 121, 158, 160, 161, 163, 173–176, 178, 194, 201
Germany, national memory, 175
Germany, Olympic teams, 174, 175
Germany, post-war expellees, 19, 194
Germany, tourists, 174
Giscard d'Estaing, Valéry, 41
Glastonbury Festival, 118
Gleneagles Agreement, 95
Globalisation, 1–5, 8–13, 15, 16, 40, 45, 47, 50, 52, 68, 81, 88, 93, 104, 107, 119, 121, 122, 126, 146, 148, 149, 152, 155, 157, 163, 180, 182, 184, 185, 190, 192–194, 200
Global Village of Beijing, 116
González, Felipe, 151
Gooch, Graham, 96
Goodness Gracious Me, 48
Gorbachev, Mikhail, 35, 45, 115
Grateful Dead, The, 145
Great Exhibition, 1851, 126, 129
Greece, 25, 34, 46, 55, 64, 66, 158, 159, 187, 197
Greece, tourism, 46, 66, 197
Green parties, 121
Greenpeace, 118, 201
Greenwashing, 111
Greer, Germaine, 100
Guernica, 129
Guinness, 162

G
Gagarin, Yuri, 139
Gatting, Mike, 96
General Electric, 140, 141
General Motors, 140
General Tso's Chicken, 49, 196
Georgia (nation), 70, 183
Georgia (USA), 182
German Democratic Republic, emigration from, 26
German Democratic Republic, Olympics, 167
German reunification, 46, 148, 202
Germans, Volga Germans, 22

H
Hackett, Roy, 31
Hain, Peter, 97
Haiti World's Fair 1949, 129
Hall, Stuart, 30
Halt All Racist Tours (HART), 95
Hanover 2000, Expo, 203
Hansen, Gracie, 141
Harrogate, 60
Hayek, Friedrich, 5
Heath, Edward, 32
Helsinki Olympics, 1952, 162, 163
Hillary, Edmund, 77
Himalaya, 76–78

Hiroshima, American destruction of, 168, 170
Hitler, Adolf, 16, 64, 160
Holocaust survivors, post-war treatment of, 163
Holt, Harold, Australian politician, 31
Hong Kong, 16, 39, 75
Hope, Bob, 100
Horizon Holidays, 63
House Un-American Activities Committee (HUAC), 102
Howard, John, 185
Howe, Darcus, 33
Humphreys, Barry, 164
Hungary, 11, 15, 16, 19, 20, 34, 36, 45, 52, 55, 56, 73, 115, 165
Hungary, refugees from, 55, 56
Hungary, uprising 1956, 36
Hurricane Charlie, 1951, 27

I
IBM, 140, 141
Immigrants, hostility to, 56
Imperialism, European, 2
India, 23, 24, 71, 74, 77, 105, 120, 161, 194
India, decolonisation from Britain, 23
Indian National Congress, 23
Integration, 3, 4, 18, 33, 46, 54, 65, 104, 193, 200
International Alliance of Women, 99
International Council of Women, 99
International Cricket Conference, 96
International Expositions, 6, 12, 13, 126, 128, 150, 154, 155, 201, 203
International Monetary Fund (IMF), 3
International Olympic Committee, 13, 95
International Refugee Organisation (IRO), 19
International Women's Suffrage Alliance, 99
International Women's Year, 102–104, 106
Intersectionality, 99, 107, 123, 124
Iran, 43, 44, 74
Irish Republic, 7
Israel, founding, 21

Israel, Jewish immigration, 20, 21
Israel, team at Helsinki 1952, 163
Italy, 1, 24, 46, 53, 57, 63, 166
Italy, emigration, 1, 25, 33, 46
Italy, national memory, 73

J
Japan, 75, 109, 145, 151, 152, 161, 167–169, 192, 202
Japan, display of art, 147
Japan, economic growth, 168
Japan, modernity, 147
Japan, national identity, 145, 146
Japan, national memory, 170
Japan Pavilion, Osaka 1964, 167
Jazz music, 132, 134
Jefferson Airplane, 145
Jewish Holocaust survivors, 20, 163
Jinah, Muhammad Ali, 23
Jobbik, Hungary, 55
Johnson, Lyndon, 143
Jones, Claudia, 30
Judo, 169, 180, 183, 204
Jurmala, Latvia, 70

K
Karelia, Finland, 19
Kayibanda, Grégoire, 145
Kazakhstan, 22, 36
Kennedy, Edward, 39
Kennedy, John F., 39, 111, 195
Khakhaleishvili, David, 183
Khrushchev, Nikita, 35, 114, 131, 137, 138, 165, 166
Killanin, Lord, 177, 179
King, Martin Luther Jr., 92, 183
King, Milton, 91
King Tribhuvan, 77
Kodak, 141
Kuoni, 74

L
Labour Party, UK, 32
Lake Baikal, 114
Laker, Freddy, 69
Las Vegas, 83

Latvia, 19, 21, 52
League of Nations, 3, 11
Leave.eu, 11
Lega Nord (Northern League), 47
Leningrad, 34, 35, 46, 72, 194
Leopold II, 127, 136
Le Pen, Jean-Marie, 41
Le Pen, Marine, 57
Lhasa, Tibet, 78
Liberal Democrats, UK, 9
Lisanevich, Boris, 77
Lithuania, 18, 19, 21, 52
Little Rock, desegregation of public schools, 134
Liverpool Pavilion, Shanghai 2010, 152
Liverpool, United Kingdom, 28, 42
London Olympics, 1948, 6, 161, 169, 203
London Olympics, 2012, 188, 189
Lord Brothers, 73
Los Angeles Olympics 1932, 160
Los Angeles Olympics 1984, 179
Lovelock, James, 112
Lübeck, Germany, 18
Lucky Dragon incident, 110
Luxembourg, 3, 24

M
Macau, 83
Macmillan, Harold, 28
Makeba, Miriam, 90
Malta, 52
Mandela, Nelson, 89, 90, 92, 93, 96–98, 108, 199
Mangrove Restaurant, London, 32
Marcellin-Fontanet Circular, 1972, 41
Marseilles Defence Committee, 41
Marshall Islands, 110
Marshall Plan, 3
Marx, Karl, 126
Marylebone Cricket Club (MCC), 96
Matthews, Vincent, 175
May, Theresa, 9, 154
McCarthy, Joseph, 39
McDonalds, 179
Melbourne Olympics 1956, 37
Melilla, Spain, 46, 54
Mendes, Chico, 107, 120, 201

Mercedes Benz, 128
Mexico City Olympics, 1968, 189, 191
Mexico, national identity, 171
Miami, 49, 50
Middle East, 21, 55, 58, 68
Midnight Oil, 185, 204
Migration, 2, 5, 9, 12, 13, 15, 16, 20, 21, 23–28, 32, 34, 35, 37–40, 44–47, 49, 50, 52–55, 57, 58, 193–196
Migration, during the economic miracle, 24
Milan Expo, 2015, 128
Mini Cooper, 144
Mini-skirts, 171
Miss America, 100
Miss World, 100
Monroe, Marilyn, 143
Mont Pelerin Society, 5
Montreal Expo 1967, 176, 202
Montreal Olympics, 1976, 176
Moreno, Mario, 170
Morgan, Robin, 100, 106
Morocco, Emigration, 46
Moscow, 34, 35, 46, 71, 72, 114, 133, 138, 160, 175, 179, 194
Moscow Olympics, 1980, 178
Mosely, Oswald, 28
Mountaineering, 77
Mount Everest, 77
Mouvement des Travailleurs Arabes (Arab Workers Movement, France), 43
Mujahedeen, 44
Munich Olympics, 1972, 173, 174, 204
Munich Olympics, 1972, terrorism, 173
Muslim migrants to France, 41, 43, 44
Muslim populations in Europe, 43
Mussolini, Benito, 64, 165, 167

N
Nagy, Imre, 36
Nationalism, 10–12, 130, 148, 154, 160, 179, 194, 204
National Party (South Africa), 13, 94, 95, 98
NATO, 11, 68
Nazi Germany, 12, 128

Neo-liberalism, 4, 5, 47, 122
Nepal, 77, 78
Netherlands, 3, 24, 26, 36, 41, 53, 54, 113, 165, 195
Netherlands, Moluccan immigration, 26
Netherlands, Surinamese immigration, 26
New Zealand, 31, 94, 177, 178
New Zealand, rugby teams, 94, 177
Nike, 157, 184
Nixon, Richard, 138, 147
Noranda Mines, 141
Norgay, Tenzing, 77
Northern Ireland, 7, 154
Notting Hill, riots 1958, 29, 30
Nuclear testing, 118

O

Obama, Barack, 57
Ogale, 119
Ogoni, 119
Oil shocks 1970s, 41
Olympic Games, 6, 13, 155, 158, 160, 162, 171, 191
Olympic Games, exclusion of women, 159, 162
Olympic Games, social cleansing, 157, 187
Olympic Project for Human Rights, 171, 172
Olympics, anti-Olympic protests, 190, 191
Orbán, Victor, 55
Ordaz, Gustavo, 170
Osaka, Expo 1970, 145, 202
Owens, Jesse, 160, 161, 172, 175

P

Pakistan, founding of, 23
Palestinian Liberation Organisation (PLO), 174
Pan-Africanist Congress (PAC), 89
Pan-American Airlines, 68
Paralympics, 169, 188
Paris Exposition, 1889, 127, 128
Paris Olympics, 1924, 160
Paris World's Fair, 1937, 128, 129

Party for Freedom, 53
Pasqua, Charles, 44
Pass Laws (South Africa), 88, 89
Patkar, Medha, 120
Pavilion of Youth, Montreal 1967, 145
Penan, 119
Pepsi Cola, 138
Pesticide use, 110, 111
Picasso, Pablo, 129
Poland, 11, 16–20, 34, 45, 47, 52, 115
Political activism, 5, 32, 123
Political Islam, 43, 44
Pollution, 108, 109, 113, 116, 117, 119, 179, 200
Port El Kantaoui massacre, 84
Portugal, emigration, 34
Potsdam Conference, 17
Powell, Enoch, 28, 32, 41, 42
Prague Spring, 71, 144
Protestantism, 7, 8, 18
Punjab, 23, 24
Puskas, Ferenc, 37, 165

Q

Queen, 96, 181

R

Rabanne, Paco, 143
Racism, 28, 32, 35, 42, 48, 91, 95, 98, 189
Railway travel, 2, 60, 61, 76
Raitz, Vladimir, 63
Reagan, Ronald, 94, 97
Reclaim the Night, 101
Red Army. *See* Soviet Army
Red Army Faction, 174
Refugees, European post-war, 19
Reggae, 30, 42, 196
Republic of China (Taiwan), 139, 167, 176
Republic of China (Taiwan), Olympic teams, 177
Republic of China (Taiwan) pavilion, Seattle 1962, 139
Rhodesia, 172, 173
Rimini, 62
Rio Olympics, 2016, 188

228 INDEX

Road travel, 2
Roberts, J. Col., 77
Robertson, Pat, 51
Rock Against Racism, 42, 97
Romania, 16, 35, 52, 70, 73
Rome Olympics, 1960, 165
Rugby, 94, 95, 177
Rushdie, Salman, 44
Russia, 1, 11, 19, 22, 46, 61, 108, 114, 186
Russian minorities, 45

S
Salvini, Matteo, 57
Samaranch, Juan Antonio, 182, 184
Sanyo, 146
Saudi Arabia, 43, 50
Saunders, Red, 42
Scarman Report, 42
Scouts, 145
Seattle International Exposition, 1962, 139
Seattle Space Needle, 139
Selassie, Hailie, 173
Selector, the, 19, 42
Selvon, Sam, 30
Seoul Olympics, 1988, 180
Seville Expo, 1992, 181, 202
Shanghai Expo, 2010, 152
Sharm El-Sheikh, 74
Sharpeville massacre, 89, 91, 93, 167
Shell Oil, 111, 119
Sierra Club, 108, 112, 117
Sinatra, Frank, 96
Singapore, 16, 69, 75, 167
Singapore Airlines, 69, 197
Ska music, 30, 42
Skoda, 136
Skytrain, 69
Slovakia, 52
Smith, Tommy, 172
Sochi, 70, 186
South Africa, 88–98, 172, 173, 177, 199
South Africa, Olympics, 95
South American identities, 149
South-East Asia, 145
South Korea Pavilion, Montreal 1967, 145

Soviet army, 165
Soviet Union, 4, 17, 18, 45, 72, 108, 115, 132, 133, 136, 139, 142, 144, 160, 165, 176
Soviet Union, Asian identity, 147
Soviet Union, dissolution, 45
Soviet Union, environmental campaigning, 108, 114, 115
Soviet Union, fashion, 138
Soviet Union Pavilion, Osaka 1964, 148
Soviet Union, tourism, 198
Spaak, Paul Henri, 141
Space exploration, 140
Spain, bull fighting, 65, 69, 197
Spain, colonial past, 203
Spain, conservative attitude to tourism, 197
Spain, constituent nations, 25
Spain, emigration, 33, 46
Spain, national identity, 65, 69, 148
Spain, tourism, 64, 65
Spas, 60, 61, 70
Special Committee Against Apartheid (UN), 94
Specials, the, 42, 97
Sputnik, 132, 139
Stalin, 21, 22, 34, 70, 71, 108, 114, 128, 133, 135, 163
Status Quo, 96
Steel Pulse, 42
Steinem, Gloria, 100, 101
Stephenson, Paul, 31
Stockholm 1912 Olympics, 159
Stop the Seventy, 96
Suez crisis, 165
Surinam, 26, 195
Sus laws, 42
Sweden, 19, 55, 113, 139, 159
Switzerland, 24, 41, 165
Sydney Olympics 2000, 188
Syrian civil war, 153, 188

T
Taekwondo, 180
Tambo, Dali, 97
Thailand, 74, 136
Thatcher, Margaret, 42, 45, 97
Thomson holidays, 72

Thunberg, Greta, 107
Tlatelolco Massacre, 170, 171
Tokyo Olympics, 1964, 204
Tokyo Olympics, 2020, 1
Torrey Canyon disaster, 111
Tourism, 5, 59, 60, 62–68, 70, 71, 73, 75–85, 125, 151, 181, 196–199
Tourism, Americans to Europe, 5, 75, 197
Tourism, Asian travel in West, 76
Tourism before twentieth century, 62, 76, 77, 83
Tourism, Cold War, 63, 64, 76
Tourism, resistance to, 58
Tourism, sex work, 82
Transatlanticism, 62, 68, 69, 81, 148
Transnationalism, 8, 10
Treaty of Rome, 25, 45
Trudeau, Pierre, 176, 177
Truman, Harry, 63
Trump, Donald, 1, 12, 57, 67, 122, 200
Turkey, 25, 56, 68
Turkey, emigration from, 18, 25, 56
Two-Tone, 42, 196

U
Ukraine, 1, 12, 19, 21, 22, 46, 115
Unboxed: Creativity in the UK, 154
UN Climate Change Conference (Paris) 2015, 122
UN Conference on Climate Change (Kyoto) 1997, 119
UNESCO, 75
Unfinished Business, 134
United Kingdom, Asian immigration, 32
United Kingdom, attitude to immigrants, 196
United Kingdom, Caribbean migration to, 26, 27, 30
United Kingdom, Chinese immigration, 28
United Kingdom, Commonwealth immigration, 27, 28, 32
United Kingdom, hostility to immigrants, 56
United Kingdom, Irish migration to, 28
United Kingdom, Muslim population, 23

United Kingdom, National Health Service, 28, 30
United Kingdom, Polish immigration, 27
United Kingdom, post-colonial migration to, 15
United Nations (UN), 3, 64
United Nations Conference on the Human Environment, 1972, 115
United Nations Relief and Rehabilitation Agency (UNRRA), 19
USA, Asian Immigration, 40
USA, attitudes towards immigrants, 50, 196
USA, Bracero programme, 38
USA, development of national airlines, 69, 197
USA, European immigration, 195
USA, Mexican migrants, 57
USA, Muslim population, 51
USA Pavilion Aichi 2005, 152
USA, Pavilion, Montreal 1867, 176
USA, Pavilion, Osaka 1964, 141
USA Pavilion, Seville 1992, 149
USA, race relations, 134, 202
USA, space technology, 139, 143
USA, undocumented migration, 38
USSR, release of Gulag prisoners, 35
USSR, Special Settlement programme, 21, 22
USSR, Virgin Lands Campaign, 35
US State Department, 162

V
Venice, 62, 83, 152
Vichy, 61
Vietnam, 45, 71, 75, 139, 143, 145, 202
Vietnam War, 191
Vietnam War, protests, 143, 191
Vorster, B.J., 95

W
War on terror, 6, 12, 50, 53, 54, 185, 196
War on terror, refugees from, 50
Wehrmacht, 19

Weinstein, Harvey, 200
West Berlin Pavilion, Seattle 1962, 139
West Indian Standing Committee (UK), 91
White nationalism, 9, 42, 51
Wilders, Gert, 53
Wilson, Woodrow, 2
Women's rights activism, 98, 100, 101, 103, 199
Women's International Democratic Federation (WIDF), 102–104, 114
Women's organisations, 105, 200
Workers Olympics, 160
World Bank, 3, 5, 11, 81, 120
World Conference on Women, 103
World Festival of Youth and Students, Moscow, 1957, 138
World's Fairs, 13, 127, 137, 142, 151, 158, 201
World War II, 3, 4, 16, 21, 25, 28, 31, 37–39, 56–58, 63, 64, 67, 87, 98, 99, 109, 123, 128, 129, 144, 145, 161, 167–169, 194, 196, 198, 205
Wu, Lihong, 116

X

Xenophobia, 53
X, Malcolm, 92
X-Ray Spex, 42

Y

Yiddish, 20
Yoshinori, Sakai, 168
Youth Hostel Federation, 64
Yugoslavia, 18, 19, 25, 34, 72, 115, 198

Z

Zádor, Ervin, 165
Zionism, 21

GPSR Compliance

The European Union's (EU) General Product Safety Regulation (GPSR) is a set of rules that requires consumer products to be safe and our obligations to ensure this.

If you have any concerns about our products, you can contact us on

ProductSafety@springernature.com

In case Publisher is established outside the EU, the EU authorized representative is:

Springer Nature Customer Service Center GmbH
Europaplatz 3
69115 Heidelberg, Germany